Eat, Drink, and Be Merry

Eat, Drink, and Be Merry

AMERICA'S DOCTOR TELLS YOU WHY THE HEALTH EXPERTS ARE WRONG

Dean Edell, M.D.,
with
David Schrieberg

HarperCollins*Publishers*

HarperCollins books may be purchased for educational, business, or sales promotional use. For information please write: Special Markets Department, HarperCollins Publishers, Inc., 10 East 53rd Street, New York, NY 10022.

FIRST EDITION

Designed by Interrobang Design Studio

Library of Congress Cataloging-in-Publication Data

Edell, Dean.

    Eat, drink, and be merry : America's doctor tells you why the health experts are wrong / Dean Edell, with David Schrieberg.

      p. cm.

      Includes index.

      ISBN 0-06-019155-4

    1. Medical care.   2. Medical misconceptions.   3. Consumer education.

    I. Schrieberg, David.   II. Title.

    RA776.5.E342   1999

    362.1—dc21   99-10112

99 00 01 02 03 ❖/RRD 10 9

Dedicated to my listeners
and viewers, the best teachers of all

CONTENTS

————————

ACKNOWLEDGMENTS

At critical turning points in my career and personal life there were people who gave me inspiration, support, and help. To name them all would take pages that I'm sorry I don't have here. My parents never wavered in their love, even in the less traditional periods of my life. My sons, Jordan, Adam, Caleb, Aaron, and Ethan, have kept me young and focused on what's really important in life.

Many others were directly involved in this book. William F. Johnson, Joe and Teresa Graedon, Penelope Dunham, and Daphne Brogdon encouraged me to quit whining and stick to it. Susan Marie Schustak, with her boundless caffeine-stoked energy, kept all the balls in the air during my lengthy periods of distraction. My sister, Erica Edell Phillips, came up with the title. Brianne M. Miller deftly made sure that my time blabbing about this book was well spent. Susan Maruyama of Round Mountain Media, through her creativity, enthusiasm, warmth and publishing savvy, conned me into believing this would be easy and then made it happen. Our editor at HarperCollins, Megan Newman, who has more medical journals on her desk than any doctor I know, held us to the highest standards. David Schrieberg—a prize-winning journalist and former *Newsweek* bureau chief (and fellow resident of the San Francisco Bay Area)—not only turned my jumbled ramblings into a real book but kept us laughing during our all-night marathons. And Sharon Johnson, even in the midst of writing her doctoral thesis, fueled me with constant love, patience, support, and encouragement, which in the darker hours stopped me from giving up.

Eat,
Drink,
and Be
Merry

INTRODUCTION

Come Join the Dance

Obviously you worry about your health. Why else are you reading this? In fact, I'll bet it's not the first health volume in your library. Will it be the last? Maybe.

Let me tell you what is *not* going to happen in this book. I am not going to tell you what to do. I am not going to sell you anything (other than this book). There will be no Dr. Dean food supplements, vitamins, T-shirts, mugs, prepackaged foods, or expensive seminars. You will not find seven, nine, or a dozen steps to anything. No paths to a healthy heart. No roads to Wellville. No guides to good health. No magic cures for disease.

Disappointed? I don't think you are. I hear from many of you every day of my working life, and you sound tired of all the health formulas, diet plans, and guru guides. I don't blame you—they are confusing and disturbing. They can make you neurotic and crazy. Many of them promise you the moon and the stars but deliver disillusion and defeat. They establish artificial systems and rules that can make you absolutely miserable with guilt. In the end, none of them work for all of you. Not a single one. How can I be so sure? Because there is nobody else with your body, metabolism, personality, genetic character, and family history.

Have you noticed how many people have a new idea to sell you about your health? Click through your cable channels and marvel at the sheer quantity of health schemes and products that rocket past your eyes. Look at the shelves of health books in the bookstore, and health-related magazines spilling off the racks at the newsstand. Health sites explode over the Internet. Newsletters by every health nag of the moment fly through the mail.

Your eyes glaze at all the contradictory advice and the advice that turns out to be just plain wrong. One day you are told that eating rutabaga is the true path to everlasting health, and the next day you hear that rutabaga will rot your brain. There is some good in all this, though—many of you at last are becoming skeptical and asking important questions. That's what brought you to me.

Are you ready for the real thing? I am taking a radical departure, so prepare yourself. Forget what you have heard about what is good for you and what is bad for you. I want to challenge your preconceived notions about all of it. Be forewarned—some of your most cherished beliefs about health may fall by the wayside.

You see, I have worked inside the media machine that generated most of the ideas you've picked up about how your body works and how to make it work better. The health gurus, preaching the latest fads, blow in and out with the seasons. Each year I watch a new crop of pretenders to the throne march through the system. I've met famous diet doctors who are overweight. I've seen the high-profile masters of mellow, famous for their sermons about inner peace, throw hysterical tantrums when they didn't get what they wanted. I have watched the food supplement kings get rich even as they accused drug companies of putting profits first.

We're going to rattle all their cages. You must keep an open mind as we search for the truth behind your health. If a jury can overturn a murder conviction when presented with new facts, then surely you can purge outdated fairy tales about your health as I submit new evidence for your consideration.

I can summarize all that I have to offer you in one word: information. I sit on a unique perch. I see pretty much all the breaking medical news. All the research, all the surveys, all the published reports, all the controversies pass my desk. I have the luxury to measure the trends, to assess the credible and the incredible, and to pass it along to you without any particular spin because I have none. See, there it is again—I have nothing to sell you. Unlike the gurus out there, I don't care who you believe as long as you believe what's best for *you*—and it makes medical sense.

I want you to leave this book with the tools you need to make health decisions for *yourself*. As long as you are of legal age and able to think clearly, logically, and coherently for yourself, you should never cede that responsibility to anyone else—not to your doctor, not to your friends, not to your family, not to the health gurus, and especially not to the media. Unlike many among the health police force, I believe that you are easily smart enough to evaluate the news. You really have no choice. People are finally realizing that they cannot trust the health industry machine anymore. That means you must come to rational, intelligent decisions based on the best that science has to offer.

Catch that word, *science*. You will hear it a lot in the coming pages, and it should not frighten you. My single bias is toward that force which has lifted us from the dust and the darkness, slain the demons and fears of yore, and brought us the world we have now. It is the application of reason and logic, of trial and error, of scientific method and experimentation. Through science, we have created our world and vanquished the great medical foes of the past.

This book is filled with commonsense choices and options but always based on science. I am not suggesting that science has made a perfect world or answered all our questions, but what has? Where it has not established definitive answers, we look for the best estimates based on what has gone before and what is known. This doesn't mean that all your decisions will be scientific, nor should they be. In all phases of life, you should go with your heart as well as your head. Ultimately, though, science is your best friend when you consider your health.

My guess is that you will love at least some of what science has to say in this book, and at times you will be happily surprised. You need real answers, and you will find them in the next ten chapters.

What *is* a nutritious diet? Is it best that we all cut our fat intake to 10 percent? How much exercise should you really get? There are many exciting avenues in alternative medicine—and some horrible trash. Do you know how to tell the difference? Many of the substances you were taught could only hurt you can, in fact, help you when used intelligently and in moderation. Sex isn't only fun—it has some terrific health benefits; you should do it more often and get better at doing it. Are all those germs out there ready to do you and your loved ones in? Do you have any clue to what goes on in your doctor's head? Shouldn't you? How about the power of *your* mind. It can be critically important to your health, yet a person's mental state is often either overlooked or exaggerated.

In the end, we are all on the same page: each of us wants a long and healthy life. But it's no good if you cannot *enjoy* it, and to do that, you must separate reality from fiction and hope from hype. I think I can help you get there.

First, though, it might help you to know how I got *here*.

*

I walked down the long corridor, its walls glowing an eerie pale green in the fluorescent light. I stood for a moment outside a frosted glass door, unable to see inside, my heart pounding with excitement at a moment I had longed for and feared for months.

My junior year in college had ended a few weeks earlier. I was working that summer of 1962 as an orderly in the New York Hospital medical center. Everything was fresh and exhilarating. I showed up early for work and left late. Cranking beds, emptying bedpans, passing pills in little cups to the patients—I loved every minute of it. But the experience I needed to make that summer complete waited for me on the other side of that door.

I opened it, and walked into the morgue.

To see a human body cut open in front of me had been an overwhelming obsession. Somehow I suspected that there I would find a view like no other, the best the universe had to offer. Given the choice between a ride through space or a ride through a human body, my decision would be easy. This autopsy was a religious, if terrifying, adventure. Every stage was unexpected, shocking, and thrilling. How could such stillness ever have been life? Had this body once been a walking, talking, thinking, feeling human being?

I had glimpsed God.

I was dizzy as I stepped out into a drizzling Manhattan evening. I had traveled to a distant place I had imagined but never envisioned. There was no doubt about what I wanted from my life. That fall, I applied to medical school.

Twelve years later, God had fallen from my gaze. I was leaning over the edge of a Dumpster behind a Safeway, trying to reach a package of expired cheddar cheese.

It was 1975. My family and I were living in a bus I had converted into a rolling home. Burned-out and fed up, I had dropped out of my surgical practice. We drove down Highway 1 south of San Francisco, stopping for months at various beaches and trailer parks along the way. My parents and friends were appalled at this turn in my life. I, on the other hand, felt rather proud. I had abandoned the Ivy League to survive on the streets, with only my wits to guide me. Medicine was far behind me, and I never expected or wanted to go near it again. I would learn that the gap between life and intention is a wide one.

Years later, we moved to Sacramento. I made a friend who was fascinated by medicine and health. For hours he would grill me with questions—bizarre and routine—and I would entertain him with the answers. One night he suggested I contact a friend of a friend who owned a radio station. "Wouldn't it be cool to have a doctor on the radio who could take calls and answer people's questions?" he asked me. Yeah, right, I answered. I gave the idea no thought.

He, though, took his idea more seriously. A few days later, he called me and said we had an appointment at KRAK, a local country music station. Looking back on it now, I figure that either I was out of my mind or delusional. Not only had I been wholly disconnected from medicine for seven years, but my last involvement had been with eyes, a highly technical subspecialty of surgery. I assumed the station manager would kick this preposterous idea where it belonged. "Sure, let's try it," she said.

I was stunned and panicked. Was I *really* going to field questions on any medical topic? I raced to the nearest medical school and barricaded myself in the library. I quickly saw it was hopeless. But something else hit me in those two weeks before the first broadcast. I had run away from my profession and never looked back, yet I found myself becoming captivated all over again. The information. The texts. The illustrations. The research. The collected knowledge of thousands of years of medical experience.

I was energized again, unlike any time since that autopsy so many summers ago. The fear of making a fool of myself on the air gave way to a genuine and insatiable passion for knowledge. It was like falling in love anew with an ex-wife, recognizing that the first marriage was all wrong but now could be all right.

Of course, I was still terrified when I sat before the radio console for the first time and saw it light up with callers. The first caller must have been a doctor or nurse having some fun—the question was esoteric and full of medical detail. The topic, though, was a godsend—an obscure eye disease. My specialty. I hit it out of the park, and a career was born. Had I been unable to answer that first query, I wonder if I would have had the confidence to continue. "I don't know" was not in my phrasebook at that time.

I did six shows, which were truly terrible, and then, by chance, the station was sold. I approached KGO radio in San Francisco, which was looking for a shrink to host a weekend show. Fortunately, the manager gave that up and settled on me.

We were living in distant Mendocino County, and I wasn't confident enough to commit fully to an uncertain job in San Francisco. I commuted four hours each way to do the show, sleeping overnight in my old bus in a campground just north of the Golden Gate Bridge. A year later, I went to TV-land and got a job as a medical reporter for Channel 7, the ABC station in San Francisco.

I still marvel at all that has happened to this medical dropout. My average weekly national audience numbers well over 20 million, a figure that still astonishes me. Among so many people are true experts on any subject. They are quick to let me know when I'm wrong, and I adore hearing from them. They may call or fax during the broadcast or write a letter. The payoff is the same—I get an instant and welcome update of my education. Imagine that every time you didn't know something or did something wrong, you were instantly apprised of the correct information or technique and in a constructive way that invigorated you. Can you see how fast you would grow?

It's great to field callers with questions I can easily answer, but early in my radio career I learned to love *not* knowing the answers. That meant I was about to discover something new. It makes me voracious for questions and the new information they bring. My staff and I buy medical books by the boatload, subscribe to scads of medical journals, track medical work around the world, and read everything we can get our hands on relating to all medical subjects. It has become a delightful, lifelong addiction.

I feel very fortunate because my job now is to feed that habit. I learn new things and pass them on to anyone who wants to share my education—at no cost. It's kind of like learning a new dance together. Consider this book a manual of the latest steps. So come and join the dance. You'll feel far better for it.

1

TRUST THE MEDIA AT YOUR PERIL

(It's Your Health, Not Theirs)

L et's start at the bottom line. Americans enjoy the best health and longest life spans in our history. Yet medical advances aside, we worry more about our health than ever before. We have become obsessed and neurotic to the point where we bounce like pinballs from one health-related anxiety and scare to another. Be honest—that's *really* why you bought this book (fortunately, you *are* that anxious). Rather than basking in triumph over the scourges of our ancestors and enjoying our good health, we live in fear and paranoia. Relax. Things are better than you think. Give me 325 pages or so, and I'll prove it to you.

Don't get me wrong. I'm not saying for a second that life is risk-free or comes with any guarantees. But from the start of this century in particular, medical science has advanced with extraordinary speed. In 1928 we had effective treatments for at most only 10 percent of the 360 most serious diseases. Nowadays we can handle most of them. Consider these numbers, culled by Harvard psychiatrist Arthur Barsky from government and other sources. If you were born in 1900, you were expected to live to age forty-seven. Through the century, life expectancy has rocketed. After the millennium, it will be over eighty. A child born today is likely to live longer than at any time since we started tap dancing onto the planet.

Isn't it strange that as things get better, we feel worse? If we're not semistarving ourselves to a slimmer body, or trudging up StairMasters to nowhere, we feel guilty that we're not doing what we should do, whatever *that* is. When the wonders of modern medicine aren't perfect, we whine and complain and sue and turn back to witch-doctor wannabes in disguise and other quacks. Barsky calls this "the paradox of health." Our concept of healthiness, he found, has not kept pace with medicine's overall gains. Although methodologies differ among several surveys, all report similar trends. In the 1920s, the average American reported having a serious, acute, or disabling illness every sixteen months. What do you think that same survey found in the 1980s? More than two a year, with each episode lasting longer than in the 1920s.

Another survey compared public concern with health between the 1950s and the 1970s. Folks were asked about specific symptoms, like breathing trouble, rapid heartbeats, palpitations, and pain. They complained of *more* poor health in the 1970s, and fewer people reported being symptom-free. Comparing the 1970s and 1980s, people said they were less satisfied with their health as time went on. So much for the comforts of science.

We report being sick more. We report illnesses as recurring. We report each episode as lasting longer. Yet in reality, we are not sick more. We don't have more recurring illnesses. And we are not sick longer.

The truth is that as a population, we seem less able to tolerate even slight discomforts. In fact, we view such discomforts as real pathology. We are faster to consider ourselves sick and run faster to doctors for everything from our stuffed sinuses to our stiff joints. The logical question, then, is have we become a hypochondriacal culture? Hypochondriacs, contrary to what many think, do not imagine their pain. But they do overreact to a multitude of common little aches and discomforts. All the attention to fitness, diets, and exercise simply means we spend more time thinking about our bodies. That's not necessarily a healthy trend.

In the two decades I've been a media doctor, I've noticed a change on my radio call-in show. Early on, the calls seemed more substantive. There were real symptoms needing real advice. Nowadays there are more calls about vague and what I judge to be innocuous symptoms. "Dr. Edell, I have this funny tingling sensation in my tummy," or pelvis, or legs. "Could it be multiple sclerosis?" Headaches are quickly presumed to be brain tumors. Chest discomfort? Must be heart disease. Routine dryness of the skin? The heartbreak of psoriasis. Normal vaginal secretions? Infection, definitely. I have never gotten so many calls from men concerned about the clumpiness or textural qualities of their semen. Even routine forgetfulness, stuff our forefathers forgot to worry about, must be early Alzheimer's. Sore muscles? Trot down to the clinic. Got a cold? Off to the doctor, even though you must know that colds taper off in a week if you go to the doctor—and in seven days if you don't.

It's understandable, considering how everyone is pummeled with diagnostic nightmares by the media. It's human nature. How can you ignore indigestion after television's *ER* features a character whose presumed heartburn turns out to be a heart attack? News of an obscure disease convinces you that you may be a victim. This isn't new. In the 1950s, my father brought home a copy of the *Merck Manual*, a single-volume compendium of the main diseases known to man. After a few months of looking up all our symptoms and convincing themselves we all had every disease in the book, my parents came to their senses and chucked the book.

After the first media reports on HIV in the early 1980s, my show was inundated by panicked callers. Some had engaged in unprotected sex, others were worried about oral sex or kissing. One woman anguished about her adult son who had gone to a topless bar where a lactating dancer had sprayed the audience with breast milk. He got splattered, his mother cried, and what of those stories about AIDS in breast milk? Then there was the frantic couple who slept all night in a hotel room only to find a used condom suspended in a lamp. Had HIV vapors attacked them overnight?

A call I found far more upsetting came from a concerned mother whose daughter and son-in-law were, in good faith, feeding a "healthy, organic, low-fat diet" to their toddler. That is a straight shot to a serious pediatric condition called failure to thrive, in which a child simply does not grow. In the past this was usually due to an intestinal or metabolic problem. Today it is mostly caused by well-meaning parents responding to media-generated fear. Simply put, kids *need* fat to grow normally.

This is all very frustrating for a radio doctor. I know they won't listen to common sense (that's one of the reasons I wrote this book. Maybe at least they will *read* it). In my view, parental ignorance is child abuse, morally if not legally.

Our obsessions have gotten the best of us. If a guest on a TV talk show discusses a lump in her breast, viewers start feeling their breasts. That can and often does trigger a positive trend as people become aware of symptoms that they might otherwise have ignored. That said, the guest cannot tell you about *your* breasts. What is a small lump versus the normal knobby texture of the breast?

When you pay greater attention to your body and your health, you tend to assess them both more negatively. Lie down and start to focus on your abdomen. Feel something strange? Maybe a little gas wriggling through your intestines on its way out. Normal peristalsis. Really focus on it, though, and I guarantee that some of you will wonder if it's normal. What is normal, after all? Did your brother-in-law feel like that before his stomach cancer? Whatever it is, you'll just as likely go for the worst-case assumption, and the resulting unnecessary anxiety can undermine your health in subtle ways we're going to talk about.

IT'S A TABLOID, TABLOID, TABLOID, TABLOID WORLD

Again, it's human nature at work, goosed along by the media. Let's look at the extremes and have some fun with the tabloids, those purveyors of the latest medical outrage, secret miracle, and discovery the government doesn't want you to know about. Why do so many of their stories deal with simians? CHIMP'S HEAD PUT ON HUMAN BODY—

WORLD'S RELIGIOUS AND MEDICAL LEADERS OUTRAGED; HUMAN BRAIN PUT
IN CHIMP—COULD BE TRYING TO SPEAK, SAY DOCTORS; SNEEZING INCREASES
YOUR BUST SIZE; CORPSE REVIVED AFTER 23 DAYS; UNBORN BABY TRANS-
PLANTED TO HUBBY—PREGNANT MAN GIVES BIRTH FIVE MONTHS LATER. You
laugh—I hope you do—but these are extraordinarily popular newspapers, and that should worry you. For many people, if it appears in
print it must be true. These same papers are full of cures and remedies—and they too feature horrifying exaggerations and distortions.

For tabloids and their respectable relatives in the mainstream, good
news is no news. In medicine, we are painfully aware of what draws
attention and what does not. A serious study concluding that a particular drug cures nothing or causes no side effects often falls into the
second category. It is unlikely even to get published in the medical
journals, let alone the mainstream media. A study of this very issue
uncovered that research on secondhand smoke was less likely to be
published in scientific journals if no link to disease was proved.

It's hard to overemphasize the dangers here. If study after study
finds that aspirin does not cause birth defects, those studies never see
the light of day. Then researchers at a lab in Podunksville think they
can prove that aspirin does cause birth defects. Watch what happens.
Even though many other better and more thorough studies were negative, Podunksville will lead the evening news. Panicked pregnant
aspirin-takers will abort. This is why it is so treacherous for you to
rely on a single, isolated study that goes against the grain of all previous research. Professionals understand this, and that's why doctors
seem so conservative about interpreting the latest cure-all or curse-all
headlines. Often you are not informed about studies that show something is safe.

Take just one extraordinary example of the wrong side of the story:
Bendectin, an anti–morning sickness pill, was safely used by millions
of pregnant women starting in 1956. It contained vitamin B-6 and
doxylamine, an antihistamine. In 1979 I had just started doing radio,
and a listener sent me a tabloid newspaper story about a child born
with only one hand. The story claimed that use of Bendectin had
caused thousands of tragically deformed infants. I was naive and new
to the industry. Regrettably I fell for it and passed along the misinformation on the air. After all, the story quoted a real researcher making
the claim. By the time I figured out the truth, it was too late.

Television and newspapers blared warnings about Bendectin. Personal injury lawyers hired publicity firms to drum up more cases. The talk shows loved it—it offered the classic dynamic of children with obviously tragic birth defects, available as studio guests, taking on the drug company Goliaths.

As the legal costs grew, the manufacturer, Merrell Dow Pharmaceuticals, got cold feet and stopped making the drug. This had been one of the most studied drugs ever used in pregnancy, and the vast majority of specialists still insist that Bendectin is safe. Yet think how easy it would be to mislead a jury. In the general population, birth defects of varying severity routinely occur in about 5 percent of births. Among millions of women taking Bendectin, then, you would expect many thousands of babies born with birth defects. Think how easy it would have been to demonstrate the truth: Compare one thousand women who were taking Bendectin with one thousand women who were not. Do children of the former have a higher rate of birth defects? Subsequent studies have shown that they don't. But juries are sympathetic to suffering children. How can you prove that a birth defect was not caused by the drug? As late as 1994, a Philadelphia jury awarded nineteen million dollars to a couple that blamed Bendectin for the clubfeet of their fourteen-year-old son.

Who wins? Today, pregnant women suffering from nausea must take drugs not as rigorously studied as Bendectin was. Morning sickness, including the severest form, hyperemesis gravidarum, has doubled because doctors are now reluctant to prescribe any drug that could help alleviate its symptoms. But the offending ingredient, doxylamine succinate, is widely available over the counter in many cough and cold medications, in doses far higher than in Bendectin—and any pregnant woman can walk into a drugstore and buy them off the shelf.

BAIT-AND-SWITCH

The tabloids are only part of the problem. In March 1991 the *Journal of the American Medical Association* (JAMA) examined the bias toward scare stories in mainstream newspapers. In a clever sting operation, the journal published two articles on the same subject: the link between nuclear radiation exposure and cancer. One story was positive, the other negative. The positive study found twenty-eight deaths from leukemia over three decades among eight thousand men hired by the federal radiation research laboratory at Oak Ridge, Tennessee. Statistically, you would expect eighteen leukemia deaths among eight thousand workers in nonnuclear-related industries, so a number of these specialized employees may indeed have suffered from the exposure.

The other story in the same journal studied cancer rates among eighteen million people living near nuclear facilities. The authors found *no* increase in cancer and leukemia deaths. That's the negative study and, of course, far more important to many more people than the nuclear-lab-leukemia story. JAMA issued carefully crafted press releases, of similar length and tone, on both stories. The editors wanted to see how newspapers around the country would handle both stories. Their sting worked.

Seventeen newspapers, and major ones at that, covered at least one of the studies. Nearly half the stories dealt only with the scarier report about the nuclear lab workers. Papers as august as the *New York Times*, the *Los Angeles Times*, and *USA Today* didn't even mention the reassuring study. The papers that did cover both reports wrote in far greater detail about Oak Ridge. The wire services, a primary news source for media around the world, were just as bad.

Why, then, is good medical news no news? People turn off the weather report when the weather is good. Walk into a cocktail party and listen to different conversations. There is one about the delicious deviled eggs. There is another about salmonella-tainted eggs at a local chicken farm. Which one are you going to join?

I think this is the intellectual equivalent of one of our most primitive reflexes, the fight-or-flight reaction. When an organism is threatened, its physiology changes in response, preparing either to stand and fight or flee. Walking in the woods, you hear or see something unexpected, and you can't help but give your full attention to the perceived potential threat. Any sudden change in the status quo and you want to know what's going on. Your nervous system is designed to adapt quickly and to react when you are threatened. The media peddle you threats because threats generate ratings and readers by triggering your nervous system's response. How can you not pay attention? How are you going to stop worrying?

Couple that anxiety with the reality that in an MTV-paced, rapid-fire world, we feed on constant stimulation—the more outrageous, the better. And to be fair to the human animal, we are, as are most mammals, just plain curious.

We in the media feed on that curiosity. For instance, surveys show that you want cancer stories. In a Gallup poll of consumers about the health stories that most interested them, 62 percent said cancer, 48 percent said heart disease, and 38 percent said AIDS. Reflecting this concern, television management once besieged me with its latest research based on focus groups (plain folks solicited and plied with free food and a few bucks to assess programming while station executives stand behind a one-way mirror noting their every burp). This time, participants held little dials in their hands to gauge interest in the stories they watched. All their input was charted on a graph. I could smell trouble as a newsroom executive darkened my door. "Dean, as soon as we showed them a cancer story, their interest meter went up," he said, his face aglow from the light bulb I imagined above his head. "You got any cancer-scare stories you can do for sweeps?"— referring to the period that stations use to measure their ratings. In very uncharacteristic fashion, I kept my mouth shut.

The sorry truth is that most of America's health information comes from television. In a 1997 National Health Council poll, more people named television as their primary source of health news than named their doctor, and most people—76 percent—had taken health advice they'd seen on a TV news report, yet only 5 percent thought the quality of the television news on health was excellent. Go figure. Polls show that the vast majority of the public wants even more media health coverage. That may mean job security for me, but I'm afraid that the demand for more coverage will lead to lower quality and even less accuracy.

ENTER TV DOCTOR, STAGE RIGHT

I was at the start of a healthy trend in television medical reporting— the TV doctor. I had started to do radio on KGO in San Francisco in 1978. Health news was getting hot, and I heard that Channel 7 news, the local ABC station, might be looking for a doctor to put on the air. I got turned down then—I didn't look enough like a doctor, they said. A little later toxic shock syndrome hit, and I was all over it on the radio. Channel 7 couldn't find a local doctor who knew anything about this syndrome yet. One of the producers heard me talking about it on my radio show and asked me to go on the evening news that night. I had been waiting for this moment. I lined up glasses of water on camera and dipped different brands of tampons in them to demonstrate absorbency, which was related to this disease. I ranted and raved about how the feds were withholding information and not telling women the whole truth about toxic shock. News management loved it. Off camera, I also mentioned that I was talking to another station across town about a job. Channel 7 hired me.

There were growing pains. Many in the business were suspicious and resentful of an outsider who hadn't earned his stripes the conventional way (medical school didn't count to these folks). How could I, a stethoscope-wielding man of medicine, report health news objectively? For example, would I ever criticize doctors?

Call it "The Education of Dr. Dean." Early on, I believed that news departments wanted real *news* (hence the title—news department), which I interpreted to mean stories no one had heard before. Instead of doing the standard—regurgitating wire-service reports—I actually scoured medical journals for story ideas. I quickly realized how far ahead of the curve my producer and I were, as the national press, the wire services, and major papers covered the same stories weeks, months, and sometimes years after we did. I thought news directors and management would love what we were doing. They couldn't have cared less. When I came to them with a story I thought was important, they would ignore me. Yet weeks later, when the wire services finally caught wind of the same story and ran their versions, management would ask me to cover it.

In those days we kept a lengthy log of all the stories on which we beat the national media. We don't bother anymore. We still do stories way ahead of everybody else. That doesn't make us God's gift to journalism. We just read a few medical journals, which almost no one in the national press corps does. Remember that big Viagra story in May 1998? It led the newscasts for weeks on end and graced the cover of every national news magazine. I did my first Viagra story in April 1997. I had to talk the station editors into running it. They agreed, but it ran late in the show.

I was a rare breed in the early days. Now we are many—actual doctors discussing health issues—and it is a good trend, in my view. There is even an annual TV-doctor convention, which draws several hundred doctors and health professionals. We fill an ever-greater public hunger for health news and a consequent need for reporters who know their stuff. My TV news stories are syndicated to seventy-five local news stations nationwide. I constantly hear doctors who want to be TV stars. I encourage them all—the more the merrier—and do all I can to help get their careers going. As far as I'm concerned, anything is better than untrained reporters doing medical news.

IT'S *SHOW* TIME: THE RESPONSIBILITY OF POWER

With news, you expect a journalistic commitment to accuracy. You cannot and should not expect the same from the *showbiz* side of television. Talk shows have no obligation, intent, or commitment to get at the truth, and because their power is so great, they are even more dangerous. Their massive audiences often do not understand the difference between the talk show and the news. I don't mind when they do their typical transvestite-whales-without-partners thing. It's trash but relatively harmless trash. I go nuts when the same talk-show titillation techniques and production practices are used for serious health subjects.

It's difficult to pick just one example when my files are bursting with them. I'll choose a show no longer on the air, because I need the talk shows to promote this book. The granddaddy of them all is Phil Donahue, the man who single-handedly invented the format. For twenty-five years, he interviewed heads of state and other elites. But Donahue realized that TV was changing, leaving him with a far different audience from the one with which he had initially earned respect. The competition was closing in. Phil, the viewer's avuncular and intelligent friend, had to react. On one such program, he never imagined the damage he was about to inflict on a gullible public.

THE ISSUE OF THE DAY: VACCINATIONS

On this particular program, Phil has invited a leading public health expert on vaccinations. Well, not exactly. Her name is Lisa Bonet, and she is a television actress. Let's roll the tape: five . . . four . . . three . . . two . . . one and cue.

Donahue: You obviously love your baby, and you are an enlightened
mother . . .

Bonet: That's why I'm here, you know, to share what information I've learned.

Donahue: Tell me, Lisa, you are not scared that you didn't vaccinate your child?

Bonet: I'm scared, I'm scared, and I'm scared to vaccinate her, which is why I didn't vaccinate her in the first place, which led me to read about the warnings that are out there. And what I've learned is that there are warnings about introducing these alien microorganisms into our children's blood and the long-term effects. Which could be trivial or they could be quite hazardous. And they could be just allergies or asthma or sleep disorders. Or they could be cancer, leukemia, multiple sclerosis, sudden infant death syndrome. It's very scary and it's very serious. I think because I felt wrong doing it, that's why I didn't do it and, uh, we have to think twice. Why are our children getting these diseases?

At this point, a normal person in this conversation might ask Ms. Bonet how she knows all this, exactly. Who told her vaccines would or could cause all these diseases? Phil doesn't ask her, because this is called the "churn" at the beginning of a talk show, when stirring the pot is the name of the game. This episode would move ahead to some significant rambling.

Donahue: And what is the biochemical legacy of the vaccination? How long does it last, and what might be its effect? You are putting something into your baby's bloodstream. Everybody ought to think about that twice. Zoe [Bonet's daughter] will not have fish or chicken?

Bonet: No, they are poisonous. No, you know even if you get organic chickens, our oceans are polluted.

At that point a fellow guest, actor River Phoenix, joins in the conversation.

Phoenix: The fish that we are feeding our chickens has estrogen in it.

The discussion continues, now focused on the horrors of additives. Keep in mind that River Phoenix later died of other additives called drugs.

I don't fault Phil for being ignorant about the subject. But he is a smart guy. It would have been easy—and invaluable to his audience—to put the other side, the informed side, on the air.

Donahue did not wander out on the antivaccination limb alone. Talk show after talk show after news program has pushed the very media-savvy antivaccine propaganda line. Personal tragedy can easily sway you and can more easily sway audiences who observe your tragedy. One woman recently attributed her child's autism to vaccines. She launched a media blitz, taking to the talk-show circuit. The *Los Angeles Times* called her "charismatic and camera friendly" and therefore persuasive to impressionable audiences.

I'll tell you here, there is no controversy about vaccinations. We've forgotten the contribution of vaccines to our modern quality of life. Most diseases prevented by vaccines are almost unknown today. There are no cases of smallpox or polio in the United States. I've never seen a case of tetanus or diphtheria in my career. I have seen whooping cough, though, in a child barely able to breathe after a prolonged coughing spell, his desperate attempt to inhale through swollen trachea and bronchi inhibited further by a thick and viscous mucus. The horrible sound created by this battle for air is a whoop, hence the name. At its peak it struck more than 250,000 American children a year and killed 10,000 of them. Consider the magnitude of the victory over that disease.

Or don't. Whooping cough is back, and it doesn't have to be. From California to New York to Northern Europe, immunization rates are down. In some countries, antivaccination hysterics got to the politicians, who then stupidly cut back vaccination drives. The percentage of the population vaccinated against whooping cough in the United Kingdom dropped from 90 to 30 percent, and within eighteen months an epidemic ensued. We media types turn our backs on these victories for the sake of ratings and sales. We have forgotten history and are doomed to repeat it. Sometimes you just cannot pile enough shame on us. I had my five kids vaccinated, and you should do the same for yours. It's simple, and the benefits far outweigh the risks, if there really are any risks.

MY TURN AT BAT

Donahue was the first of an increasingly dangerous breed. Most producers and hosts of talk shows have neither journalistic nor science backgrounds nor scruples. They book guests with the explicit aim of teasing and thrilling you. The truth does not figure in their thinking. If ninety-nine scientists say black is black, they'll go out of their way to book the one kook who says black is white, and they'll put him on stage alone. Even if they do go for balance, the "balance" is usually a classically unappealing nerd who plays straight man to the slick, media-savvy charmer. The producers know the audience is more likely to stay glued for the iconoclast, the guy who touts the easy way out of your problems without any of the hard work.

How do I know all this? I was probably the first physician in America to be given his own daily network TV talk show. At the time, in the early 1990s, NBC soap operas weren't doing so well. Health was hot in the media. I was established in a local market, with a considerable national radio following. The network decided to put me up against the biggest guns: Oprah and Phil.

You barely heard me go pop against the cannons.

The start-up and management of a daily network talk show is a truly remarkable process. Offices to rent; producers, writers, directors, accountants, assistants, and messengers to hire; theme music to be composed; sets to be designed and built; money to be spent; network executives to be pleased. We checked our scripts with the network every day. As strange as it sounds, every question on these programs is preplanned and run first by network suits. Even the guests' answers were to be scripted. How were we to know what a guest would say in response to a question, I would ask? We guessed anyhow, and made the network happy.

Despite a grueling personal schedule—I kept my daily radio program and television medical reporting job as well—I stayed current with the medical journals and tried to slip responsible medical information into the typical TV talk-show format.

But we had to bow to the genre. Little by little we got sucked into doing the schlockier subjects, but with a medical angle. When we teased sexier topics, we got ratings. I was told to make guests "squirt"—or cry—for the same reason. Nevertheless, I am proud of every second of tape we did. We had the best producers in the industry, so the shows were superbly crafted and looked as good as anything on the air. But the handwriting was on the wall.

From the start, the competition was fierce. I'll go back to my files and blindly pick a date. September 8, 1992: Donahue does older men with teen girls. Geraldo features homosexual parents. And Dr. Dean? Teenage plastic surgery, my friends. We had very clever ways of putting medical spins on everything. We booked comedians and did segments on humor and healing. We booked rock 'n' roll acts with self-piercers. There was a fellow who let his girlfriend stand on his face in a box of cut glass, accompanied by a segment on pain and the mind. We did plenty of sex, from sexually transmitted diseases to prostitution. But we always began with a monologue summing up medical news and always ended by taking medical questions from the audience. I still survive in some offbeat venues. Fly to Australia and you might yet catch me in reruns.

The show was a runaway train. Early on we realized we were not going to dominate the ratings. But it was naive even to think that we could broadcast responsible health information and compete, for instance, with another newcomer named Jerry Springer, who went on the air around the same time. We lasted 125 shows. Springer is still around.

I worked to stay on top of the bookings to make sure our guest experts were credentialed. It wasn't easy, and I'm sure everyone who worked for me thought I was a pain in the gluteus maximus. If I had problems overseeing the quality of the guests and the show, you can imagine the difficulties encountered by a typical talk-show producer. I must say that part of me was glad when the network pulled the plug.

NEWS—NOT FACTS

May 7, 1998. The pickets outside KGO studios are back. "Hey, hey, ho, ho, Dr. Dean has got to go," they chant. "Hey, hey, ho, ho, breast implants have got to go." Here we go again, I thought. The angriest folks are often those with diseases that don't exist. This time, women with silicone breast implants.

In fact, I always had a bit of antipathy for the breast implant. Weren't these women submitting to men's obsession with breasts?

Although my opinions have changed a bit, when breast implants started to take off I thought it was crazy for women to have this plastic surgery. The breast implant craze really began with prostitutes in postwar Japan trying to appeal to American GIs. At first wax and then silicone gel were injected directly into women's breasts. Silicone is remarkably inert in the human body. That means it is tolerated well, without inflammation and reaction, which is why doctors use it in so many surgical prostheses, from penile implants to heart valves. But direct injection was an inferior technique. The first silicone breast implant in bag form was invented in 1962 in the United States. Since then, roughly two million women have had the surgery.

I trace the beginning of this tidal wave of aversion to implants to a CBS broadcast starring Connie Chung in 1990. It featured characteristically mindless bashing and blaming, poorly supported by the facts. Women with breast implants claimed that their autoimmune diseases—including arthritis, lupus, scleroderma, and fibromyalgia—were caused by their implants. The next day I found myself trying to calm callers to my radio show. There was no evidence, I told them, that women with implants had higher rates of these diseases than the general population.

My opinion was shared by every expert I tracked down. Despite that, I quickly became subject to the worst harassment and vile hate mail of my career—including death threats and petitions to remove me from the air. Out of the blue, Dr. Marcia Angell, executive editor of the prestigious *New England Journal of Medicine*, flew unwittingly to my aid with a book entitled *Science on Trial*, which documented this travesty of science and law. Not to be egocentric here, I took it as personal vindication. In early 1992 the federal Food and Drug Administration banned silicone implants. That made it still more risky to report on the first major studies exonerating implants as a source of autoimmune disease. Female anchors with and without breast implants chided me for ignoring the plight of women. News directors doubted my credibility.

Yet, as is so often the case, the science was simple. If you claim a disease is more common in one group—in this case, women with implants—then simply compare that group to women without implants. Study after study has shown the same rate of autoimmune disease in both groups, about 1 percent. That means ten thousand cases for every one million women. If those women have implants, however—well, that was enough for the lawyers, who had a field day.

The media became their witless allies and dupes. Every major national talk show and news program did the typical implant episode, with "victims" (and their lawyers) complaining about how sick implants had made them. Juries awarded millions of dollars in civil trials. A Houston woman won a record twenty-five million dollars. Reported symptoms got wilder as time went on. I ran into one of the big winners at the airport one day, lugging her heavy bags and berating me for my stand. She had claimed crippling arthritis and fatigue in her successful multimillion-dollar suit. As of this writing, as much as four billion dollars are up for grabs in a class-action suit representing 170,000 women. All this, and there is absolutely *no* direct evidence that autoimmune diseases are more common in women with implants.

It should be said that surgical complications can occur with implant surgery, just as they can with any plastic surgery. Only a small percentage of cases in the implant lawsuits revolve around surgical side effects, and I don't know if those effects are more common than normal. Surgery is not perfect. In most cases, implant patients wanted bigger breasts (most cases are not postmastectomy reconstruction), and such patients must assume some small risk to have this surgery.

In July 1998 two major government panels in Europe vindicated breast implants, saying that not only is there no evidence that they cause diseases, but, according to the UK Independent Review Group on Silicone Gel Breast Implants, that "no further studies into the issue . . . can be justified." I rest my case, and so should you.

If a person is falsely convicted of a crime, we become justifiably upset. Yet when a company or a product is falsely convicted, we tend to shrug our shoulders. But take another look. These junk-science lawsuits scare the companies that supply raw materials to manufacturers of medical devices. Supplier A sells seven cents worth of medical-grade silicone to manufacturer B, which uses it in an implantable medical device. When manufacturer B gets sued, supplier A gets dragged into the suit. It isn't worth it for supplier A, which can make more money with less hassle by selling the product for industrial uses.

Why should you care if you don't have pumped-up breasts? The list is long of people with silicone components in many types of implants: over 2 million heart patients with pacemakers, grafts, and catheters; 600,000 orthopedic patients with joint prostheses; 1.5 million eye-surgery patients with lenses and oils; 2.6 million urological patients with catheters, stents, and testicular and penile implants; 75,000 neurosurgical patients with shunts. That is an incomplete list, and it should worry you. In 1994 more than one-third of the biomaterials suppliers stated they would not sell raw materials to American implant manufacturers. By 1997 three-quarters had stopped sales to manufacturers because of fear of liability. Dupont spent eight million dollars defending itself over five cents' worth of biomaterial in a jaw implant. This is enough of a crisis that Congress has stepped in to limit the liability of the suppliers.

Hey, hey, ho, ho, junk science has got to go.

THE TERROR HIT PARADE

The implants alarm is just one among countless examples of media-whipped-up terror based on a distorted reading of science. The fogies out there will remember just a few golden oldies like the cranberry scare of 1959, cyclamates in 1969, hormones in beef in 1972, saccharine in 1977, Alar in apples in 1989, benzene in Perrier water, and amalgam dental fillings in 1990. And this is the short list. Eventually all were acquitted, but not until the media had scared the bejesus out of the public, often for nothing, and at a cost of millions of dollars to taxpayers and industry.

There is no media conspiracy here. (Don't forget—I'm one of them, even if most of the time I feel like a voice in the wilderness.) The biggest threat out there is wrong or distorted information. It's just gossip when it concerns your favorite star or politician. It's a real danger when it concerns an important medical treatment, useful medication, industrial process, or basic diet staple around the world.

Humankind has been manipulating its food supply through plant and animal breeding for thousands of years. The tomato you slice and throw into your salad bears no resemblance to nature's original model. In days of yore, farmers and plant breeders painstakingly cross-bred plants to develop desirable characteristics, from disease resistance to better taste. Today we do it in the lab, with high-tech gene manipulation techniques, among others. But genetically modified foods scare people. The media know this and love it.

On August 10, 1998, I was on the TV news set before my daily segment, when the anchor read the following to half a million local viewers: "Before we get to Dr. Dean, a new study is calling into question the safety of 'genetically engineered' foods. British researchers fed genetically altered potatoes to rats, which they say stunted the animals' growth and weakened their immune systems. The results of the study have renewed calls to take genetically modified products off store shelves. But supporters of such foods say the study doesn't apply to products now on the market."

Livid, I turned to the anchor, live on the air, and said that our audience should not believe this story. There have been thousands of reliable studies attesting to the safety of genetically altered foods. This *single* report was based on a mere *five* rats that the researcher claimed were only *slightly* stunted. The anchor looked away.

That same night, this story was heard or seen by millions of people around the world via the usual satellite news distribution systems. ABC's version, fed instantly to all its stations including ours, was based on a European wire story. It featured visual images of caged rats and suspicious-looking potatoes.

Of course, the media cannot track down every source in every story, particularly when fed from overseas and network sources. But when a story even on its face is so obviously bogus, it should raise suspicion among supposedly seasoned news veterans. In fact, the next day the truth came out. The source was one Arpad Puztai, a researcher at an institute in Scotland. He had published nothing in the usual scholarly journals about his findings but announced his discovery on a British television documentary. Asked to supply complete data on his five rats, he disappointed his colleagues. "Some of the claims he made could . . . not be substantiated by the data," said the head of the institute, expressing his deep embarrassment and announcing the suspension of Dr. Puztai.

ABC never ran a follow-up, correction, or retraction. The network let it stand, and millions of people will remember—wrongly—that potatoes may keep their children from growing and weaken their immune systems.

BEARERS OF IGNORANCE

Medical reporting in this country is for the most part inept. I have been archiving such examples for years. As I look them over, I find that the common denominator among news writers and anchors is a lack of fundamental scientific knowledge. Even on the basics, the truth is shocking. For example, a University of Wisconsin biology professor surveyed the staffs of daily newspapers and found that half the managing editors believed that humans and dinosaurs walked the planet at the same time (dinosaurs were gone more than sixty-five million years before humans came ambling along).

Legitimate journalists would never report something that they knew to be untrue. But in science and health, they are often out of their league. While there are reporters who train and specialize in sports, weather, and business, for instance, health news is often covered by general assignment reporters. What do reporters and anchors know about science and medicine? Not much usually. To be fair, the health beat is a tricky one. A reporter who is not knowledgeable will buy a lot of bull. Reporters are people, after all.

Does it seem as if experts keep changing their minds? On some topics, they do; that's the nature of science. But they don't do it as much as it seems to you. Inexperienced reporters often have little context for the news they are expected to cover. How can they? And when they give every story equal weight, the *coverage* is misleading. Reporters have to know the prior research before they can put a story in perspective. To spot a trend, you have to know what has gone on before in that particular field. That's tough when the eleven o'clock news team doesn't bother to check what the six o'clock news team wrote in its story. Even forewarning doesn't always help.

A CURE FOR CANCER! MORE AT ELEVEN

A small example on a local level: I remember a story that ran on an early newscast claiming that sharks don't get cancer. I saw it and warned management that I had done a story weeks earlier concluding just the opposite, that sharks can and do indeed get cancer. Our team had confirmed it with the recognized authorities. (I'm going to ignore here the entire bogus nature of the story they were doing: eating shark cartilage will cure cancer.) What do you think happened? The story ran again at eleven, teasing with the lead that "sharks rarely, if ever, get cancer."

That incident was relatively innocuous. Sometimes, though, one media personality with a lot of power and little knowledge can cause a lot of trouble. On September 30, 1996, a press release was issued to the media. I reproduce selected portions:

Publisher Kathy Keeton Says Inexpensive Experimental Drug Has Reversed Her Cancer and Saved Her Life . . . The American cancer establishment may be dismissing the drug because it is too inexpensive for its own good and none of the entrenched medical, governmental, and pharmaceutical interests can make any money on it. . . . The reason the drug is dismissed is perverse [says Ms. Keeton]. "It's because the medical establishment can't make any money on it."

I'm not going to bother to pick this apart. But can you really imagine a cancer cure that is so cheap no one wants it? This is the height of conspiracy theory nonsense. I don't blame Kathy Keeton, who happened to be the wife of *Penthouse* publisher Bob Guccione and a ranking executive in his empire. Rational thought can be difficult for anybody who is fighting for her life. But here's the part that really caught my attention: "My recovery from cancer is all due to Dr.———" (I refuse to give him more publicity). "All my tumors have shrunk or disappeared. I have three tiny ones in my liver still, but there were six originally." Medically, that admission is not a good sign. The cancer was not truly gone. That did not stop the *Penthouse* publicity machine from gunning full speed ahead. Ugly articles followed about greedy doctors and Kathy's cure. Patients were solicited for lawsuits against the National Cancer Institute via full-page ads in other magazines in Guccione's stable.

The truth is that the particular drug—hydrazine sulfate, a component of rocket fuel—has been tested and failed the test. Indeed it is cheap, but it definitely does not cure cancer.

Why let a fact get in the way of a good story? It didn't for Paul Harvey, an icon of American radio. Three months after the *Penthouse* press release, Harvey, with his unmistakable delivery, read the following report to his audience:

If you are suffering from cancer or love someone who is, may I have your undivided attention for one minute. More than a week ago, I related the experience of Kathy Keeton. . . . Kathy Keeton's breast cancer had spread to her stomach, lymph nodes, aorta, and liver. She was given six weeks to live and that was two years ago. Instead of chemotherapy or radiation, she tried two pills a day of hydrazine sulfate. She is now virtually free of cancer and is back at work, leading a normal life.

Harvey goes on to tell his listeners how to contact her doctor.

If she and Paul Harvey could use their media power to deceive the public, I would use my own to set the record straight. I filed the Harvey transcript. Clearly she was dying of her cancer; if she still had any tumors, as she herself admitted, she was not cured. In sad fact, Ms. Keeton died on September 19, 1997, nine months after Paul Harvey announced that she was "virtually free of cancer" (even her own press release had not gone that far). She died as surgeons representing the conventional medicine of which she was so criticical tried to save her life. It may sound morbid, but I made sure that my listeners, at least, heard about it.

WHERE FEAR IS MANUFACTURED

In 1965 not one health or diet book made the Top Ten best-seller list for hardcover nonfiction. These days that list is dominated by such books. Just look over the covers of the national news magazines in one year alone and count the looming heads of the latest medical gurus peddling their own separate paths to health nirvana. Diseases themselves are staple cover stories: herpes, AIDS, cancer, chronic fatigue, germs. The esteemed cover-doctors have usually made no great scientific breakthroughs or discovered a cure for anything. They simply feed our desperation for everlasting wellness, a need that springs from our deeper sense of everlasting illness.

For that, you can blame the media. That's why you buy any health-related product or service, including those offered by your doctor. If you're worried about various routine aspects of your health, you become a potential customer for a massive range of products and services. After all, who doesn't want to believe that good health can be bought at the corner drugstore or health food store? Or that it comes with just the right tests from your doctor. Or from the right exercises with the right shoes and weights at the right fitness club or with the right exercise machine. Your worry may be the reason you bought this book (and thank God you did because now I have a shot at convincing you that you're in better health than you think).

There is no way to assess the magnitude of this convergence of media, health, and marketing, but it touches almost every aspect of your daily life. Medical care itself is an enormous industry, worth five hundred billion dollars a year. Every choice you make, from the water you drink to the food you eat to the air you breathe, taps into your efforts to live a healthy life. You are barraged with tales of the dangers around you as well as advertisements for the purported solutions. Organic, fat-free, low-cholesterol, and high-fiber foods; bottled water, water filters, and air purifiers; exercise machines and health clubs; diet books, fat farms, and shrink shows; an avalanche of supplements, nostrums, and potions. Where do I stop? The purveyors of all this, in one form or another, are the media.

Why did NBC give me a daily network television show? I'm no Oprah, but I do communicate medical information to a broad audience. The network was feeding the monster. The more medical media we consume, the more worried we become, the more health information and products we buy, and the more we want. The money flows and everyone goes home happy—except you.

When someone famous gets sick or dies, we are treated ad nauseum to reams of stories about their illness. There is an entire infrastructure of publicists and consumer groups representing different diseases. They try to get studios, as well as television show and movie writers, to incorporate their diseases into story lines. Greater public awareness translates into more money for research (that's not necessarily a bad thing, but it leads to vast distortions in public policy decisions concerning research). It all takes on a life of its own in a frenzy of paranoia and fear. On the surface, maybe some of this leads you to take better care of yourself or to get the right test. On another level, though, many folks will worry needlessly.

More than a decade ago, Arthur Barsky, the Harvard psychiatrist I mentioned earlier, rightly blasted the medical media hype in a prescient piece in the *New England Journal of Medicine*. He accused it of inducing "a cultural climate of alarm and hypochondria, undermining feelings of well-being." He is well worth another quote here:

It is harder to feel confident about one's health when sensations and dysfunctions one had assumed to be trivial are portrayed as ominous, the herald of some heretofore unrecognized or undiagnosed disease. Feelings of ill health and disability are amplified when every ache is thought to merit medical attention, every twinge may be the prodrome of a malignant disease, when we are told that every mole and wrinkle deserves surgery.

While many of you walk away freaked out over these supposed threats, the media get their ratings and readers. They are never held accountable, because they hide their ignorance behind the protections of free speech. All attempts at recompense by individuals and industries hurt by shoddy health reporting have failed.

WHO FEEDS THE MONSTER?

Where does the news come from? The wire services, first, have a stranglehold because only a few of the country's news organizations have the time or expertise to develop their own stories. When they do, they often foul things up. A Gallup poll in 1990 found that "the most prevalent sources of medical news on television are the wire services and network feeds used by 98 percent of all TV news directors surveyed." What you most often hear on the air are wire stories read straight to the camera with only a word or two cut or changed.

The power of a wire service health writer is astounding. I have never in my twenty-year career seen a reporter first look for and then read the original medical journal report or research project on which a health story is based. My staff does it every day and does it well, without medical training. Believe me, it can be done, and some are starting to do a very credible job in medical reporting. At the moment some, like Reuters, are developing high-quality operations.

Give me a choice and I will take the wire story over the alternatives—industry-generated public relations material masquerading as news. This process is nothing more than an attempt by special-interest groups or individuals to get free exposure by making their spiel sound like news. On some occasions it actually qualifies. My day begins with literally hundreds of such press kits and pitches. It's become our office game to predict which will get some attention and which will not. It's just as upsetting to see legitimate detailed press releases get ignored because they are not written at a low enough level to quickly capture the attention of editors and reporters.

Let me give you a specific example of how all this gets handled by lazy news departments aiding and abetting junk science. Here's a trade term you need to know: VNR, or video news release. *TV Guide* has correctly dubbed it "fake news." It's a videotape story supplied by a public relations firm representing a manufacturer, lawyer, nonprofit organization, or other interest group trying to induce a news department to put it on air. It's a lot easier for a station to use this free footage than to send an expensive camera crew out to cover real news. VNRs were first used in the late 1970s by Hollywood to promote movies; the studios would send movie clips to TV stations that welcomed getting stars into their news broadcasts. The practice then spread beyond La-La Land to become one of the most insidious and dangerous in the news business. Many thousands of different VNRs are sent to stations every year.

Now, I have used video from VNRs many times, but only very carefully and for a very specific purpose. If I need tape of an operation, say, or a generic shot of people eating, I might use such a stock video rather than fight with the assignment desk for a scarce camera crew. It would be unconscionable to use the words that accompany the tape, and I never do. But with all the satellite feeds and videotapes that descend on news departments these days, VNRs are routinely put on the air wholly intact, using the exact words supplied by the interest group. Let's look at one.

A product appears on the market, made from crab shells and promoted as a weight-loss pill. Oh yes, it also cures acne, lowers cholesterol, treats constipation, helps deter tooth decay, slows tumor growth, and lowers high blood pressure. Its function as a fat blocker, though, obviously offers the greatest potential for sales. On June 17, 1997, my station records a satellite feed of an obvious VNR from the manufacturer. It's clearly labeled as what it is—"THIS VNR IS FREE FOR UNRESTRICTED USE." There is a chemist in the piece who mixes a batch of crab-shell powder. "The gel completely envelops the fat, and therefore the pancreatic enzymes that digest the fat can't get at the fat," he intones. "So the fat passes right through the digestive tract and is never absorbed into the body." A writer in the newsroom actually adds his own touch. "If you're looking for a quick and easy way to lose weight," the anchor dutifully reads, "the latest diet trend comes straight out of the sea." The tape, with the quote from the chemist, runs intact and unchallenged. I've got news for you—munching on powdered crab shells will not help you lose weight.

I wish I could say that it's only cub reporters who get fooled. One

VNR went out to stations around the country, generated by lawyers representing women who claimed that their breast implants made them ill. Not only was it totally untrue, inflammatory, and one-sided, it also promoted a bogus and discredited blood test that purported to detect silicone in the bloodstream. We monitored stations nationwide to see if they would question any of this. We were horrified as we reviewed video-tapes of their broadcasts: all the news anchors read the lines—each and every word—as supplied by the lawyers' public relations firm. Worse still, a well-known TV doctor on a New York City news broad-cast, who clearly should have known better, committed the same crime.

WHO'S THE PITCHMAN?

There are lots of people who play doctor on TV. At a cocktail party, I was chatting with a well-known star who played a neurosurgeon on a popular soap opera. A woman approached us and asked him a specific medical question about her health. He and I both rolled our eyes. He told me it happens all the time. It frightens me that I need to remind you, but think of it as a bonus for the hard-earned money you paid for this book: these people are just acting. Why do we believe actors about important health matters? Have reality and fantasy really become so confused?

But I'm not acting, and that creates all kinds of problems with my advertisers. The way radio works is that two or three of the commer-cial time slots on my national show are owned by the company that syndicates the show. We sell those ads to national sponsors. Often they are the first and second commercial you hear in the show. The rest of the commercials are sold by the local radio station that airs the broadcast. Sometimes you can tell which is which. If it is an ad for a local car dealer or pharmacy, you know it came from the local station. I get into a tough spot when a product that I don't feel has merit wants to buy a national slot on my show.

The advertiser wants the air time because those of you who listen to my show are more likely to buy health products. When I tell him I don't like his product, he flips out, sends nasty and threatening let-ters, and sometimes brings out the lawyers. A worse situation is when a caller asks me specifically about a product advertised during the show. Once when that happened and I told the truth, the agency pulled the ad and made a lot of trouble for me.

These things affect me deeply, tie my stomach in knots, and can make my daily life miserable. Even worse is when an advertiser manages to slip through the system, gets on the air, and I'm faced with pulling the ad. Most of the time these products are not dangerous. The only damage is that you waste your money. Very often some of my sharper listeners pick up on it and take me to task. "Hey, Doc, I thought you said to beware of any product that promises to 'burn or melt fat away,'" they'll fax or write. "Well, there's one being advertised on your show."

My latest solution is to tell potential advertisers what I think of their products and therefore what I would say if asked about them on the air. So I can honestly say that anybody advertising on my show nationally has passed muster at least to that extent. But I can't control what happens at the local level with the more than three hundred radio stations that carry my show. If KRAP in Palookaville sells a spot for Dr. Shrunkenkopf's Feel-Good Pills, I won't know about it until the mail starts rolling in.

PLAYING THE SUCKERS: IT'S SO EASY TO BELIEVE

Why do so many people believe so much nonsense? From psychics working the phone lines, to astrology predictions in the newspaper, to the health supplement saviors, we turn to superstition and pseudo-science because they offer such black-and-white alternatives. It's exciting to think you can see past our present reality into strange and astonishing worlds, worlds denied to those nerdy scientist types.

But it takes work and study—lots of it—to earn the real privilege to peer into the wonders and glories of the universe. I promise you the view is invigorating, and I wish I could convey the awe it inspires. If you have ever been moved by great music or art, I offer the tantalizing proposition that to look into the science of our universe is easily as inspiring. One of my listeners once said something that makes sense: Although the twentieth century has catapulted us into a new world, our dark and superstitious past is still very much with us. We are living in the overlap between our future and our past. While we live in the modern world, many of us really have no idea how it all works. The basics of seventeenth-century science baffle most people in the twentieth century. I once had a heated discussion with a secretary at work. "I don't believe in modern chemicals," she declared. I tried to get her to see the difference between fact and belief. No luck.

We fear the involuntary, unfamiliar, uncontrollable, acute, artificial, and undetectable. No wonder we believe those weird urban legends— the poodle in the microwave, the blind alligators in the subway, the Chihuahua that was really a rat, the welder who fused his contact lenses to his corneas. Every few weeks someone calls this one in to me, a legend that has been around for a decade. In a single day, I had to fend off efforts by a veteran assignment desk editor, an assistant news director, a producer, and a promotions director to put it on the air.

It starts with a victim having a drink, passing out, and waking up in a bathtub full of ice. A note is scribbled and left on his chest that says to call 911. A scar creases his back. Paramedics pick him up and tell him his kidney was ripped out by a roving band of bad surgeons because kidneys are worth a lot of money on the street. A variation is the-tourist-and-the-missing-kidneys tale (in fact, murder for organs is a story that continues to circle the globe, usually rich Americans snatching and killing Third World children for their organs). Just think about it a bit and you'll see how preposterous this is. If it makes perfect sense to you, there is hope—you can apply for a job in a major market news department.

At its core, a big part of the problem is our fault. We have become scientifically illiterate, and it will get worse as long as our kids lag in science and math. According to a survey by the American Museum of Natural History, only about one-fifth of adults scored 60 percent or better on a simple twenty-question test of scientific literacy. We're talking questions like: Does the sun go around the Earth, or does the Earth go around the sun? Which travels faster, light or sound?

How about the high school biology teachers instructing your children? Well in another survey, one-third of these teachers said they believed that people with psychic powers could read their thoughts. More than one in five believed in ghosts.

Sorry, but I'm not done finger-wagging yet. More blame goes your way. The media feeds you this junk because you buy it. Have we lost faith in science itself? I guess some things are the same as it ever was, as David Byrne might put it. "The public we are trying to reach is in the cultural state when three-headed cows, Siamese twins, and bearded ladies draw the crowds to the side shows. That is why science is usually reported in short paragraphs ending in 'est.' The fastest or the slowest, the biggest or the smallest, and in any case the newest thing in the world." That was penned by E. E. Slosson, editor at a science news service. He wrote it in 1924.

YOUR HEALTH IS FAILING! YOUR HEALTH IS FAILING!

When the media plays Chicken Little, you're likely to see the sky falling at any moment. In medicine it's called a nocebo. You know what a placebo is—if you believe something or a substance will make you better, it will. If you believe something will make you sick, it will—that's the nocebo. It's an extremely important concept. Once you understand it, you might be able to lighten up and enjoy life just a little more. Here's an easy illustration of how that works: Researchers studied a group of women who believed that one day they would have a heart attack. Over two decades, they turned out to be almost four times as likely to succumb to cardiovascular illness as those without that belief. Sometimes believing can make it so.

Which brings us to the fascinating, sad, and upsetting phenomenon of mass sociogenic illness (MSI), or mass psychogenic illness, or group conversion reaction or, as you know it, mass hysteria. This is how the media has made many of you sick. It is a subject that triggers my ugliest, most threatening hate mail. Many of the diseases we are now going to discuss have taken on cultlike status. Patients approach these illnesses with a religious fervor that defies explanation. Anyone challenging their view of the world, even if only to help, is one size short of Godzilla on the monster chain.

Sociogenic illness has a long history. In the Middle Ages an epidemic of Tanzwuth swept Europe. Sufferers listened to stimulating music that led to wild dancing, seizures, and, eventually, fainting. People got a kick out of this, looking for musicians who could play the right music to bring it on. Descriptions in the seventeenth century documented hyperventilation, rapid heartbeat, palpitations, and sleeplessness. Young single women seemed the most affected. The Italian equivalent was called Tarantism and was supposedly caused by the bite of the tarantula. After the imaginary bite, peasant women would run to the square and begin to dance riotously. Animal-like squealing, obscene shouting, and a desire to be lifted into the air followed. This could go on for days, and evidently the tarantella was written to cure it. The modern-day equivalent might be mass fainting at rock concerts.

You know the sound your finger makes rubbing the rim of a champagne glass? Lay different-sized crystal bowls on their sides, spin, and you have a glass armonica. Ben Franklin is credited with the invention in 1761. Mozart even wrote a short adagio for glass armonica. The sound is eerie and the instrument enjoyed a certain popularity until it was claimed in the early 1800s that it made women faint and become sterile and caused dogs to foam at the mouth. Anton Mesmer played it to help induce trances (that's right—mesmerize). Some said that it even woke the dead. By 1839 most European countries had banned it.

Who can forget koro, or shrinking penis syndrome? The victim panics in the belief that his penis is shrinking into his abdomen and that he will die (to be nonsexist, there actually is a shrinking nipple version for women). Communities go hysterical over this one, and various remedies are desperately tried. As fear spreads, more cases are registered, and massive outbreaks occur. It happens primarily in Southeast Asia but has been documented among Africans, Jews, Canadians, Americans, English, Greeks, and especially Chinese. Medical and psychiatric journal descriptions are fascinating. Thousands of people get swept up in it, and injuries are widespread due to the many methods evolved for cure. Rope burns of the penis are common. An outbreak in Singapore was blamed on eating pork from pigs inoculated with anti–swine fever vaccine. Later it was clearly demonstrated that the number of cases correlated with the number of media reports. In January 1997 an outbreak in Ghana grew out of control when crowds beat twelve supposed sorcerers to death, convinced they had made men's penises shrink. Police with automatic weapons were called in to quell riots, and doctors appeared on state television to explain that penises naturally expand and contract.

Before you laugh at the Third World for its superstitions, look at our own culture. Hundreds of incidents have been reported in this country in recent decades:

- Like the 1968 "June bug outbreak" in a southern textile mill, where victims complained of nausea, fainting, and headaches attributed to bites of bugs that came in on imported fabric. Nobody could find anything.

- Like the "cable lice" allegedly living in computer cables and causing skin problems for Delta Airlines reservation agents. Again, nothing turned up.
- Like the students in a California high school gym class in 1995 who were told that spraying (with a safe, nonvolatile herbicide) had been reported near the school. The spraying never actually happened, but by the time that event was over, thirty-two students had been rushed to three hospitals with the same symptoms.
- Like the Naples, Florida, high school class in 1997, for which a kid baked a white cake and joked that he had included cocaine among the ingredients. Three ambulances and twenty-two kids to the hospital later, tests showed that it was a joke. No cocaine in the cake.

Now that I have your attention, let's investigate. These are all classic cases of mass sociogenic illness. The characteristics in these cases are almost always identical: a triggering event, stressful situations, rapid spread of the symptoms, no deaths, lack of illness in others who shared the environment, a preponderance among females, absence of laboratory or physical evidence, similar symptoms, victims positioned to see each other's reactions, and benign course of the illness. The most common symptoms in all these incidents are dizziness; light-headedness; hyperventilation; nausea; headaches; dry mouth; irritation of eye, nose, and throat; fatigue; drowsiness; weakness; numbness; tingling; chest discomfort; rapid heartbeat; breathing trouble; itchiness; and rash.

WHEN GOOD BUILDINGS GO BAD

I've seen literally dozens of these outbreaks reported over the years by my station alone. The images on your screen feature employees lying on the lawn or sidewalk outside their office building, paramedics and firefighters administering oxygen. It is often attributed to "sick building syndrome." Sure, toxic fumes *could* enter a building's ventilation system. But if that were the case, the problem would spread in a pattern consistent with air flow in the building. That's not what happens in most situations. In at least 75 percent of cases, according to the *New England Journal of Medicine*, no fumes are detected. But the telltale signs of MSI are there. It spreads, again, by line of sight. One person in accounting feels funny, maybe smells something. A coworker sees or hears about it and starts feeling weird. No physical abnormalities are found in the patients or in the building. The symptoms are typical. The diagnosis: MSI.

The syndrome itself is one thing. It's another when it becomes a chronic problem, when workers at one building after another complain of the symptoms. This is no small issue. Surveys of nine thousand workers in European countries uncovered as many as 80 percent reporting symptoms. Experts in occupational medicine estimate that between ten million and twenty-five million American office workers will complain of symptoms characteristic of sick building syndrome. I'll pick just two significant studies on this. One report in the *Journal of Occupational Medicine* found a direct link between the rate of these symptoms and the level of individual stress and job unhappiness. The other study, by Canadian researchers, was still more direct. If, as some believe, the syndrome is caused by undetectable toxin–contaminated indoor air, fresh air should alleviate symptoms. Yet the study found no decrease in symptoms even when the amount of fresh air pumped in from outdoors was *quadrupled*.

So what's going on here? I know a fellow, a heating and air-conditioning contractor, who decided to find out. I will protect his identity for reasons soon to become obvious. One day his company gets a typical call: a sick building and no cause found after $20,000 in tests. Air samples found the indoor air to be cleaner than the air outside. But the employees are threatening to sue anyway. The building owner invests another $105,000 in tests. Still nothing found. The contractor hears one of my radio shows about sick buildings. He mulls it over, talks to the employees in the building, and discovers that symptoms seem to worsen after they see media reports about the syndrome. It's nocebo time.

The contractor calls in all his techs and ladders and fancy-looking equipment. The crew pops a lot of ceiling tiles, makes a lot of noise, and declares to the workers that the problem is finally found and finally fixed. Everyone's symptoms disappear in twenty-four hours. That was a decade ago, and the contractor has used the technique successfully on the most stubborn cases and gone on to teach it to major corporations. He always runs extensive tests first to rule out a legitimate problem, which he says he does find on occasion.

Now that you understand sick building syndrome, consider a related condition. You know it by various names, and you've seen it on the talk show circuit. Its victims appear with masks and oxygen tanks, telling their woes to sympathetic hosts and clucking studio audiences. They call it multiple chemical sensitivity, or environmental illness, or twentieth-century disease. Here's a typical story, as reported by the Associated Press in April 1993. The piece leads with a profile of a married couple in upstate New York. She cannot be near newsprint or magazines without gasping. All her clothes must be aired out before she can wear them. Her husband, suffering from sore knees and arms, is reduced to medical disability. They work in the same building and are diagnosed as "chemically sensitive." Along with forty-one fellow employees, they sue four corporations for $82 million. In 1997 an additional seven hundred employees in the same building file claims for worker's compensation.

When people think their building makes them sick, it can get expensive. In San Rafael, California, federal officials put up money in 1994 to build "ecology housing" for these folks, using government housing money for the disabled. The apartments cost $1.8 million for eleven units. Steel framing, rather than wood, aluminum wrap on everything to prevent chemicals from escaping into the air, ceramic floors, and special "airing rooms" for perfume-laden magazines. Some scientists were outraged at tax dollars spent to accommodate a disability they consider nonexistent. Local and national television reported it straight. I did not. We interviewed the local representative of the federal Department of Housing and Urban Development, who said on camera that he didn't care about the absence of scientific evidence. I went on record on TV and in local newspapers to declare that none of this would work. It may have been a chemically sensitive haven, but soon tenants were complaining of mysterious fumes. They started sleeping in their cars.

Repeated studies of people claiming chemical sensitivity have found no physiological abnormalities or reactions to the allegedly toxic chemicals. They have, however, found high rates of current or past mental disorders.

THE MEDIA MAKES THE MALADY

People get upset about all this. But remember, always look at the *science* behind the hype. Psychiatrists at a Toronto hospital studied a group of patients claiming to be chemically sensitive or to suffer from environmental illness. Nine out of ten reported at least one other media-popularized condition. Some said they had as many as eight of these diseases du jour. The five most frequent conditions were chronic fatigue syndrome, food sensitivity, yeast hypersensitivity syndrome, hypoglycemia, and severe premenstrual syndrome.

Do you get the connection yet? The line of sight spread here is your television. The symptoms are vague and no different from what many of us often feel and shrug off. "These diseases have filled radio and television talk shows, magazines, and newspapers," said Dr. Donna Stewart, the Toronto psychiatrist who led the study. "In some cases the very existence of the condition is doubtful." She considers this to be somatization, or the tendency to experience psychological distress as physical symptoms. "Two-thirds of patients said they first learned of environmental illness through media reports," she adds, "and they sought out practitioners who would confirm their self-diagnosis."

This is where I may lose you or you may hate me, but I'll take the risk. The basic symptoms of breast implant disease, environmental illness, chronic fatigue syndrome, Gulf War syndrome, electromagnetic field syndrome, yeast syndrome, and sick building syndrome are all similar. All defy diagnosis. There are no consistent abnormal lab findings. All emerged suddenly with massive and uncritical media coverage. All respond well to cognitive behavioral therapy. Until proved otherwise, the most logical explanation is that they are all variants of somatization or mass sociogenic illness. Present me with reliable information to the contrary and I promise that I'll change my mind. For now, unfortunately, poor reporting and media distortion affirm my view. To those who believe still, it comes down to the p-word. Prove it.

That's the fundamental beauty of science. Most scientists will change their minds with the evidence. At the moment the best evidence out there tells us that these are media-created epidemics. We have worried and introspected ourselves until we are good and sick. Many "victims" do not want to get well. They enjoy all the attention. And believe me, there are doctors who love this stuff. It's exciting. It makes them feel they have landed at the cutting edge of something new instead of the daily humdrum of life in an HMO (medicine, despite *General Hospital* and *ER*, is mostly not glamour and romance). Of course, many doctors are genuinely concerned and are searching for answers, as they should be. And we always need to make certain there is no physical basis for these conditions. But as of this writing—plain and simple—nothing has convinced me.

THE RISK OF MISCOMMUNICATING RISK

We all measure life in terms of risk. You should not accept "percent rise in risk" as a true judgment of danger. Do you feel better knowing real risks? Statistically, walking is the most unsafe mode of transportation per mile, a hundred times riskier than traveling in a car or a plane. Your annual chances of death by car are 1 in 3,000. Air travel is far safer statistically than road travel. Yet which do you fear more? We feel in control in our cars yet doubt the ability of the pilot who flies the plane.

You need to understand the real odds. For instance, if I told you that the risk of death from leukemia increased 50 percent or even doubled because you lived near power lines, would you worry? (This is not true, by the way, but was once reported as truth.) Look at the real numbers. Your annual chance of death from leukemia is 1 in 12,500. A 50 percent rise in that risk would be 1.5 in 12,500. A full doubling of that risk would mean 2 in 12,500. Doesn't sound so scary, does it?

Reporting risks as a percent change is a common media technique used for dramatic effect. Of course, if your chances of something are 3 in 10, a doubling of risk is very significant. The problem is that numbers are tricky and hard to get across, especially in a land of math illiterates. What is one in one million (1 in 1,000,000)? A disease that occurs that frequently will produce 270 cases in the American population. Three of them on a talk show will make you think it's an epidemic.

I really want to pound this point home because if I'm lucky, you will calm down. When you see a child with neurological damage on TV, and the parents claim it resulted from a vaccination, you get no *real* information. If you knew a child who almost died from a near-fatal allergic reaction to penicillin, would you abandon penicillin for your child?

The communication of risk also appears around clusters of disease, a regular staple of the media. A random distribution of cases can easily be transformed into a dreaded "cancer cluster." A few extra cases of cancer in a town and, bingo, panic. This is very difficult to sort out for reporters and researchers alike. In my experience, most clusters of cancer cases turn out to be due to chance alone. I once explained it this way: A cluster of cancer cases was detected in one neighborhood of a California town. I spread a map of the town on the floor and counted one bean for each case of cancer. I threw the beans on the map. On my first throw, sure enough, the beans randomly distributed themselves with more beans in the neighborhood in question. In addition, all the cancers were of different types. An environmental cause should have induced similar types of cancer. So if you see leukemia, stomach cancer, breast cancer, and melanoma, it is most likely a random distribution of events. Take a nickel and start flipping. You can get many heads in a row.

We look for ominous causes of disease-related clusters. But when the outcome is happy, we tend to accept coincidence as the cause. Recently, when an Omaha hospital registered the births of five sets of twins in one day and a New York hospital had six sets on another day, everybody thought this was charming. Nobody looked for a toxic trigger.

DR. DEAN'S CONSUMER GUIDE TO THE MEDIA

We are going to get down and dirty. This is what you need to know, based on my experience in the media and medicine. For this alone, you can be happy you coughed up the dough for this book.

Expert Credentials Are Almost Never Verified by the Media

Degrees can be bought. No one has ever asked to see mine. That should be your warning. And even having an alphabet soup of degrees after a name doesn't necessarily mean credibility. Credentialed people can lie, cheat, steal, and be greedy as well as the next guy.

Beware of the Breakthrough

Penicillin was a breakthrough. Polio vaccine was a breakthrough. Doctors don't talk breakthroughs. News anchors do. True breakthroughs are rare and can only be judged with the passage of time.

Major Claims Require Major Proof

One study never tells all. Casual investigation doesn't count. Press releases by publicity seekers don't count. Hundreds of experiments by the best scientists and institutions in the business *do* count, and even then, firm conclusions can be elusive.

Two Events at the Same Time Do Not Constitute Cause and Effect

Most people killed in a car crash ate french fries during the previous week. Nobody would suggest a connection. Get the picture?

Some Research Is Better Than Others

In medical investigation there is a clearly defined hierarchy in reliability. Laboratory and animal research is lower in relevance than research on humans. Thalidomide did not cause birth defects in dogs, on which it was first tested. Many of the scary reports you hear on the news are based on epidemiological studies, next on the ladder. But these can only suggest relationships—they never tell us true cause and effect. For instance, people who shop in health food stores are healthier, but not because of their shopping habits. That's because they usually have more money and healthier lifestyles overall.

Most studies you hear about are either case-controlled, where sick people are compared with healthy people, or cohort studies, where huge numbers of people are observed for many years, their lifestyles and habits carefully charted. Yet even these studies rarely give us the definitive answers we crave. The best we can do is the controlled study, where some subjects get a treatment or substance and others don't, and the subjects don't know which group they're in.

Even with all this, controversies linger and are settled by the weight of many, many studies—not by the six o'clock news. Keep in mind that size and quality matter. Lots of subjects in controlled studies sets the gold standard. Don't fall for the tyranny of the anecdote, the last refuge of the insupportable claim.

To be fair, an informed media can actually help you with your health, and it does happen. There *is* a lot you can learn, as long as you pick your resources with care. But in the end, remember that man bites dog is news. It's not news that polio and smallpox are gone. It becomes news when some mom thinks—mistakenly—that her child's illness was caused by the vaccines that were administered, and she runs to the nearest television station to talk about it.

In my business, fear is the name of the game. So don't be a sucker. Don't live your life scared.

2

NUTRITION MADE EASY

Eat What You Want and Still Be Healthy

———

You are what you eat. Is it really that simple?

Well, yes and no. Because you ask, the expression that haunts us seems to originate with an eighteenth-century French linguist, musician, and judge. You might never know of him but for two traits that make him relevant here. Like any Frenchman worth his passport, Jean Anthelme Brillat-Savarin had a love of good food—and an inexplicable lifelong fascination with medicine and its practitioners. "I am above all a lover of doctors," he once said. "It is almost a mania with me." In his 1825 book, *The Physiology of Taste, or Meditations on Transcendental Gastronomy*, he left as his legacy the follow-ing line: "Tell me what you eat, and I will tell you what you are." Slightly more eloquent than its descendent. Of course, if you prefer, he also left us this: "A dessert course without cheese is like a beautiful woman with only one eye." All right, one more, just to get your day going: "One can learn to cook but one must be born knowing how to roast."

Roasting aside, a little circumspection would be wise as we cast about for perfect nutrition. It might not exist. After all, it would not serve the survival of the species. A slight change in the environment or the weather and things could go haywire. Imagine northern European Cro-Magnon man unable to digest meat. Yet when people decided to stop roaming and settle down, grains and plants seemed just fine.

I've watched passionate vegetarians try to convert their dogs to meat-free diets. As carnivores, dogs are beautifully designed for meat. When a primary source of game disappears, carnivores die. Unlike them, our omnivore physiology gives us flexibility that allows us to endure in an incredible variety of environments. Our choice of foods *does* affect us, but those choices figure among many factors that determine health and longevity. Some you can control; others you can't. Otherwise, how to explain those centenarians who eat fat, get no exercise, and smoke? Jan Breslow of Rockefeller University calls it the Winston Churchill syndrome, referring to the prime minister's ninety-one-year-long stay on earth despite a lifetime of unhealthy habits: "some sort of natural immunity to cardiovascular disease, despite the worst that the environment, or they themselves, can do." After all, people with *low* cholesterol also die prematurely of heart attacks. But food is one of the few things we can control that is very likely to alter our bodies. After all, besides air and water, what else do we put *into* our bodies?

BOW BEFORE HIGHER POWERS

There is more to food than personal choice. Other forces are at play. Yes, my vegetarian sons gobble their greens, and they definitely have their favorites. But there is a logic to our different food preferences. We can learn to like lots of things we think we would never touch, and that's good (later I'm going to ask you to do just that). The reason for all this? From the biological and evolutionary point of view, if we all liked the same thing and that food source dried up, we'd be in deep doo-doo. So it seems there is some genetic programming here.

Programming for food preference happens early in life. In 1928 pediatrician Clara Davis wondered whether kids, free of Mom's intervention, would instinctively figure out the best foods to eat. Back then, parents waited until Baby was at least a year old before introducing solids. Davis asked whether infants could handle real food and, if so, which foods. She assembled orphans between seven and nine months of age who, until then, had been exclusively breast-fed by wet nurses. She offered them a choice of thirty-four fresh, unseasoned foods selected from meat, seafood, cereal, eggs, fruits, and vegetables. She excluded premixed dishes and supersugary foods. Heavily processed foods didn't exist then.

What suited the infant palate? Nine out of ten times, they chose fourteen of the thirty-four foods offered. Of those fourteen, nine were the favorites by far: bone marrow, raw milk, eggs, banana, apples, oranges, cornmeal, whole wheat, and oatmeal. Davis conducted the experiment for a year. Throughout that time, the kids grew normally and were just fine. (By the way, I'm not suggesting your kids should eat whatever they want. Most kids today would head for the sweet sodas, fruit drinks, potato chips, and candy that were not among Davis's menu options.) Within a restricted range of unprocessed natural foods, it appears that kids can make the right choices. You should not let go of your authority, but the research is intriguing. It seems that we come hardwired for certain foods from the time our parents unwrap us.

At least part of our ability to taste sweetness and bitterness, for example, is inarguably genetic. The taste for sweets is complex, probably involves many genes, and is harder to study than the taste for bitterness, which has fewer gradations and may depend on one simple gene, just like the color of your eyes. You can plot your family tree with this. Some people cannot even taste certain bitter-tasting chemicals because they lack the appropriate gene. I remember an experiment with one of these chemicals called PROP (6-n-propylthiouracil) in elementary school science class (yes, once schools did such things). I was amazed that my best friend couldn't taste its bitterness, while I had to spit out the foul-tasting stuff.

Many foods have naturally occurring PROP-like chemicals as part of their flavor molecules. In adults the ability to taste PROP has been correlated with food preferences. If you have that gene, caffeine tastes more bitter. The taste of some salt substitutes, as well as white sugar and saccharin, is stronger. Even milk and certain cheeses taste more intense. If you are sensitive to PROP, you will probably not like certain foods. If you cannot taste PROP, you will probably prefer certain stronger-tasting foods. In a 1954 study, PROP-tasters did not like sauerkraut, turnips, spinach, strong cheese, cottage cheese, buttermilk, kale, kohlrabi, pumpkin, curded cheese, and whipped cream.

PASS THE MUD, PLEASE

I can't pass up the temptation to digress here into the How-Weird-Can-Your-Body-Get Department. I love when I can out-tabloid the tabloids and still be faithful to the facts. The body is a wondrous thing, and it's worth taking a moment to explore one of its stranger secrets. Let's talk *pica*.

Never heard the word? It's Latin for "magpie," a bird that likes to carry off and eat strange things. Medically, it is a compulsive and unusual craving for nonnutritive substances, but it may be more complex than that. Medicine names picas by tacking the Greek suffix *phagia* to the back of whatever weird stuff the patient eats. Thus eating dirt is called geophagia; eating ice cubes is pagophagia; eating dust is coniophagia; eating cigarette ashes is stachtophagia. Those are the tasty examples. Try some of these for dinner, compiled from the medical literature: stones and pebbles, hair, air freshener, baking soda, cardboard, cement, chalk, coal, paper (ranging from toilet paper to the pages you are now reading; I hope you'll taste the difference), plaster, rubber (one of my callers once said her child chewed bicycle tires), plastic, toothpaste, and wood.

The condition is usually listed in psychiatric texts, but probably erroneously. From a cultural, historical, and even nutritional perspective, eating soil, for example, is not as abnormal as it sounds. In fact, it is a common—and global—practice. A typical case history is a Houston woman who craved certain soils and clays. She would drive 200 miles for her favorite types, hiding her spot from other geophagic friends. The Pomo Indians of California and Italians in Sardinia traditionally mixed clay with acorns to make bread. Acorns contain a lot of tannic acid, which is neutralized by the clay, thus making the bread palatable. Archaeological sites in Zambia show that Homo Erectus was a clay eater. Some Africans prefer soils from termite mounds. Chemical analysis has discovered high levels of kaolinitic clays in these soils. The locals used it for stomach upsets. Think about the name. The Kaopectate you take for your bad tummy uses these same clays as a base.

We're not talking seasoning here. Clays and soils can nullify toxins, and they can also supply specific nutrients. A team of chemists and physical geographers examined soils in Zimbabwe, China, and North Carolina that were said to be medicinal. The soils from China and North Carolina contained minerals like iron, potassium, and calcium, all commonly missing in the local diets. These are specific soils from specific regions. I am not suggesting you head for the backyard to gobble soil from the garden.

Iron deficiency can push people to eat weird things. In fact, pica may occur in up to 50 percent of iron-deficient individuals—and that translates into millions of people. You can be lacking in iron because you don't eat enough of it. Far worse, though, is that some people with iron deficiencies have internal bleeding—mostly from an internal polyp or undetected colon cancer. Any patient with pica needs to be checked for iron deficiency. If it is present, iron supplements will cure the pica where there is no bleeding.

Medical journal case studies show how serious pica can be. A twenty-two-year-old woman walked into the emergency room after three interminable weeks of nausea, vomiting, and back pain. The attending physician discovered a hard ball in her stomach. She had been self-medicating, chewing half a sock per day. She was cured with iron supplements. How about the forty-year-old man who chewed and swallowed forty toothpicks a day. If his supply ran short, he gnawed on matches.

Then there was the thirty-five-year-old man bleeding from both ends, his nose and his hemorrhoids. He had perhaps the most common of all picas, pagophagia. He was chewing five trays of ice a day. Iron and blood transfusions fixed his problem. Every time I mention this condition on the air, we save lives. You surely know people who chew ice; they should be checked by their doctors for iron deficiency. Curiously, nobody knows why a lack of iron can drive people to chew frozen water. When your body talks, even if it sounds like gibberish, it is usually trying to tell you something.

EAT RODENTS, LIVE FOREVER?

What can we learn from the diets of one-hundred-year-olds and other remarkable seniors? Does what they eat contain the secret to their longevity? Consider the Wu Zhenglu Nutritional Guide. An octogenarian in China's Jiangxi province, Wu discloses his dietary secret to long life: rats. He makes his living catching and selling the little critters to eager customers who want to turn them into . . . crispy critters. Before you toss this book in disgust, consider that Wu swears by them as a food staple, and Wu runs as fast as a young man, can carry 110 pounds on his back, and boasts a clear mind and fast reaction time. So start a fad.

Many people naively embrace any diet and health program, automatically believing that it will produce results. Not so. I wish I could say we have observed something consistent and statistically verifiable in long-lived people. Then I could recommend it to the world, as do so many food, diet, and health gurus. That's not what this book is about. I just cannot tell you that a healthy diet will guarantee you a long life.

I had a friend who began each day with a thick slab of bacon, eggs, whiskey, and tobacco. He hardly exercised and died well into his nineties, comfortable in his favorite chair. Bir Narayan Chaudhuri of Nepal passed on recently at the unconfirmed but nonetheless impressive age of a hundred and forty-one. He was a regular smoker and lived on a diet of pork, vegetables, and rice.

At this point, you should be saying that these isolated incidents prove nothing. You are right, of course. So I submit for your critical (I hope) consideration one of the few studies of folks over the age of one hundred. A University of Georgia investigation of mentally intact centenarians found that they went on diets less often and therefore were less likely throughout their lives to experience fluctuations in weight. They relied less on the news media for nutrition information and more on their physicians and family. Although they ate breakfast more regularly and ate slightly more vegetables, they were less likely to eat low-fat diets or to comply with nutritional guidelines designed to prevent chronic illness. Finally, they generally did not shovel in vitamins or other supplements, nor did they meet the government's recommended daily allowance for calcium. They did meet it for vitamins C and A and protein.

OK, so we're not exactly discovering the fountain of youth from these eating patterns. What else could be going on?

IT'S NOT FAIR, THEY GET PARIS, TOO

Call it the French Paradox. Despite all those creamy sauces and red meats and cheeses and pâté and croissants and pastries and cigarettes, the French have almost the lowest rate of heart disease in the world, just a notch above the Japanese. They also live almost as long. Yet they have higher blood pressure and higher cholesterol levels than Americans. Their rate of obesity rivals America's, and they gobble many more pills than we do, especially antidepressants.

Researchers are still scrambling to explain this one. Every few months, a new "definitive" study claims to have the answer. One declared that the French are genetically resistant to heart disease. Another found that they underreport heart disease. Another said that different regions of France have different rates of heart disease. Of course, what you hear most is . . . the wine. Oh, the wine. They drink a staggering amount per capita, more than three gallons of pure alcohol equivalent per person per year.

Researchers got the bright idea in 1996 to assess how the French measure up against U.S. federal nutritional guidelines, including daily intake of cholesterol, carbohydrates, and fat. The French flunked miserably. For instance, nine out of ten Frenchmen exceed our guidelines for fat intake. Our French friends fall into what American nutritionists would call a "high-risk population with a poor diet." But they get the last laugh as they dodge our rates of cardiovascular disease.

The diet nags—if you'll permit me the expression—tell us that if we eat this and don't eat that, we all will live long and healthy lives. My point, as always, is that it is not so simple. My belief, as of this writing, is that there are many, many factors that are beneficial to your health. No single magic diet will give you a second century. Nor will you get there simply by avoiding certain allegedly bad foods.

The answer may lie not in what you eat but in how many different things you eat. The University of Michigan and L'Institut Scientifique et Technique de l'Alimentation in Paris together hit it on the head: dietary diversity. Americans are among the least creative eaters in the world. We exist on a narrow range of foods. It always amazes me how many different species of edible fruits and vegetables there are in the world and how few of them you find here. On top of that, we slide into deep ruts concerning food choice, eating the same foods over and over again.

This is what both schools found in their jointly conducted survey: Nine out of ten French people ate a "highly varied diet," representing all five food groups (FYI: Cookies, candy, cake, chips, and Cheetos are not the basic five food groups. Meat and fish, grains, fruits, vegetables, and dairy are). Only three out of ten Americans can make that same claim. Unlike Americans, the French routinely consume ten different kinds of meat and fish, fifteen different milk and cheese products, ten grains, fifteen fruits and vegetables, and five alcoholic and four non-alcoholic beverages.

Sorry, you can't count brewskis and beer as separate items in *your* diet.

The more diverse your diet, the more likely you are to be getting all the important nutrients, including some about which we are only just learning. For instance, lots of you take a multiple vitamin supplement, which undoubtedly contains beta carotene, a form of vitamin A. I've heard it a thousand times: "I can't eat right, so I'll take vitamins to cover myself." I've got news for you: beta carotene is only one of many carotenes, like gamma and delta and lycopene. These others are available in natural foods and not in pills. The best available studies suggest that beta carotene may actually *increase*, not decrease, the risk of cancer. Meanwhile, other studies show that fruits and vegetables, with all their naturally occurring vitamins and phytochemicals, can prevent cancer. I made my choice long ago.

EATING THE RIGHT WAY

Go ahead, blame it on Mom. We develop our eating styles when we're young. Think about how you eat now—bolting down your coffee and bagel on your way to work—and I'll bet you could follow it backward to bolting down your cereal and milk on your way to school. The family table is often a battleground, where Mom dispenses bribes, threats, and rewards along with the broccoli. There is growing research suggesting something called an "intergenerational transfer" of eating styles. Obese parents may apply eating practices that foster obesity in their children. Of course, obesity is partially genetic, but only partially. According to a University of Illinois study, controlling mothers who prompted their kids with pats on the back, praise, or criticism made things worse. These kids ate faster and ate more. Fatter moms tended to be more like this. Their kids were fatter.

Now, how many hours have I just saved you on a therapist's couch?

Mother might have done you a bigger favor by teaching you some basics about what your body needs from the food she was trying to shovel into you. Food is relatively simple, from the chemist's point of view. Your body derives energy only from fat, protein, or carbohydrate. Your digestive system quickly breaks down those substances into fatty acids, amino acids, and simple sugars, respectively. Your body cannot tell whether an amino acid came from corn or from a cow. Or whether a sugar came from a lollipop or a lemon. Try this metaphor: A construction crew tears down a magnificent cathedral into a pile of bricks, then does the same to the tenement next door. All the bricks are dumped together. The foreman picks one. From which building did it come? A difficult call.

Nutrition really is not more complicated than that. We only make it that way.

SECRETS OF THE CENTURIES

There is nothing new under the sun as far as health fads go. We've been there, done that for every diet fad that comes along. We just keep changing the names, and they just keep coming back. A few years back, the biggest diet going was the cabbage diet, supposedly created by doctors at a midwestern hospital for good health and weight loss. Cato the Elder and his cabbages actually beat them by a couple of millennia.

Hundreds of years before Christ, wealthier Romans ate mostly meat and fish. Scurvy, from a lack of vitamin C, was rampant. Cato, a Roman dignitary, grew cabbages, wrote about them, and really and truly cured fellow Romans with them. Of course, the secret was that cabbages are a good source of vitamin C. Foodism was born.

Possibly the godfather of foodism in our culture was a fellow named Sylvester Graham, born in 1794 in Connecticut to a family of passionate gospel preachers. Graham had a force of personality that made him both unlikeable and charismatic, a dangerous combination of character traits matched today in many of his modern counterparts. To Sylvester, eating right could save the sinner's soul. White flour, alcohol, and meat were the devil's work (meat, by the way, triggered sexual excess). The Sylvester regimen featured cold-water baths, hosings, firm beds, chew-chew-chewing food, no liquids with meals, and chastity. Vegetarians' bodies did not rot when dead, he taught. His most famous gift to the future was the graham cracker.

There were others. Father Kneipp in Bavaria and his water cures (which you can still find today in Germany); James Caleb Jackson, inventor of granola and the first to put that hose right in Toxin Central, the colon; C. W. Post and his magic grains. But these gentlemen paled alongside Dr. John Harvey Kellogg, the first modern media health faddist. At the time, he was both a Grahamite (certainly better than being a Graham Cracker) and a water man. Then twenty-five, he was hired by an Adventist health institute in Battle Creek, Michigan, and the Battle Creek Sanitarium was born. (You may have seen some of this in the movie *The Road to Wellville*.) Kellogg attacked his patients with a few new twists on the whole-wheat-vegetable mania of his forebears. The sanitarium grew into a lush resort with animals and orchestras and a constant stream of his inventions. It drew the elite of the day. Rockefellers and Fords mixed with congressmen, actors like Eddie Cantor and Johnny (Tarzan) Weissmuller, aviator Amelia Earhart, and explorer Admiral Byrd, the gelatin Knoxes with the baby-food Gerbers. They all fell under Kellogg's ever-evolving spell of diet and health. No sick or infectious patients were admitted.

All of this will ring bells with you still. Kellogg put a big priority on roughage and fiber—he coined the term *nature's broom*—but believed they weren't sufficient for the job. Meat putrefied inside us and clogged our bowels, he insisted. Those bowels required not only multiple daily cleansings, but sometimes surgical removal. On any given day, Kellogg himself performed as many as twenty partial colectomies. His fascination was unwavering—he is said to have shared with guests a sample of his perfect stools, wrapped in a dinner napkin.

It should be no surprise that he developed a practice of which you no doubt have heard: colonics, or enemas. These were *real* enemas, the cleansing, 30-quart kind. He took his own medicine routinely. Many of his inventions pumped water into the bowels of his patients at ever-increasing flows. But his sanitarium also made some less purging discoveries. His wife, Ella Eaton, came up with meatless recipes and toasted wheat and grain products that led to today's breakfast cereals. Kellogg's brother, Will, began Kellogg's corn flakes. Though hundreds of eat-right-get-rich schemes ensued from copycats, nutritionists today would approve their emphasis on whole grains.

Kellogg's concepts of colonics are still with us. I get many calls from people who have been warned that their colons are clogged and poisoning them. Colonic therapists are a mainstay of contemporary diet and health faddism, despite the fact that modern colonoscopy has shown us that our colons, in fact, are not encrusted and clogged. I once interviewed a colon therapist who insisted, ridiculously, that he could see ten-year-old corn flakes in the outflow from clients' colons. Kellogg would be appalled at the fate of the flake.

Other fads blew through prewar America. As fast as scientists unraveled the basics of nutrition, the faddists came up with new ways to exploit them. In 1912 Casimir Funk found that pigeons recovered from beriberi by eating wheat bran. He named this new substance vita-amine, and others ran wild with the discovery. Mucusless diets, raw foods, acid and alkaline eating systems, food combining—they all swept across the landscape and should sound familiar because they are very much with us still. The last great health titan of the mid-century was Gaylord Hauser, the first to popularize liquid diets, juice bars, and laxatives as the route to beauty and health. He rubbed shoulders with Hollywood's elite who bought his nonsense that physical beauty was somehow linked to liquid diets, elimination diets, and raw foods.

If you've never heard of these people, that's fine by me because maybe you'll realize that in a few years no one will have heard of today's nutrition gurus. They'll be footnotes in some doctor's commonsense guide to how to oil your bionic colon.

YOU SAY YOU WANT A REVOLUTION

Food fads faded in the years after World War II. The country was wrestling with other issues. The revolution was coming, though, and no one could have been prepared for the upheaval. The sixties were more than Vietnam, politics and drugs, music and art, hair and clothes. Along with the cultural eruptions, there was much to make Kellogg proud. The hippies didn't invent whole wheat, natural foods, or vegetarianism, but they resurrected everything "old" they could find. Anything was worth a try, as long as it was not dictated by the "system."

American medicine and all other "straight" institutions were mistrusted. Nature was in vogue—farewell to chemicals and processed foods. I went for it all, grew organic and went vegetarian. I ate granola. Food co-ops, whole foods, whole wheat, brown rice, and brown sugar were happening. White sugar and white flour were the cause of all the world's problems.

Diet health mania took off. Diets to combat hypoglycemia. Diets to prevent aging. Diets to pump up energy. High-protein/low-carbohydrate diets. Low-protein/high-carbohydrate diets. Like the basic law of physics—for every action there is an equal and opposite reaction—nutrition books and their promises kept us following the bouncing ball back and forth. Almost four decades later, the boomers have aged and taken these ideas with them into the mainstream. But the ball still bounces back and forth. I hope I can keep you from getting dizzy.

WHO YOU GONNA TRUST?

As I may have ranted—I mean mentioned—once or twice in the first chapter, most of your health information comes, inaccurately, from the media. Nutrition is no different. One survey recently found that 80 percent of women polled relied on the media as their primary source of nutrition information. Slightly more than half also took information from food packaging, about one-quarter, from Mom, and 11 percent, from the Internet. A physician as the main supplier of nutrition information figured way down on the list.

You would expect to turn to the professionals, right? The problem is that the most meaningless term in medicine is *nutritionist.* The National Council Against Health Fraud ran a thirty-two-state survey of nutritionists listed in the Yellow Pages. Nearly half had spurious degrees, claiming to be doctors of nutrimedicine, food counselors, or certified nutritionists. All these are meaningless titles. The institutions from which they graduated sounded reputable, but it ends there. Diploma mills abound. Dogs and cats, literally, have been awarded degrees by some of these outfits. Anybody can hang out a shingle as a nutritionist and not worry about regulation.

When I started doing radio, I retrained myself. I read the nutrition books and subscribed to all the respected scientific nutrition journals as well as lay publications. I can tell you two things: First, the amount you need to know about nutrition to eat right and stay healthy is easy to find and can be quickly mastered by anyone. Second, if you need help, you can do what a physician does when he or she needs help with nutrition: consult a registered dietitian, or R.D. Dietitians do know more about the subject than the average physician. These nutrition specialists have bachelor's and master's degrees and may have medical degrees as well.

Because the basics of nutrition are so easy and straightforward, the impostors and promoters must keep you intimidated and confused. If they cannot convince the public of some new twist, how are they going to sell books? So the cyclical waves of "nutritional" diets just keep on coming. As soon as one generation forgets the high-protein mania of the past, out comes an "improved" version by a new name. We are a culture that hungers for the latest model, and health and diet fads are no different.

So who you gonna trust? As with everything else in this book, we'll use nature, common sense, and science as our guide.

TIME FOR FAT, THE BIG ENCHILADA

I watched one night in awe and admiration as Bob Pritsker, an old college chum, worked his magic. In his legendary Manhattan restaurant, this master chef cooked for the stars, but on this particular evening I had corralled him into creating an extraordinary dinner on my stove. At the moment he was preparing a secret sauce to pour over micron-thin slices of radish. He sprinkled and dashed ingredients with the care of a seventeenth-century Chinese apothecary. Then the cherished container of clarified butter. His blue eyes glinted as he poured forth his liquid gold and uttered the ancient wisdom that plagues us today: "No fat, no joy."

Why does fat haunt us so? Why does it maintain its stranglehold on our bellies and coronary arteries? Because it *tastes* good. It *feels* good. It gives that melt-in-your-mouth sensation that elevates so many dishes to another level. That word *melt* implies the essence of fat: smooth, rich, moist. Fats have flavors all their own, whether olive oil, butter, or meat fat. Fat allows cooks to heat food evenly to temperatures above that of boiling water, which in turn creates entirely new flavors. Then there's that crispy, crunchy, brown thing. It prevents sticking and seals in moisture. Have you had enough? Do you succumb to this savory seduction? Can you escape? Should you?

Welcome to Dr. Dean's (In)Complete Course in Nutrition in four words. Without fat, you die. It's more than mere blubber around your waist. Fat enables you to absorb fat-soluble vitamins, like A, D, and E. Certain fatty acids are necessary for life, growth, and healthy organs and skin. Fat is compact energy. You need fat on your frame for insulation and padding. Your body uses it to manufacture sex hormones, estrogen, skin oil, bile, cell walls, and even the coverings of nerves.

All fats, though, are not alike. Unsaturated fats are oils that become liquid at room temperature. They come only from the vegetable kingdom. Saturated fats, like butter, are usually solid at room temperature and come from the animal kingdom, with a couple of exceptions (coconut and palm oil). We can take an unsaturated, liquid vegetable oil, pump it with hydrogen—saturate it—and turn it into a solid, like margarine.

Once upon a time, we thought that the key to good health was simply eating unsaturated fats and avoiding saturated fats. As we learned more about the third fatlike substance that concerns us—cholesterol—things got more complicated. So let's take a cholesterol break.

A quick run through the rudiments. Cholesterol is a waxlike, fat-like substance found only in animals—in fact, in every cell in every body. You cannot trim it off the meat you are planning to cook tonight because it is bound in the very cells of the beef. Bad press aside, your body needs cholesterol to make hormones and to perform other critical functions. The liver manufactures between 1 and 2 grams of cholesterol each day, which is then circulated through the blood-stream.

There is good cholesterol, HDL (high-density lipoprotein), which goes through cells and tissues and then heads back to the liver to be processed, destroyed, and removed from the body. That's a good thing, and you want high levels of HDL in your blood. Then there's LDL cholesterol (low-density lipoprotein), which goes to the cells where it is needed. But some of the LDL, for reasons we don't completely understand, gets stuck to certain spots inside your arteries before it can get where it is supposed to go. Higher levels of LDL in your system means that you are more likely to have cholesterol clogging your arteries. HDL is such a good guy that it can even clean up some of the LDL from your arteries and push it back to your liver. But it is always better to have low LDL levels rather than rely on HDL to clean up the LDL.

Ready? All together now: High HDL, good. High LDL, bad.

Now that you're ready for the medical board questions on the science of cholesterol and fat, how are you going to adjust your diet? Most scientist agree that too much saturated fat (animal fat, cheese, and dairy) increases your risk of heart disease. There is an easy solution for that one—just decrease the foods you eat that contain saturated (animal) fat. If you do that, though, your body will start craving calories from sugars and carbohydrates, foods like pasta, rice, potatoes, and bread.

Here's the problem. You will then tend to consume more calories with these foods because the fat you gave up was more satisfying per calorie—remember Chef Pritsker? Studies confirm that in fact that's just what people do. One investigation showed that those on low-fat diets—less than 30 percent fat—overcompensated for that reduction by eating more calories from carbohydrates than they had cut out as fat. Net results: lower fat intake, more calories overall. How about those no-fat wonder potato chips fried in fake fat? Studies found that people simply ate more of them. Even when they were not told that the chips were no-fat, the body somehow increased the appetite to adjust for the fewer calories in the chips.

Just to complicate your life further, you actually *lower* the level of good (HDL) cholesterol by eating more carbohydrates. Remember, low HDL levels raise the risk of heart disease. In response, the diet mavens recommended that you add polyunsaturated vegetable oils to make up for the reduction in saturated fat. Ah, but then scientists discovered that by doing that, you also lowered your (good) HDL.

Worse still, a 1998 study of sixty thousand women in Sweden found that polyunsaturates increased the risk of breast cancer. That study found that heart-healthy fish oils *also* increase breast cancer risk, while saturated fats—the original villain for heart disease—turned out not to boost the rate of breast cancer.

Confused? You should be. The medical profession is just as confused. Because, once again, diet and health are not so simple.

Here's where we are now: You will lower your HDL when you decrease saturated fats, increase carbohydrates, or increase unsaturated fats. One day we may know which of these strategies is better for your heart. Unfortunately, no one can tell you now.

WHAT'S IT ALL ABOUT, DEANIE?

What should you do about your cholesterol levels? Should you get them screened regularly? Should you even worry about it?

In 1991 the *Journal of the American Medical Association* (JAMA) concluded that there was "no direct evidence that a nationwide cholesterol screening program for the elderly would lessen overall morbidity and would be worth the cost." If all Americans over the age of sixty-five—the group most affected by all this—followed the recommended cholesterol screening program, it would cost billions of dollars and possibly not offer any dividend.

In 1994 JAMA tried again: "High cholesterol levels appear not to be important risk factors for coronary heart disease in people over 70." If we can be sure that cholesterol levels are of no use after age seventy, that should help allay some fears about the issue. Indeed, it may be reasonable to try to lower cholesterol levels in middle-aged people with heart disease or in people who have high blood cholesterol. But it has not been shown that anybody else would benefit from lowering their cholesterol.

In the late 1990s, a succession of studies emerged that challenged the idea that your cholesterol level automatically determines your mortality. One study in Boston looked at 2,535 patients entering the hospital. Of them, 42 percent had good cholesterol levels (under 200). Yet 64 percent of *those* folks had angiographically documented heart disease (narrowing of the coronary arteries). Of those patients with heart disease, 32 percent had *desirable* cholesterol levels.

What should you conclude? Try this: that when you rely too much on the numbers game, you could lull yourself into a false sense of security or generate a false panic. Your risk for heart disease is way more complex than a cholesterol test. You cannot rely on either a low cholesterol value to protect you or a high value as an automatic death sentence. Over large populations, there are shifts in certain directions, but no individual can know whether such shifts in the blood will mean anything to him or her.

. . . AND NOW, THE BACKFIRE REPORT

Enough with the cholesterol already. Let's get back to fat. We should take a look at the best research out there, then maybe we can figure out what would happen if everybody managed to get on a low-fat diet. Suppose that over a lifetime, every American ate a diet where only 30 percent of the calories came from fat, as recommended by the American Heart Association. As a country, we are very far from that level. Some high-profile doctor-gurus say we won't see much effect until we get down to an impossibly low level of *10 percent*! In 1991 researchers at the medical school of the University of California at San Francisco mathematically spun out the 30-percent-for-all hypothesis. What would happen?

Life expectancy for women would increase by an average of three months. Life expectancy for men would increase by an average of four months. That's all, folks.

You can imagine, or maybe you can't, the ruckus this kicked up in the medical community. The authors understood the reaction. "These results may be disappointing to those who believe that following a healthier diet will protect them from early death," said Warren S. Browner, the lead researcher. "For people who feel better about themselves by focusing on diet or exercise, that's wonderful. But not everybody is like that and I worry about patients who say they feel so badly and are so guilty because they've cheated on their low-fat diet."

Some doctors focus on saturated rather than total fat. In 1994 a study published in the *Archives of Internal Medicine* reported a similar mathematical calculation for 10 percent saturated fat intake levels. You ready? In healthy men, it would extend life from eleven days to five months; for women, from three and a half days to two months. The same study, by the way, found that quitting smoking would extend life between two to four years.

Dr. Ronald Krauss, head of the American Heart Association Nutrition Committee, says it better. "We now know that individual responses to food cannot be predicted reliably on the basis of studies of large populations of people." The reason the clinical studies are so confusing and inconsistent is that each of us is unique genetically and we respond differently to various nutrients. Believe it or not, there are genetic differences in the way people react to low-fat diets. Those with a metabolic and genetic profile that puts them at high risk may respond positively to very-low-fat diets. "But the remaining two-thirds of the population," says Krauss, "would show minimal benefit and for some it would be harmful." He summarized his conclusions:

Drop fat below 30 percent of calories, and one-third of you *may* benefit, one-third will experience neither help nor harm, and one-third will be harmed. Stick that in your no-fat yogurt smoothie and smoke it, although I don't endorse smoking.

Oh, one other thing, just in case you're on the fence. Two reliable studies by the U.S. Department of Agriculture found that half of the women they examined who managed to get those fats down to 30 percent did not get the recommended daily amount of vitamins A and E, folic acid, calcium, iron, or zinc. In the quest to reduce fat, many low-fat foods sacrifice nutrients. If you still insist on low fat, you should look for those nutrients in fruits and vegetables, whole grains, and skim milk.

What, you want more? I offer this next one not to scare the hell out of you but to keep you skeptical of diet kings claiming to know all the answers about anything as complex as nutrition and disease. In 1998 a Harvard Medical School research study appeared in JAMA and dropped a bomb still ringing in the ears of cardiovascular specialists. It seems that saturated fat—that villain of villains—reduced the risk of stroke. Each 3 percent *increase* in total fat was accompanied by a 15 percent *decrease* in stroke risk. It's not completely surprising news— low-fat diets in Japan are associated with very high rates of strokes. This is not genetic, because Japanese men living in Hawaii eat more fat and have fewer strokes. This study continues to be the subject of heated debate and is sure to be repeated. But once again, it is important never to change your lifestyle on the basis of one study.

If you do decide to pursue the way of low fat, don't count on those friendly low-fat food makers for the straight skinny. Especially on their labels, which are grossly misleading. Take my luncheon meat, please. The label says 95 percent fat-free. Yet one-half of the calories are fat. How do you explain that? Let's do some math together—honest, it's easy. Just remember that the real way to calculate fat is as a percentage of total calories, not as a percentage of the weight of the food.

If 5 percent of the weight of the luncheon meat is fat, 95 percent is not fat. That's how they can legitimately claim the meat is 95 percent fat-free. Water is heavy, though, and products like luncheon meat contain a lot of water. By weight, 5 percent is actually a lot of fat. Suppose this luncheon meat weighs 30 grams, or just over an ounce. Well, 5 percent of 30 grams is 1.5 grams of fat. Because all fat has 9 calories per gram, that 1.5 grams equals 13.5 calories. Now go back to our package and you'll see that the total for all the contents is 27 calories (hey, be glad I didn't make you do this with Spam). If 13.5 calories are fat, we're now up to 50 *percent fat.* Get it? The label's 95 percent fat-free just blimped into 50 percent fat in reality. Go collect your Ph.D. You're a nutritionist.

Man doth not live by luncheon meat alone. If the rest of your diet is low in fat, this doesn't matter. Just don't believe everything you read on those labels.

MAMA WAS RIGHT: YOU SHOULD EAT (WELL) AND STOP TALKING SO MUCH

Most experts agree that our biggest problem isn't what we should cut *out* of our diet. Rather, it's what we're not including *in* our diet. Sorry, but Mom had it nailed. Whether or not you significantly reduce fats, the single most successful dietary improvement you can make is to increase your intake of fruits and vegetables. Remember the French Paradox? If you hike up that good stuff, you'll probably spontaneously lower fat percentage anyway. Oh, you say you can't get fresh produce where you live? That won't wash as an excuse not to get the five servings a day that you should be eating. Canned and frozen are sure better than none. In fact, they can even be better than fresh.

It's true. Massive recent reanalyses of canned, frozen, and fresh fruits and vegetables uncovered lots of surprises. Researchers at the University of Illinois documented that for nutrients like fiber, vitamins A and C, folate, carotenes, and protein, canned and frozen for the most part were equal to fresh. In some cases, they were even better. Canned pumpkin, for instance, blew away the fresh competition. Canned tomato sauce? Better than fresh tomatoes for lycopene, a very important carotenelike micronutrient especially important for men's prostate. Canned tomatoes have more fiber, potassium, vitamin A, vitamin C, calcium, and iron than their fresh cousins, perhaps because they can be picked closer to ripeness. Also, there is no risk of infectious disease from canned produce.

Want to know the most nutritious vegetables and fruits? In all fairness, I can't tell you. Various groups have tried to determine the "healthiest" fruits, for instance by rating their nutritional values. But every group differs on the priority of the nutrients. For instance, which counts more—vitamin A or vitamin C? Silly question, isn't it? Kind of reminds me of the kids' game: Which would you rather have—poor vision or poor hearing? Scurvy or rickets? Rutgers University puts watermelon at the bottom of its list of recommended fruit, while the Center for Science in the Public Interest rates it number two. Frankly, I don't care where it's ranked. Just eat it, and all other fruits and vegetables that you like.

Want to know Americans' favorite and least favorite veggies, according to surveys? Top that list with the tomato, then string beans, potatoes, corn, mushrooms, carrots, broccoli, onions, spinach, asparagus, cauliflower, green peppers, peas, zucchini, sweet potatoes, beets, cabbage, squash, brussel sprouts, and at the bottom, lima beans, my absolute favorite.

All right, it's just *spilling* out of me now. I've decided finally to give you your money's worth of advice: Vary your diet as much as possible. Adding fruits and veggies is one thing everyone can do, and unquestionably it will pay dividends. Not only will you automatically decrease the amounts of other less healthful foods you're chawin' on, you'll get a whole range of beneficial phytochemicals. So far we have identified at least forty separate micronutrients in fruits and vegetables that are not found in vitamin pills—and the list is growing.

By the way, if you still want to get yourself on a lowered fat diet, research shows that you can splurge on a super-high-fat meal on alternate days without altering blood fat profiles. So there's incentive if you need it. Be a good egg and you can have your cake and eat it too.

How are you going to cook these healthy foods? You can nuke 'em. Microwaves are quick and easy and I promise you that your food won't end up glowing in the dark, whatever you may have heard over the years on Phil, Oprah, or Jerry. Cornell University reminds us that one of the best uses of your microwave is to increase veggie consumption. In fact, when you microwave vegetables in a teaspoon of water, the food retains between half and all its vitamins, compared with only 40 to 60 percent on the stove.

If you push me, I have to admit that as a diet, I still like vegetarianism. I have a certain affection for it, and I marvel that it still gains converts so many years after its popularization by hippies and baby boomers. The moral, animal-friendly part will keep you motivated to stick to it. It offers a graceful simplicity—there's no eat-this-in-the-morning-eat-that-at-noon dogma. In a flash, you know what to eat and what not to eat. It's adaptable to all cuisines. Of course, it also separates you from your social network and can be isolating. Some people like that; some don't. It's a great rebellion diet for teens. Their parents call me in droves. I can't count the number of times I've heard the question "Where are they going to get their protein?" We've been sold so hard on protein, parents panic that their children's bodies will dissolve somehow from a lack of it. They won't. It is true that certain deficiencies—zinc, iron, and vitamin B-12 among them—are more common in young vegetarians, but a little knowledge will take care of that. In any event, you don't have to give up the joys of flesh, at least not for your health. Your body is finely tuned to handle a wide variety of foods.

By the way, you can satisfy your body's need for protein with vegetables alone. Any individual vegetable, by itself, will not supply all your protein needs. By combining veggies, though, you can easily get all you need. Here are some good, nutritious combos: lentils and corn, rice and beans, peanut butter and bread, corn tortillas and pinto beans. Daily protein requirements are easy to remember: 1 gram per kilogram (2.2 pounds) of body weight. So a 70-kilogram (154-pound) person needs 70 grams of protein. If you add up your current consumption, most of you get more than enough—maybe too much.

Several studies have confirmed that by adding one fish meal to your weekly menu, you can cut your risk of sudden death by a whopping 50 *percent*. That's a huge reduction. You choose—fish once a week or rice cakes every day. Better yet, fish really may be brain food after all—dementia appears less commonly among those who eat more fish.

New research is pointing the way toward other heart-healthy foods. For instance, many people avoid nuts because of their high caloric content. In fact, as part of a balanced diet, subjects who ate nuts four times a week experienced half the normal rate of heart attacks. Ditto for whole wheat bread.

Then there's the nibbling thing. Is it better to gorge like a piggy or nibble like a mousy? Doctors at the University of Toronto compared seventeen meals—snacks, really—versus three meals a day. Metabolically, these were the same diet. The nibblers, they found, had lower LDL cholesterol, and their insulin decreased, which is a good thing.

For weight loss, earlier studies found that nibblers actually did worse because they ate too much with each nibble and ended up gaining more weight. This latest study gave the same total calories to the nib-blers and the three-meal feasters.

If you want to eat less, eat alone. One study documented that those who ate with others increased the size of their meal by 44 percent compared to when they dined by their lonesomes. Want weird? Certain kinds of music boosted the amounts eaten. Bites per minute increase with the tempo. Listeners to *Stars and Stripes Forever* clocked 5.1 bites per minute, finishing their meal in thirty-one minutes. Those eating to the strains of a flute instrumental chewed 3.2 bites per minute and took an hour to finish. The louder the music, the more sugared soft drinks people consumed. Finally, if you *play* the flute dur-ing dinner, I think you'll eat less. Take it up.

IF YOU TAKE ANY ADVICE FROM THIS CHAPTER, LET IT BE THIS

One final nutritional thought, possibly the biggest, least controversial of all. But I'll bet it will surprise you. One nutritional strategy emerges from all the animal research I have seen, and it really and truly may prolong our lives.

In the 1930s, researchers at Cornell University found that restrict-ing the number of calories eaten by lab rats resulted in the rats living longer—a lot longer. A 40 percent reduction in food intake below that which the animal would have eaten on its own led to a remarkable 50 percent increase in its life span. Applied to humans, that translates into another forty years for your eighty-year-old aunt! All the basic age-related changes in the rodents were retarded, from cataracts to bone deterioration to immune problems. It's as if the body wears out processing all that food it doesn't need. Simplistic but reasonable.

Since those early Cornell studies, caloric restriction has been found to extend the lives of protozoans, fleas, spiders, even guppies. Chick-ens and every mammal examined have shown this remarkable effect. Autoimmune disease is unknown in calorie-restricted mice. There are some ongoing monkey studies, but because they can live forty years, we won't know the results for a while. So far, their organ systems are staying young. Pig research has shown the same thing.

There don't seem to be many downsides here. I'm not ready to build a bandwagon, but if you want to jump aboard, make sure you get all your basic nutrients. All the current confusion about nutrition and health can be reduced to this: Eat whatever you want, just eat less of it, and add some veggies. Some researchers believe that protein restriction is the key and have accumulated lots of evidence to support this contention. The body must work extra hard to process protein that it does not really need. That's why I worry about the current high-protein fad diets.

Meanwhile, before you move on to the next chapter, take a break. Go nibble a carrot, or even two.

3

THE TRUTH ABOUT YOUR WEIGHT

You Can Be Fatter Than You Think

---

*D*octor Edell? Not on your life.

I had abandoned medicine and opened a small art, antique, and jewelry gallery in downtown Sacramento. I really wanted to be an artist, but I had a family to support. So I took up smithing silver and gold. I wasn't making a living at that, either. My then wife and I decided to pack it all in and move up to the wilds of Northern California's redwood country.

But I could never quite go the whole way of giving up my medical license. One day, just before leaving Sacramento, I was casually glancing at the help wanted ads in the local paper. Not usually the place to find someone soliciting physicians—not that I was looking, mind you. There it was. No night calls, no weekend calls, no emergency calls. Some travel. Didn't sound like medicine. Just what *this* doctor ordered. I called.

"How much weight would you like to lose?" a female voice chirped.

"I'm answering the ad in the paper, ma'am," I said, unnerved by her question.

"Yes, I know. How much weight would you like to lose?"

"I don't want to lose any weight," I insisted. "My name is Dr. Edell and you're looking for a doctor."

I had called the then-largest chain of weight loss clinics in California. This was 1977, before the days of the major national chains like Weight Watchers, Jenny Craig, Nutrisystem, and Diet Centers. She asked me to come down and meet the founder. His centers were strewn throughout Northern California—seventy of them—and he was poised to take over the south. His advertising was all over TV, radio, and the newspapers. He had built an empire, probably putting more women on diets than anyone in history up to that time (men were rare in these clinics). He was intense, fast-talking, and smart, a radiologist by training, and I wondered if he was eating his own diet pills. He could spout Shakespeare's plays from beginning to end and had a bizarre habit of reciting long soliloquies to reinforce a point.

He hired me. My assignment: cover ten clinics in a day, two days a week. Not so bad, especially at four hundred dollars a day, a lot of money to a broke silversmith/disillusioned doctor. We had moved back to the land in rural Mendocino County. Making a living wasn't something I had figured into that equation. Becoming Dr. Fat Farm would suit me just fine.

I began my work day at 5 A.M., running the exhausting circuit to clinics in towns with names like Willits, Ukiah, Clear Lake, Redding, Marysville, and Yuba City. I can't remember them all, but I learned a lot in those clinics.

My job was to conduct a quick physical on the new patients, take their blood, and administer two shots, one of human chorionic gonadotrophin, or HCG, and the other of vitamin B-12. I also handled any patients with problems and did follow-up visits. The offices were all exactly alike, right down to the placement of the medications and syringes on the card tables in the examining rooms. The formula was consistent and successful.

It was a slick and well-run operation. The physicals were brief. I sat in front of bare chests all day and placed my stethoscope at those special places on the anterior thorax where doctors listen to heart sounds. You breathe in, breathe out. I poke here, poke there. These were healthy women.

Then I drew the blood, an important ritual that could have been done by others but added the crucial medical spin. I never got truly comfortable drawing blood in medical school. It takes practice, which I was about to get, and on fat people no less. Drawing blood—called phlebotomy—from fat people is every medical student's nightmare. But I had originally practiced eye surgery and figured that if I could learn that, I had the hand-eye coordination to draw blood. After plenty of fumbles—"My goodness, *your* veins *are* hard to find"—I actually got good at it. Eventually, to relieve the boredom, I would keep score. When it reached the point where I never missed, I would do it with my eyes closed. Any good phlebotomist will tell you that when you're on top of your game, you do it by touch anyway.

Then there were the shots. HCG is a hormone normally produced in the placenta and found in the urine of pregnant women. There is a rare hormonal disease in which young boys do not develop mature sexual characteristics. One symptom is a chubby, feminine, baby-fat appearance. Injecting them with large doses of HCG will stimulate their testicles to produce testosterone and reverse these symptoms. In the 1950s it was theorized incorrectly that the hormone would do the same in weight-conscious adult women. All this started with a doctor named Albert Simeons, who started his own chain of clinics. They took off despite studies showing that HCG did absolutely nothing for weight. Years later, in our clinics, we told women that it decreased their appetite. We used teeny doses, and once when one of the clinics didn't get its shipment of HCG, the staff used saline—plain water—without telling the women. It worked just fine. When patients complained of hunger, they were given a double shot of placebo. They walked away happy.

The shot served another important function. The patients had to get it every day and therefore came to the office, faced the staff, and got weighed. That was additional incentive to stick to the diet, which was low enough in calories that the patients couldn't help but lose weight if they stuck to it. Patrons were told that the vitamin B-12 shot gave them energy. We doubled up on that one in stubborn cases of fatigue. It worked as a placebo as well. We also used real drugs—amphetamines—to depress appetite. Most patients got them, and they worked in the short term. All these, including HCG, are still in use today in weight-loss clinics across the country.

With ten clinics to cover every day, I couldn't spend too much time at each one. I would drive 500 miles each run and get home at 4 A.M. In those days, I drove a 1962 Cadillac Fleetwood that someone gave me in payment of a one-hundred-dollar debt. Actually it was made from two Cadillacs, the front half purple and the back half blue. It had no muffler and must have been a sight as I rumbled up to these clinics. "Oh, here's the doctor now." I started parking around the block. I wonder if any of those patients ever recognize me on TV and radio.

I must say that this many years later I still have mixed feelings about my time on the fat farm. Accompanying these women on literally thousands of diets and listening to the staff in the offices was better than medical school for teaching about diets, weight loss, and the desperation to be "slim." This is not experience most doctors have had, and I offer it as part of my credentials for this chapter. I want to pass the benefits of that education on to you.

FORGET THE MEEK

From nature's point of view, chubby folks are the blessed ones who will surely inherit the earth if famine ever makes a comeback in the Western world. Fat has been with us since the beginning, and for good reason. The oldest sculpture of a human being is a very fat woman, the Venus of Willendorf (in Austria). She is twenty-thousand-plus years old and very typical of sculpture of that period. Today she resides in the Kunsthistoriches Museum in Vienna. She is all butt and stomach. Her stubby arms rest on gargantuan breasts. Her head is bowed down to hide her face. She always appeared bashful to me, but I'm sure there was no such intent by the sculptor, because obesity was much admired in Stone Age culture. There is a reason, after all, that today she is known as a Venus.

Throughout civilization, obesity has almost always been the desired norm. You would be hard-pressed for examples in the art world of a female form that resembles today's fashion models. Even in the Orient, where we think of women as smaller framed, fat had its day. In the Tang dynasty of China, A.D. 618–906, tomb pottery buried with the deceased reveals the beauty standard for courtesans. They have round, cherubic faces with tiny puckered lips peeking between swollen cheeks. Their bodies bulge beneath their robes. These women were fat, plain and simple, and highly prized for their beauty.

Western art and sculpture also betrays our penchant for chubby women and men. From the Renaissance to Rubens, from the Victorians to Renoir, where are all the skinny people? Right up to today, take a look at Fernando Botero's many delightfully fat figures. In the fifteenth and sixteenth centuries, Albrecht Dürer published standardized ratios for beauty, carefully annotating the exact mathematical formulas for perfect body shape. They were not skinny.

The standards of the past were far different from ours now. Fat was positive and good. Societies recognized that fat was, in reality, stored food energy. As such, it was a sign that the bearer had access to food, a sign of power and stature. Fat men were considered smart and powerful, fat women fecund and sexual.

As the twentieth century dawned, we had plentiful food supplies and distribution systems. We needed new aspirations. Women before World War II reflected their new freedom and status by tending toward boyish and unfeminine fashions. In the constant search for novelty, fat was passing from style. While most fad diets of this period were about health, the major diets after the war were about weight. Then Twiggy hit the scene, setting an altogether new standard. Despite the institutionalization of that image, subcultures persist in the United States that continue to resist these trends. African-American women are more accepting of larger sizes, as are black men. Black women weigh more than white women, leading some to suggest that in this case, beauty standards may match a genetic propensity toward greater weight.

It's all programming. We accept the prevailing beauty standards of our culture in our time. Unfortunately, Madison Avenue has sold us an unrealistic standard, which, of course, reflects what we cannot have. Check out the endless pages of anorexic models in the women's magazines, followed by pages alternating diets with recipes for lusciously photographed food. Be honest: Do you think you can ever really look like the average fashion model? Would you *really* want to?

IS IT A MAN THING?

Lesbians don't show up often in eating disorder clinics.

That's a simple and easily documented empirical observation. But behind it lies an interesting insight into how we view our bodies and, maybe, why we see them the way we do. Researchers at the Massachusetts General Hospital decided to explore.

They showed a series of twelve different outlines of women's bodies to groups of heterosexual and homosexual women. The outlines are standard images used in tests to determine a subject's body image. The figures range from skinny to obese. The women were told to select the outline that reflected their own body; the body they would like to have; the body they felt would most appeal to a sexual partner; and the body to which they themselves were most attracted.

First, the homosexual women on average were heavier. Of the heterosexual women, 16 percent were overweight compared with 44 percent of the gay women. Of the heterosexuals, 32 percent were underweight compared with 11 percent of the gays. Even if you exclude the overweight women, three-quarters of the straight women wanted to lose weight compared with less than half of the gay women. Twice as many straight women as gays were concerned about their overall appearance. When looking at the body outline images, heterosexual women chose ideal weights *below* normal, while gay women chose bodies almost right on the norm. In picking the figures they thought partners would choose, homosexuals chose larger bodies than heterosexuals.

The researchers concluded that "homosexual women have a different standard of 'ideal' weight and body shape, and are more satisfied with their bodies than are heterosexual women." What's the explanation? Lesbian ideology rejects the standard of beauty set by straight society, freeing these women to worry less about their weight.

JIGGLING IS JUST ALL RIGHT WITH ME

Of all the tissues in the human body, adipose tissue—fat—must surely be the most precious. It's an extraordinary example of our clever bodies. You eat, and your onboard computer takes some of that extra food, knowing how scarce and important it is, and stashes it away for a hungry rainy day. It acts as an energy bank account, there for you to draw on any time you want. If your account runs out, though, you die.

On the other hand, if your account balance is high, you outlast everyone else if there is no food around. Imagine if your car could do the same: take several gallons of the gas you pump, stow it in a secret tank, and then draw on it when the needle hits empty. Fat is that remarkable. You are not only protected if food becomes scarce, but also if the weather turns cold. Fat supplies a blanket of insulation.

As I was ruminating on all this recently, I broke away for a family celebration. My fiancée, Sharon, had just earned her Ph.D., so we took family and friends to a local Moroccan restaurant, a place where the food is great and you eat with your hands and lounge about in tentlike rooms. Authentic it was, including one more Middle Eastern custom between the appetizers and main course: a belly dancer. She knew her art well. As we all sat mesmerized by her gyrations, I found myself fascinated by her, well, flesh.

How many generations of men over the centuries have watched that same jiggle? There is a quality to the bounce of human adipose tissue that comes from within the tissue itself. The dancer was more plump to the casual eye than the slick stick-figure models in Western magazines. Yet I thought to myself that a little jiggle is a good thing. This appreciation comes from deep in my brain, despite a lifetime of antifat programming. I wish I could tell every woman in the world that it's OK. Jiggle never hurt anyone.

The point is that we've been conned, and the effect is nothing short of an endless, ongoing sickness. We can be easily and quickly manipulated into accepting something as attractive when it's not. Regardless of how your sexism needle moves over belly dancing, that jiggling woman in the restaurant was extraordinarily refreshing. I suggested that Sharon, who is svelte, gain some more weight. She laughed but said she welcomed the aesthetic latitude it implied.

This cultural collision course is playing itself out wherever American culture gets transmitted around the world—in Latin America, Asia, the Middle East—affording a unique opportunity to examine the selling of skinny. Consider one Third World country—Egypt. Traditionally, the Egyptian beauty standard for women has been basically more bounce to the ounce. But glamour in Egypt is now associated with whatever comes from the West. Increasingly, print and broadcast advertising in Egypt revolves around skinny Western blondes. Yet the women to whom it is selling are generally dark and chubby.

It's not an easy sell, despite cultural currents from the West. Middle Easterners are offended if a guest refuses offers of food. Sooner or later, though, Egypt will yield. The head of Egyptian TV ordered twenty overweight female newscasters to slim down. "Look at Oprah Winfrey," one prominent newscaster countered defensively in an interview. "She's talented and fat." When told that Oprah is now thinner, she mused for a moment. "She must not be too beautiful anymore," she concluded.

SELLING SKINNY

Back here, we just won't give up. In the 1950s, 14 percent of America's women and 7 percent of the men were trying to lose weight. Four decades later, the figures were 42 percent and 25 percent, respectively. There are some recent encouraging signs that more people are throwing in the towel and getting off the diet train. A major poll in 1998 found that although 58 percent of you want to lose weight, somewhat fewer—46 percent—are seriously trying. And various statistics show that we are more overweight than ever. In 1980 one-quarter of the adult population was 20 percent over standard weight guidelines. In 1998 that figure had risen to one-third of the population. Some of these trends may seem contradictory, and indeed, experts aren't sure what it all means yet. For instance, as a country we consume less fat, even as we get fatter. That may be because we are eating more calories as we substitute carbohydrates for fats.

Perhaps a measure of our desperation is how we suspend our good sense, do some pretty outrageous things, and fall for some incredibly dumb scams to beat the stuffing out of our fat cells. We spend forty to sixty billion dollars *every year* to lose weight. Most of it is a waste of time and money that only leaves us poorer and feeling worse about ourselves.

In vain we wrap ourselves in Saran Wrap. We rub our tummies with "belly-buster" and "inches-off" creams, "maxercise" lotions (which claim to draw out and extract excess fluid from fat deposits so your body can burn stored fat. Huh? One listener asked me if she should wear rubber gloves when she uses it "so my hands don't shrink"), thigh creams, all types of "spot reducers" (including patches you attach wherever you want to slim down. But be careful, the manufacturer warns—if you leave it on too long, you'll get too skinny. Worse yet, if you're not careful, you'll end up lopsided).

Most recent is "fat soap," imported from exotic China and a big seller. I didn't think even Americans would fall for this one. "It can discharge the underskin fat out of the human body very successfully," it promises. "Please use the soap for some time and you will be surprised to find that your body will become slender and fit." Don't want to wash? Try wrapping your fingers with surgical tape to stimulate weight loss through acupressure points. Japan's biggest surgical tape manufacturer, Nichiban, isn't complaining about tripled sales. In case all else fails, I authorize you to fall back on this one: *Lose Weight by Breathing* (nothing to buy but the book). The author claims to have lost 10 pounds just by breathing differently.

My personal favorite, though, remains Slim Skins. This was in the good old days before liposuction, so I forgive you this one time if you fell for it (although maybe you should refund the money your parents paid for your education). They were a pair of tight-fitting pants similar to the kind worn by bicyclists today. On one side there was a fitting that attached to . . . your vacuum cleaner. I quote the instruction manual: "Your Slim Skins are a marvel of ease and simplicity to use. Their ingenious design allows you to convert your own household vacuum cleaner into the most exciting and effective inch-reducing machine imaginable. Plug in your vacuum and slip on your Slim Skins directly over your bare skin, tie the waist and knees firmly, not too tight. . . . Any garment such as pants, slacks, shorts, even light underwear coming between your skin and the Slim Skins will detract from the real inch-trimming potential of this marvelous reducer." Just hook up, turn on your vacuum, and—slurp—away with the fat. This prompted one of the great letters from a radio fan. "Doc," she wrote. "The instructions didn't tell me: how do I get the fat out of my vacuum?"

The National Council Against Health Fraud has its own Greatest Hits list. In 1998 it announced its annual Slim Chance awards. Worst Product: DHEA cream gel, applied to pulse points on inner thighs and wrist. Most Outrageous Product: Phenadrene MD pill (turns ugly fat into water and shrinks a full size within twenty-four hours). Worst Claim: Herbal Cleansing and Detox Program laxative (control weight by ridding body of toxins). Worst Gadget: Elysee Body Toner Belt (battery-powered, total workout reduces sagging and cellulite).

WHAT YOU SEE IS WHAT YOU GET

So much of this has to do with how we see our bodies when we look in the mirror—and when we look at those around us. In a 1994 speech to the American Psychological Association, psychologist Debora Burgard described her study of ninety women weighing up to 485 pounds. She found that the women most accepting of their bodies tended not to try to lose weight. "Those women who accepted themselves and their weight," she said, "were more likely to believe their weight was determined by factors outside of their control and felt greater self-esteem, competence, personal power, self-confidence, and overall self-control."

Society and marketers have a lot to do with it. Choke on this one next time you thumb through the clothing ads: *half* the women in the United States measure size 16 or over. The average clothing size in stores is either 6 to 8 or 8 to 10. Burgard wonders how women would feel about themselves if the average clothing size were 14. Women are simply made to feel bad if they don't meet an artificially determined ideal weight. Burgard also found that the women who did not accept their bodies put more energy and time into trying to lose weight.

Physiologically and in some ways psychologically, dieters are no different from people who are starving. Like sex, breathing, and thirst, food is necessary for life. Eating is a basic instinct that will not yield easily to our machinations. Obsessive behavior over weight and dieting creates all sorts of havoc that we still don't really understand. I once interviewed a former World War II fighter pilot. He was shot down over Berlin, and we spoke about his fourteen months as a German prisoner of war. What did he and his fellow POWs spend their time contemplating? "You'd think we were going to talk about women, about the war, or our flying experiences," he told me. "No. We talked about food twenty-four hours a day. We were concerned only about food."

After the Liberation, the fixation stuck with him. "I knew I had an obsession," he said. Studies of other prisoners of war found high rates of binge eating not only after they were freed but long after they had recovered their normal body weights. During World War II, an experiment was conducted on American conscientious objectors. Their food intake was restricted for six months so that their body weight would drop by 25 percent. They became obsessed with food, upset and irritable, apathetic and lethargic. They lost all interest in sex. As soon as the experiment ended, they started gorging. They remained obsessed and out of control.

The same phenomenon is seen routinely in dieters. Normal eaters will decrease their food intake after a high-calorie meal. In one study, dieters were given one high-calorie meal. They immediately felt the diet was over and began to overeat, even to gorge.

The amount of personal pain is enormous among Americans trying to be something they cannot be. It stalks them every day, everywhere they go, in everything they see. The effects of the stress and depression are impossible to evaluate. As we learn more about the mind-body relationship, we may realize that constant upset over our bodies can negatively affect our health.

There is irony in the fact that usually health is not the reason people try to diet. Americans love food, and most would never put themselves through something as painful as denying themselves food just to be healthy. They want to "look good" by conforming to someone else's standards. Studies consistently show that we think we are fatter than we are and that we think the opposite sex likes bodies thinner than they actually do. Remember the point of it all? To enjoy your life, not to suffer needlessly over something that may be unobtainable. When you do have to suffer, it should be over things that are *really* important.

THE MAXI-MERMAIDS CLUB

Journalists are supposed to be the toughest of nuts. Since I'm a doctor as well, I should be pretty well uncrackable. After all, I've seen it all, if not in ER or surgery, certainly in the news department. So I was unprepared for how deeply I would be moved by a small group of courageous women I met on a story. I left that interview with my view changed forever.

Most of us, if we're honest with ourselves, have deep prejudices and bigotry about fat people. The obese suffer blatant discrimination in every walk of life. The bias is ingrained in our culture. In the nineteenth century, Phineas T. Barnum filled his sideshow with the likes of the midget General Tom Thumb, Siamese twins, bearded ladies, and of course, the Fat Lady Baby Viola. We are sensitive to racial and religious bigotry, discrimination against the handicapped, physically impaired, and developmentally challenged. Political correctness surrounds us—not an entirely bad thing, in my view. Politicians, executives, and sports and entertainment figures can ruin their careers with bad-taste jokes. Yet against the overweight and obese there is a resistant, rampant sexism and discrimination that goes unchallenged. That's why I decided to look at an exclusive set of women.

The place felt strange from the moment my camera crew and I passed through the lobby. This was a large public pool in the San Francisco Bay Area, normally bustling with swimmers. Today the lobby was empty as we made our way toward the entrance of the pool. There were the distant echoes of splashing and laughter. As we rounded the final corner, we saw a remarkable sight, one I immediately realized I had never seen before and I doubt you have either: a large pool full of very—extremely very—fat women bobbing in the water. There were a couple of dozen of them scattered in the pool. These women were a minimum of 300 pounds. I was struck by their ebullience and giggles, their relaxed faces and shrieking laughter. They didn't notice us right away. Like elves, normally out of sight during the day, they had come out to play. They frolicked and cavorted like kids at recess.

I was taken aback. I had never seen so many fat people at once anywhere, much less in bathing suits. They were unabashed and unashamed. They took turns sailing gleefully off the diving board.

One by one, they noticed us. They stopped splashing. A hush fell like a blanket over the group.

I had been invited to videotape and interview these women for a story. But I'm sure that didn't make it any less traumatic for them to have their sanctum invaded. For some, as I would learn, it was the first time in their lives that they had swum before "outsiders." I knelt at the side of the pool and held the microphone over the water as the women gathered around. They called themselves the Maxi Mermaids.

The obvious leader of the group moved forward and became the enthusiastic unofficial spokesperson. "These women are swimming," she told me, her voice both defiant and proud as she nodded to the woman at her side. "My mother hasn't been in the water for thirty years. We're heading for the water because it makes us feel beautiful. We have to stop feeling like we have to judge ourselves by our size. Self-acceptance does not depend on physical dimensions."

I asked about discrimination. "The only 'in thing' to be a bigot about is size, so we've been hurt a lot," she said. "Our goal is no longer to lose weight but to feel good about ourselves." She described how hard it had been to find a pool that would lease to them and allow them the privacy they knew they needed.

Did they, then, feel that they belonged to a minority group? I was immediately chided.

"First of all, I don't think we are a minority," she said. "I think we are a whole heck of a lot more of a majority than people suspect. We hide only because we are self-conscious, most of us. A lot of us are overcoming it. I, personally, have been called every name in the book. I've been told that I am stupid. The worst thing that someone can say to me is 'Oh, how pretty you would be if you lost weight.' They are saying to me, 'You are not pretty.' People hurt us unintentionally. Our main goal here at Maxi Mermaids is to change the way we feel about ourselves because that is much more important than changing the way other people feel about us."

She ticked off her countless diets, the sickness and resultant hair loss and hospitalizations triggered by near-starvation.

"I'm now going to live and I'm going to be healthy," she concluded, pausing finally for a long breath. The whole group erupted in cheers. They seemed less afraid of me now and nudged closer to the edge of the pool where I was perched.

I asked about men. Could they get fat men to come out and swim? Dumb question. As if only fat men would want to be near them. There are many clubs and groups of men, skinny and not skinny, that adore fat women.

"How many of us here have husbands and boyfriends?" she called out to her friends.

Most raised their hands. "Girlfriends?" a couple of voices volunteered shyly. She talked about the baby steps she took to overcome her own discomfort. A few had graduated beyond this and taken giant steps toward security.

"A lot of these girls have gotten to the point where they can go out and do whatever they want to do," she said. "They can get out of the water. They are overcoming their self-consciousness, and they are going to public swims. My mom and I have started going to the public lap-swims early in the morning. It's like doing something that was impossible. That's what this is about. This is not an exercise group."

We talked about the myth that all fat people are gluttons and overeat. "I have a boyfriend who can eat six times as much as I can," she explained. "I could not hold as much as he does, and he doesn't gain anything. I am tired of people telling me that it's a cop-out. It's not true, and we know it. Discrimination? All my life. Jobs. Grocery store turnstiles are uncomfortable. Seats are uncomfortable. People on the street harass me constantly. People just take it upon themselves to feel they have to comment upon you, no matter where you are. I am who I am, and I like who I am. I like my body, and nobody's going to tell me what I can or can't do. They can harass me, but that's from their own craziness, not mine. It's been a real hard road, and I have decided that I am going to be healthy and I am, you know. I don't need to be thought of as ill."

I reached the microphone out to another woman who had slowly inched to the side of the pool.

"You are blamed for being fat," she said, her arms treading water gracefully. "If you are fat, you are morally disgusting. You are a bad person if you can't control what you eat. It's not a question of what you eat. It's a question of your metabolism and your genetics."

I was ashamed for the medical profession and the damage it had inflicted on these women. "I went to the doctor," their leader said. "I was still up on the table after he examined me. He turned his back to me and said, 'You're pregnant.' Then he turned around and faced me and looked terrible. He said, 'I don't know how anyone could stand to get close enough to you to get married to you, let alone get you pregnant.' I was still draped and I felt very vulnerable.

"I don't remember how I got home," she said, now crying. "I think I had a breakdown then."

We gathered our equipment, left, and drove back to the station. But I felt changed. The story we put together was very pro-fat. "This is the largest minority group in America," I said in the voice-over, and closed by saying that "sooner or later, we are going to learn that the value of a person has nothing to do with the color of their skin, or the amount of it."

That piece has lingered with me probably more than any other story I've ever covered. It helped me develop an attitude based on the belief that in many cases you may as well learn to like yourself rather than fight a losing battle to be liked by adhering to someone else's standards of beauty. A tidal wave of calls flooded the station after that broadcast. I won a Distinguished Achievement Award from the National Association to Advance Fat Acceptance. Journalists would not call it prestigious, but I cherish it.

WHY WEIGHT MAKES SENSE

Sail with me to Polynesia, a location with unique conditions for studying the origins of obesity. Samoans and other Pacific Islanders have the highest rates of obesity in the world. The latest research finds their obesity made worse by modern lifestyle. Explanations for it all lie in evolution and genetics. Studying modern Samoans, geographic medicine experts from Brown University uncovered further evidence for the "thrifty-gene concept," which holds that efficient metabolisms conferred a great survival advantage on early explorers in these Pacific Island cultures (an efficient metabolism is one where the body easily stores excess calories as fat for use at another time). This is evolution at its best.

Centuries ago, explorers risked long sea voyages in order to settle this region of far-flung islands. They knew neither where they were going nor how long their journey would last. As food on these small boats dwindled, who starved? Not those with efficient metabolisms. Overweight individuals had a better chance. They could go longer without food, and it helped to have some insulating fat on your bones during those cool nights on the water. There is evidence of grand feasting ceremonies before these expeditions to fatten everybody up. It seems possible that those who gained weight faster were chosen for the crew.

After landing on new islands, those with efficient metabolisms would enjoy distinct advantages. Food shortages from storms and cyclical famines would only serve to accent the expediency of the right metabolism. Even the advent of modern agriculture may have added selective advantages to the right genes. It would take time to learn the most efficient agricultural techniques, and the many failures would favor those with fat genes.

Today, though, scientists think that the prevailing degree of obesity among Polynesians is higher than in the past, that modern lifestyles and diet have accentuated these ancient genetic predispositions. For instance, in his log, Captain James King, one of the first outsiders to see Hawaii, describes the hefty natives as "well-made; they walk very gracefully, run nimbly and are capable of bearing great fatigue." Reverend William Ellis in 1823 says the "natives are well formed, with fine muscular limbs ... their gait is graceful and sometimes stately. The chiefs in particular are tall and stout, and their personal appearance is so much superior to that of the common people."

As expected from their obesity, high blood pressure and diabetes are common among modern Samoans. Unexpected, however, are their strikingly low cholesterol levels and low mortality rates from heart disease. This tells us that nature, through genes, can make human beings fat *and* resistant to heart disease. We mistakenly assume that all obesity translates into health problems. What we learn from the Samoans is that people who are genetically fat may be healthier than people who eat themselves fat. In Western medicine, we have no way of distinguishing the genetically fat from the self-induced fat, thus we generally lump all fat people together. As a result, we may overestimate ill health in the entire group. I'm not implying that the high blood pressure and diabetes in this population cause no problems, just that they trigger fewer health problems than are experienced by other obese groups.

Time to sail home, where we find that women have higher levels of body fat than men. We've always assumed that this is nature's way of protecting the species' ability to reproduce. Women need to survive better and already do (they live longer). And when things get out of hand for whatever reason, women will do better than men. Says who? Try the Donner party.

It's not good to be in California's Sierra Nevada Mountains come October, when the weather can turn fickle. The worst happened on October 1, 1846. The infamous Donner party—settlers on their way to California—was stranded by a snowstorm. All eighty-seven pioneers spent the harsh six-month winter in horrendous isolation. They resorted to everything they could think of, including cannibalism, to stay alive. The group still experienced a high death rate, which 150 years later offered anthropologist Donald Grayson of the University of Washington a rare opportunity to demonstrate the physical routes of survival.

Among the Donner party, most of those over fifty died, mainly because older folks lose more heat through their skin due to less responsive vascular systems. And more than half of those under five died because youngsters have less fat.

But what struck Grayson was that twice as many men as women died. In the small party that tried to walk out on snowshoes, *all* the men died while *all* the women survived. In a story about Grayson's work, the *New York Times* noted that "calamities are a disaster for men." Others have challenged Grayson on this, arguing that men take greater risks in such situations. Hunting, chopping down trees, and other male activities tapped precious fat resources, contributing to their earlier demise. Grayson concluded that women, with twice the body fat, or insulation and stored energy, are simply better equipped than men for tough times.

BORN HEAVY—OR JUST MADE THAT WAY?

It has only recently been demonstrated that many people are overweight because of a different metabolism. But we have long overlooked an obvious clue. While we have refused to believe that some fat people can eat like birds and gain weight, we easily accept that some skinny people can eat like horses and stay skinny. Although you should always question the anecdotal, I am among the latter. From childhood until today, I can eat at will and not gain weight.

Earlier we told you that moms can influence how we learn what to eat. But many studies have clearly shown that when identical twins are adopted at birth by separate families, they still wind up weighing the same. Still society doubted the pleas of generations of fat people that they were not pigs or contemptible moral failures. No one wanted to believe them. Only laboratory science would finally end this myth.

The first study that demonstrated the physiological truth was published in 1992. Through newspaper advertisements, Australian researchers solicited two types of women: those who claimed, "I can eat anything and not gain an ounce," and those who claimed, "I eat like a bird but still put on pounds." The subjects were given scales to weigh their food and asked to record their daily activities as accurately as possible. To the nearest five minutes, they described how long they spent sleeping, sitting, relaxing, sitting erect, standing, strolling, walking, jogging, running, or sprinting. Swimming, cycling, aerobics, even vacuuming—all were itemized.

Previous attempts at these experiments had all failed because of all the unaccounted-for variables involved. In this one, every aspect was controlled as carefully as possible. The field was narrowed to eighteen women. Half were identified as "large-eating females," women who were proved to eat a lot routinely, and the other half as "small-eating females." After the arduous selection process, they were now to be put through the paces. As part of the test, the large-eaters on an average day ate more than twice the number of calories (2,857) as the small-eaters (1,262). But here's the part you'll hate. The large-eaters had a lower body mass, less body fat, and, at an average of 118 pounds, weighed *less* than the small-eaters, at 134 pounds.

I knew you'd hate it.

The hunt was on for an explanation. The researchers found that the large-eaters consumed more oxygen and produced more carbon dioxide than the small-eaters. Just sitting there, their engines idled faster—their bodies were burning food at a higher rate rather than putting it away as fat. With light activity, these thinner yet larger-eating subjects burned away still more food. Another clue: the oral temperatures of the big-eaters were slightly higher—a sign that these women were converting their energy to heat instead of stashing it away as fat.

It seems obvious that nature ensures our survival by endowing us with great metabolic variability. We are all different from one another, not only for the betterment and survival of our species but also to help us adapt to our environment. We all accept the fact that the skin of Africans is better adapted to the sun, a genetic legacy of geographic heritage. Why would it be any different for fatness and body size? Of course, as we watch America's collective weight increase, we see how easy it is to override this adaptive machinery with too many potato chips and too little activity.

Biologists have observed that animals living in the north tend to be heavier and have shorter limbs than animals in the south. These adaptations are designed to help the body either retain heat or cool itself. Humans have migrated a lot, but we also obey these rules. The Massa and other Africans of the upper Nile Valley live in a very hot climate and are the tallest people on earth. Arctic circle Lapps live in the coldest climate and are among earth's shortest.

WHAT YOUR FAT CAN TELL YOU

What the scale shows is certainly important. Where the fat *is* may tell you more.

Canadian researchers engaged twelve pairs of identical twin men and overfed them by 1,000 calories a day. The men were housed in a dormitory so that the researchers could prevent activities that might have thrown things off, such as smoking. As you might guess, the average guy ballooned by 17 pounds. But there was tremendous variation—some gained 9.5 pounds, others 30 pounds.

Wait a second, though. The variation diminished within the pairs of twins. If one twin gained, so did the other, and at remarkably similar rates. If a twin put on 12 pounds, for example, the other gained close to 12 pounds. Even more amazing—they gained in the same places. When one put weight on his belly, so did the other. Twin A's body shape mirrored Twin B's expansion. This is extremely important because abdominal fat is more related than fat on your butt and thighs to the risk for diseases like diabetes, high blood pressure, and heart disease.

While not saying that genetics determines everything and environment nothing, the researchers in this study conclude that up to 70 *percent* of our total body weight may be genetically determined.

We should have suspected this all along. The answer has long been there in the field of physical anthropology. Think of the Hottentots in Africa. The women have buttocks that by our standards are enormous. These cellulite-riddled mounds protrude with such audacity that anthropologists call it "Hottentot bustle." Doctors call it steatopygia, and it is an entirely genetic trait.

Current theory holds that the body has a mechanism controlling weight. This is known as the set-point theory. It hypothesizes a kind of "adipostat" in your brain that somehow knows just how much fat you are carrying. Just as the thermostat in your house reacts to the temperature, your adipostat senses the amount of fat in your body, and when that fat runs low, slows your metabolism.

It has been proved that the body obsessively guards weight within narrow guidelines. Studies that involved overfeeding have offered some surprises. If you overfeed a fat person and a thin person, who will gain more weight? Give up? Thin people gain weight more easily, but they lose it more easily, too. Thin people initially gain weight primarily as lean mass—or protein—rather than as fat. Fat people gain, well, fat.

What happens when you overeat, then stop? In the northern Cameroons, being overweight is a highly valued condition among the Masai population. They celebrate a traditional fattening period called Guru Walla that adds prestige and social status to participants who consume three times their normal food intake. The fattening period is preceded by a tough agricultural cycle of hard work and more sparse diet. Then they spend two months eating almost 7,000 calories a day of carbohydrates. Researchers investigating the tradition found that the pumped-up diet led to a body weight gain of 25 percent. The researchers returned two years later and reexamined the same men. Lo and behold, they had returned to almost their exact preholiday weight.

A less energy-intensive way to reach this conclusion examined one of the oldest traditional sports of Japan, sumo wrestling. These men reach extraordinary proportions, 500 pounds and up, by a rigorous training schedule and what *we* would call diet food—fish, rice, and veggies eaten in gargantuan quantities. They skip meals, then gorge. Skipping is like dieting. The body thinks it is starving, so the metabolism slows, and then you hit it with a truckload of food. More fat gets deposited. It is not surprising that the largest champions have been Polynesians. The most massive sumo champion ever is Konishiki, who in his prime tipped the scales at 625 pounds and could down a hundred beers at a sitting. A Samoan native of Hawaii, he has quit the ring and is reported to be on a diet. Buy my next book to find out how he does.

MESSING WITH THE THERMOSTAT

If you do manage to lose weight, in order to maintain that weight loss you must go to war with your body. This marvelous machine automatically responds to your efforts by making itself more efficient and burning fewer calories per unit of body weight. To keep that slimmer you, you must work increasingly harder at it, eat even less and exercise more. You're thinking slim, but your body is thinking starvation and—cleverly—makes it ever tougher to lose more precious energy as fat.

Are you getting the picture yet? Weight loss just isn't natural.

And don't think you can fool your body by substituting exercise for food. In 1995 Temple University doctors looked at women losing weight through exercise. As you would expect, because they now weighed less, their bodies needed less energy for movement. Think of it like this: heavy cars get worse fuel mileage, right? Cut the weight of the car in half, and mileage obviously will improve. But as these women lost weight, their bodies inexplicably used even less energy than you would expect from the weight loss alone. Our car is using less gas not only because it weighs less but because the engine has mysteriously transformed itself to run more efficiently.

HOW TUBBY IS TOO TUBBY?

First we have to figure out how fat you are. Put your scale back in the bathroom—it's not that easy anymore. Remember the height and weight charts on the penny scales? Yes, I am *that* old. In case you're not, they had three columns for "frames"—small, medium, and large. I never knew what that meant or which I was. My mother said it meant small, medium, or large bones.

We finally got off that kick when someone figured out that your percentage of body fat was more important than how much you weighed. How do you calculate that percentage? One way is to get weighed underwater with a cumbersome device that you still see in health clubs. You change into a bathing suit, sit on a big swinglike scale, get lowered into the water, hold your breath, and get weighed. Because fat floats, you can figure your percentage of body fat with some fancy mathematics.

Another method is TOBEC: total body electrical conductance. It's determined fairly accurately by a machine originally devised to determine the percentage of fat in hogs going off to market and still used by a lot of weight-loss clinics. Then there was "pinch an inch"—remember that one?—where we pinched various body sites that seemed to correlate in general with overall fat percentage.

The current trend in obesity research is something called body mass index, or BMI. Simply put, it is your weight and your height factored together, reminiscent of those old height-weight charts. If you're not metrically inclined, this won't be easy. The formula is this: Take your weight in kilograms and divide it by your height in meters squared. Or take your weight in pounds, multiply it by 4.89, then

BODY MASS INDEX (BMI)

HEIGHT	19	20	21	22	23	24
	WEIGHT IN POUNDS					
4'10"	91	96	100	105	110	115
4'1"	94	99	104	109	114	119
5'0"	97	102	107	112	118	123
5'1"	100	106	111	116	122	127
5'2"	104	109	115	120	126	131
5'3"	107	113	118	124	130	135
5'4"	110	116	122	128	134	140
5'5"	114	120	126	132	138	144
5'6"	118	124	130	136	142	148
5'7"	121	127	134	140	146	153
5'8"	125	131	138	144	151	158
5'9"	128	135	142	149	155	162
5'10"	132	139	146	153	160	167
5'11"	136	143	150	157	165	172
6'0"	140	147	154	162	169	177
6'1"	144	151	159	166	174	182
6'2"	148	155	163	171	179	186
6'3"	152	160	168	176	184	192
6'4"	156	164	172	180	189	197

Source: World Health Organization.

BODY MASS INDEX (BMI)

25	26	27	28	29	30	35	40
W	E	I	G	H T	I N	P O U	N D S
119	124	129	134	138	143	167	191
124	128	133	138	143	148	173	198
128	133	138	143	148	153	179	204
132	137	143	148	153	158	185	211
136	142	147	153	158	164	191	218
141	146	152	158	163	169	197	225
145	151	157	163	169	174	204	232
150	156	162	168	174	180	210	240
155	161	167	173	179	186	216	247
159	166	172	178	185	191	223	255
164	171	177	184	190	197	230	262
169	176	182	189	196	203	236	270
174	181	188	195	202	207	243	278
179	186	193	200	208	215	250	286
184	191	199	206	213	221	258	294
189	197	204	212	219	227	265	302
194	202	210	218	225	233	272	311
200	208	216	224	232	240	279	319
205	213	221	230	238	246	287	328

OVERWEIGHT   OBESE

divide it by your height in feet squared. Or you could just look at the chart on pages 92–93. (If you're off the chart, don't bother with a pencil because you're . . . off the charts.)

There are exceptions to such a simplistic description of something as complex as human body mass, but most researchers use BMI in their work because it's easy to calculate, so we're stuck with it for now. It is limited, though. BMI could appear to be high for a healthy bodybuilder, for example. Nor does the formula apply to kids and pregnant women. And, as we'll soon see, some doctors feel that other ways of measuring fat better predict your risk of disease.

How do you establish your most desirable BMI? Forget what you may have heard, because it's just not possible to arrive at an absolute number for everybody. Yet we are hung up on numbers, even though the standards are constantly changing—and we all go crazy. One widely used gauge holds that a BMI over 27.8 for men and 27.3 for women means overweight. The World Health Organization, however, says that anything between 25 and 29 is overweight, while over 30 means obesity.

In the past, the U.S. National Center for Health Statistics set the overweight bar at 27 for women and 28 for men. Then in June 1998, they lowered that bar to a gender-neutral 25 for all. From one day to the next, millions of Americans found themselves overweight. Although doctors love numbers, these obviously should be taken with a large grain of salt.

WHEN IS FAT UNHEALTHY?

We have no simple way to tell those who are genetically fat from those who are eating themselves fat. I suspect—remember, without proof, nothing rises above suspicion—that if we could separate the two groups we would find better health in the genetically fat compared with those who ate themselves fat. We have also shown that some fat folks do eat like birds.

Now we have to tackle the big one. With all this surprising support for fat from Mother Nature and her genes, how *unhealthy* is it to be fat? Generally, very fat people have higher rates of cardiovascular disease and some kinds of cancer, among other disorders. But nothing is automatic, and there are various exceptions and degrees within the generalizations. Even if you are extremely fat, as an individual you may beat the odds. Or you may make a decision just not to worry, that a shorter life well lived is better than a longer life spent miserably obsessing about diets and fat. (Of course, one also has to consider the possibility of a shorter life lived with illness as part of the equation.) In either case, you should be pleasantly surprised to know that you can be fatter than you think and still be as healthy as the rest of us. This is not just kindly Dr. Edell telling you what you want to hear. As you should expect from anybody's medical conclusions, all this is based on the biggest and best research out there.

Harvard Medical School took on a breathtaking project in 1976—a sixteen-year-long study of 115,195 Caucasian women. At the start they were between thirty-three and fifty-five years old. Over the years slightly fewer than one in one hundred of these women died of heart disease. While the skinnier women had the lowest mortality, mortality actually did not begin to increase substantially until a BMI of 27. That is pushing 160 pounds for a 5-foot-4-inch woman. The risk of mortality doubled at a BMI of 32, or nearly 200 pounds. Remember, the odds of dying from a heart attack over the sixteen years of the study were one in one hundred. The odds doubled means two in one hundred. How worried should that make you? That's a personal choice. Look at it another way: The very obese women had a 98 percent chance of not dying. The skinny women had a 99 percent chance of not dying.

When we are talking about millions of people, these seemingly small shifts are meaningful. But I'm trying to get you to chill out a little, look at *your* actual odds, and enjoy life. These figures included many women with high blood pressure, diabetes, and high cholesterol levels, all linked to obesity and premature death. Remove those women from the analysis, and fat people without these diseases look even healthier.

Which brings us to the Mother of All Fat Studies. It began in 1959 with one million American men and women and wound up being published on January 1, 1998, just in time for everyone's list of New Year's resolutions. First, the increased risk of dying from being fat was even more modest than in the previous study and was very age related. In fact, that risk declined with age and disappeared with senior citizens. That's right—being fat as a senior citizen did not increase the risk of dying. Obesity's effects were felt in the younger age groups. Of course, deaths in this group were much more rare than among their elders but still increased for the very overweight.

A headline about these findings in the *New York Times* said it suc-cinctly: OBESITY'S LINK TO EARLY DEATH FOUND LESS THAN SUSPECTED.

We have transformed obesity into a disease. What we are really doing is "medicalizing" behavior of which we disapprove, rightly charge the editors of the *New England Journal of Medicine*:

> In this age of political correctness, it seems that obese people can be criticized with impunity because the critics are merely trying to help them. Some doctors take part in this blurring of prejudice and altruism by overstating the dangers of obesity and the redemptive power of weight loss. On the other hand, some who object to society's prejudice against obesity engage in an overly rigid biologic determinism. They assert that obesity is no more within a person's control than eye color and thus has nothing to do with habits. Either way the result is to see overweight people in medical terms rather than as ordinary people who happen to be heavier than average, probably from some mixture of nature, nur-ture and choice.

Please don't get me wrong here. I and all the good doctors trying to get some perspective on this are *not* saying go out and get as fat as you want. Nor are we saying that losing weight automatically translates into improved health. "We simply do not know whether a person who loses 20 pounds will thereby acquire the same reduced risk as a per-son who started out 20 pounds lighter," the *New England Journal of Medicine* editorial noted. "The few studies of mortality among people who voluntarily lost weight produced inconsistent results; some even suggested that weight loss increased mortality."

We cannot answer this question, because there are not enough peo-ple who keep their weight down long enough for us to determine if they have less heart disease. It remains one of the critical unsolved mys-teries. That said, it appears that weight loss *is* healthier for overweight folks who suffer from diseases associated with obesity—diabetes and hypertension, to name two. There is a definite and increasing risk for heart disease and some cancers as you gain weight. But the risk may be lower than we have long thought, especially for middle-aged and older folks. There are so many other factors in the equation that it gets very difficult for an individual to gauge his or her exact risk.

If we start to change our thinking and accept that fat may not be such a bad thing, the query logically follows: Can you be fat and fit? Some experts have no doubt that fit-and-fat is better than out-of-shape and thin. That approach sends shock waves through the halls of weight-loss clinics. At least one study of twenty-five thousand men and seven thousand women, conducted by the Cooper Institute for Aerobics in Dallas, offers some clues. These folks were plopped on a treadmill and rated for fitness, then tracked for eight years. The least fit were twice as likely as the others to suffer fatalities from heart disease. It didn't matter how much fat they carried or where it was on their bodies. Thin, unfit men fared worse than big-bellied men who were fit!

THE WAIST BONE CONNECTED TO THE LIFE BONE

In fact, how *much* you weigh and your BMI may be less important than *where* you carry the weight. This is, perhaps, *the* critical point. It now seems that more fat at one site of the body is worse than at others. Basically, there are two body types: apple shape (abdominal obesity) and pear shape (thigh and buttock obesity). Generally, women are pears, men are apples. As you may recall, where you put weight is believed to be genetically determined.

OK, go get your tape measure, but promise you won't go crazy with these numbers. Take the smallest distance around your body below your ribs and above your belly button. That's your waistline. Now take the largest measurement around your butt and hips. That's your hip figure. Divide the waist by the hip and you now have your waist-hip ratio, another number about which to worry. Any figure above 1.0 and your risk increases for heart disease, diabetes, and stroke.

Does this represent the trashing of BMI as a measure of the fat-health connection? It's too early to tell, but we seem to be heading in that direction. "Mortality from coronary heart disease was even more strongly related to the ratio of the waist circumference to the hip circumference than to the body mass index," the *New England Journal* has noted.

There have now been a number of studies confirming the priority of shape over BMI. As a matter of fact, some doctors have gone a step further in simplifying this whole mess and come up with one single number: your waist. A recent analysis of 13,000 Europeans found that measurement still more preferable. The researchers said that it directly measures abdominal fat, is uninfluenced by height, and eliminates more "complex indices of adiposity."

Their guideline says heart disease is more likely in men with waists over 40 inches and women with waists over 35 inches. If that's you, they recommend you start slimming.

THE UGLY TRUTH

Diets don't work.

I'm trying to save you needless pain here. They don't work for a simple reason. Sooner or later, you'll go off them. Once you lose the weight—assuming that you do—you have to keep if off. If you drift back to your old patterns of eating, what do you think happens? You gain it all back, of course. Your only chance for success is permanently altering what and how you eat and your exercise patterns. You will need to find a new lifestyle and a new way of eating that satisfies you and that you can stick to forever. Otherwise you're just kidding yourself, and your body may make it harder to lose weight each time you try. And that's without considering the hazards and side effects of dieting itself.

We've already agreed that being fat is not automatically that big a deal. Major studies have found that "yo-yo dieting"—the rhythm method of girth control—is downright bad for you. In a study of eleven thousand Harvard graduates, researchers found a link between heart disease and weight changes. The lowest risk was among those with stable weights. The risk of death from heart disease rose 57 percent for those who lost more than 11 pounds and 26 percent for those who lost between 2 and 11 pounds. The researchers concluded that weight cycling adversely affects longevity. In truth, though, the yo-yo studies have not yet separated out those who lose and gain weight because of disease or stress from those who deliberately lose and gain weight for their own reasons.

Extreme dieting—roughly 1,000 or fewer calories a day—itself carries very specific and surprising side effects: high levels of blood cholesterol during rapid weight loss; altered reaction time, including deficits in hand-eye coordination that led one study to conclude that driving under the influence of a diet is hazardous; decreases in memory and mental performance; and irritability and depression.

We were taught in medical school that gallstones were specifically linked to the f-words: female, fat, forty, and fecund. Yet rapid weight loss itself, and not just being fat, could be the major cause of these gallstones. Subjects in one study were put on one of two daily diets: 520 calories and low fat (2 grams) or 900 calories and high fat (30 grams). Both diets produced the same 22 percent weight loss. But those on the lower-calorie diet had poor emptying of the gallbladder compared with those on the higher-calorie diet. Gallstones developed in four of the six low-calorie subjects and in none of the others. The researchers speculated that the greater quantity of fat might actually help, but other studies find higher rates of gallstones among people losing over 3.3 pounds per week.

In young women, there is no question that dieting inhibits ovulation, in turn stopping periods and causing bones to thin. We're not sure why, although most physiologists see a link with the amount of body fat. The body figures "Uh-oh, starvation again. I'd better not let her get pregnant, because there isn't enough food around." Click—ovulation turns off. This artificial menopause, especially in young women, creates some of the same problems experienced by older women, bone thinning among them. If your period stops while you're losing weight, take the hint.

Look at it this way: Would store mannequins menstruate? Women need at least 17 percent of their body fat in order to begin menstruating and a bit more—around 22 percent—for their cycles to stay regular. Mannequins from four decades (1920s and '30s, 1950s and '60s) were compared by measuring their shapes to estimate their percent of body fat. Would they ovulate if they were real women? Perhaps a silly question—but not when you think how women emulate these dummies on a regular basis. It turns out that before the 1950s, such bodies would indeed have menstruated—but not in the last two decades measured.

STARVING ON THE ROAD TO HAPPINESS

Eating disorders have become a plague, and international studies are finding the plague now sweeping even into the Third World. These disorders are the extreme endpoints of our cultural obsession with appearance. I'm not going to dwell on them in this book, but it would be irresponsible to talk about dieting without even a glance at this horrible phenomenon.

Anorexics see themselves and food differently than other people do. You cannot tell an 85-pound woman she looks too skinny. Where you see skinny, she sees only fat—literally. Her actual visual sense is distorted, and it can be proved. At an Australian university, women with anorexia and normal women sat down before two television sets. Only one set really worked. The screen on the other had been removed and replaced with a shelf on which real objects were placed. As a video image of the same object appeared on the working set, the subject used a zoom button to match its size to the real thing. Videotapes were made of neutral objects—a tennis ball, a notebook, a jewelry box. Videotapes were also made of a cream bun, a chocolate bar, and a sausage meat pie.

Everyone agreed on the size of the neutral objects. But the anorexics greatly exaggerated the size of the food. They zoomed the video version of the sausage pie until it filled the screen and insisted it was identical to the far smaller, real sausage pie. Just as their sadly skinny bodies look huge to them, so does a burger on a plate.

But we've all had our views distorted to one degree or another. How many diets do we have to go through before we figure out we've been scammed? Diet promoters need a new gimmick with the start of each new diet season. When February rolls around, we begin thinking about bathing suits and skimpy clothes and the stampede starts. It's not easy to come up with a dieting revolution every year. First, there are only three basic nutrients to play with—carbohydrates, protein, and fat—which greatly limits the number of diets. In other words, if you eat lots of carbohydrates, fat and protein levels will drop. If you eat a lot of protein, carbohydrates will drop and fats will rise.

Have you figured out yet what that means? There are only two diets with which to fiddle: (1) high protein–high fat–low carbohydrate or (2) high carbohydrate–low protein–low fat. I know the diet-book industry isn't going to like that.

WELCOME TO THE NUTRITION ACADEMY

Take out your notebooks, class. You'll want to remember this for the quiz.

Calories, which are heat energy, measure the amount of energy provided by any given food.

Now, 1 gram of any fat or oil has 9 calories. That's more than twice as many calories as proteins and carbohydrates, each with 4 calories per gram.

A pound of fat equals approximately 3,500 calories.

If you eat 500 fewer calories a day, at the end of a seven-day week you could lose a pound.

Exercise away another 500 calories a day and you could lose 2 pounds by the end of the week.

Anyone who tells you you can lose much more than that is kidding—or conning—you, and even if you could, it would be unhealthy. Nutritionists say that 3.5 pounds a week is the most an average human body can lose. Some diets can cause a diuresis, or water loss, and because water is heavy, you think you're on one whale of a diet. Start drinking water again, though, and—oops—the weight is back.

Finally, the Golden Rule: You will lose weight on any diet where you consume fewer calories than you burn. I have never seen a diet— and I have reviewed many hundreds—that did not obey that principle. No matter how seductive the claim, take the time to add up the calories and you'll see I'm right. Almost all will come in under 1,500 calories.

End of class. You have now graduated from Dr. Dean's Nutrition Academy. Go outside and play.

DIET GRADUATE SCHOOL

There is a very important caveat here that we do not teach undergraduates at Dr. Dean's Nutrition Academy because it might discourage our students from paying their tuition. You are all different, each with a separate and unique metabolism. No two people will react the same way to a given diet. I doubt that will stop many of you from buying diet books and throwing money away on the latest fat cure (if you buy Slim Skins, I will come and personally turn on your vacuum cleaner). Diets have turned into health cults, with all the trappings. Only religious zeal can help keep a diet alive, which may explain why so many are continually resurrected and spread by believers to a public with a short memory. Whenever I slam the diet-of-the-day on my shows, the vitriol that floods the studio is almost overwhelming. Hate mail pours in from folks who just don't want to believe the calories-in, calories-burned dictum.

I continually struggle over the best ways to convince you that most fad diets are bogus. Logic and nutritional science are no match for a good huckster. They come marching, one right after the other. High-protein diets have been condemned by dieticians since they first started emerging in the nineteenth century. They produce initial water loss, which gets you excited and turns you into a believer. But they also increase work for your kidneys, promote stones, thin your bones, increase gout, raise blood fats, and according to some research hot off the press, may shorten life span. You know their names—Dr. Atkins Diet Revolution, Dr. Stillman's Quick Weight-Loss Diet, Dr. Tarnower's Scarsdale Diet, the I Love New York Diet, Dr. Taller's Calories Don't Count. Protein powder diets were big-time, too. The Last Chance Diet, the Cambridge Diet. All were giant mega-hits in their day.

It's all just marketing twists and turns. There's nothing creative in the diet—it's in the packaging. Pick a food, make it magic. The Grapefruit Diet, the Cabbage Soup Diet, the Water Diet, the Grape Diet, the Rice Diet, the Candy Diet. Just like the seasons . . . Or you can combine those foods, a concept also dating back to the nineteenth century. Remember the Beverly Hills Diet? Eat only one food type at a time, like fruits, or it'll clog your intestines. How about the Fit for Life Diet, which warned you not to combine proteins with fat or you would get fat. Ten years ago, the immune system captured everyone's imagination and—voilà—Dr. Berger's Immune Power Diet, where fat was nothing more than the response of a hyperactive immune system to food. That one really frustrated me. True believers saw me as a typical doctor feeling threatened by the breakthrough of a great genius. The talk show hosts gushed. Dr. Berger died shortly after, at age forty. He weighed 365 pounds.

I must concede genius at work. Not of the nutritional kind, however. I still admire the inspiration behind the Blood Type Diet. If your blood is type O, which is most people, you are descended from hunters and therefore should eat fat and meat.

Time for some simple truth. If any of these diets or scams really work, why aren't they around anymore? Wouldn't all doctors—even obese doctors themselves, and their spouses and loved ones—use them? Obesity is one of the major health problems of the Western world, although I've narrowed the spectrum of its wrath. We are now experiencing the highest rate of obesity in American history. A Harris poll in 1998 found that 76 percent of adults were heavier than recommended for their height and body frame. In 1983 the figure was 58 percent. Anything that could really and truly beat this enemy would be on the front page of every newspaper, lead the evening news, and make the media circus over Viagra look like a small-time carnival. The inventor of such a diet would win the Nobel Prize. The cure for this curse is not a P.O. Box in Florida, or your neighbor's multilevel marketing scam, or the latest hardcover best-seller.

AND YOU BELIEVE THEM?

In this age of science and reason, we want evidence good enough for a court of law. We want evidence that our cars and airplanes are safe. We want evidence that our drugs work and won't hurt us and that our food is not poisoned. Yet we require *no* evidence that a diet works before we make ourselves miserable trying to follow it. True, many fat farms and diets will give you results over the short haul—and misery for the long haul once you escape the regimentation of the program. Why would you subject yourself to that work and commitment with no evidence other than what some shyster feeds you? Unfortunately, there are few long-term studies of diet farms and other commercial weight-loss programs. They are not likely to open their doors to research when they can get customers without a seal of scientific approval. It doesn't matter if research proves the diet works, because the clients have already made that assumption.

So what research *do* we have? One investigation studied a program that used one of the more popular combinations of liquid and solid food diets. At the start of the diet, the average weight in the group was 233 pounds. On average, group members lost 48 pounds during the intensive dieting phase. After three years, though, the average weight in the group was 225 pounds. About one out of ten of the subjects maintained 75 percent of the original weight loss, about half maintained only 5 percent of the loss, and more than one-third gained back more than they had lost during the diet.

The same researchers examined lifestyle factors, searching for predictors of success in maintaining weight loss. They found that frequency of exercise after the diet foreshadowed a better outcome. Television viewing translated into a gain in weight. Their rather sobering conclusion: "Given the apparent lack of substantial long-term success at weight reduction, perhaps greater emphasis should be placed on prevention of obesity."

As you can see, the bottom line is maintenance. There are plenty of diets to get your weight down, but help in making it permanent is scarce.

The largest known study of successful long-term weight loss is called the National Weight Control Registry, compiled by the University of Pittsburgh. It included 629 women and 155 men who lost an average of 66 pounds. They maintained a minimum weight loss of 30 pounds for five years. Slightly more than half lost that weight through formal programs. The rest did it on their own. Almost all relied on diet and exercise. Current consumption averaged 1,400 calories a day and 24 percent fat. Here's an important hint: 77 percent reported that success was preceded by a triggering event or incident, either of a medical nature (back pain, fatigue, sore legs, varicose veins, sleep apnea) or an emotional nature. The trigger for 11 percent was just a look in the mirror.

That is one tough approach to life to maintain.

DR. DEAN'S HIGH-PROTEIN-HIGH-FAT-HIGH-CHOLESTEROL-EAT-SUGAR-AND-STARCH-PUT-ME-ON-A-TALK-SHOW-I'M-THE-KING-OF-THE-WORLD DIET

So, what can you *really* do? Well, you *can* lose weight, but it takes hard work. Those few who have been successful in the long term swear it's worth it, but I can't tell you whether they had the metabolisms to make it happen easily and keep on happening. There is plenty of legitimate research to feed your fantasies. One of the more legitimate pieces of advice concerns fiber, which has no calories at all. You can fill your tummy with fiber-rich foods like whole grains and fresh fruits and vegetables while minimizing the number of calories that tag along for the ride. Avoid calorie-dense foods like potato chips and deep-fried foods, which pack a maximum of calories into a minimum of space.

Other advice seems a little less weighty. For instance, the National Institutes of Health calculates that if you fidget—tap your fingers and toes and chew your pencil—you can burn from 200 to 850 calories a day. The intrepid researcher does warn, however, not to rely on such knee-jiggling antics as your only source of exercise: "It's possible to be fat even if you're a fidgeter." Thanks.

Harvard University, meanwhile, tells us that 100 milligrams of caffeine—a weak cup of java—six times over a twelve-hour span burns up to 150 calories. The researchers conclude that coffee may promote thermogenesis, or heat production. I guess maybe you could be a thinner fidgeting coffee-drinker.

Tufts University says that several small meals a day are better than one big one, especially for older women. Fits in with those sumo wrestlers, who put on their pounds by gorging at one meal. The wrestlers say it's not what you eat but how and when you eat. At 500 pounds they ought to know.

In my kind of business, I come across many tasty morsels of advice that make no scientific sense for someone who is serious about long-term success. But I have never had to go on a diet. Maybe these kinds of tricks help some folks get through the night:

- Chew your food well. You'll spend time chewing instead of shoveling it in.
- Use chopsticks. Each bite will be smaller.
- Don't eat with fast music, because you eat more.
- Use tiny plates, demitasse spoons, and shellfish forks.

See what I mean?

As you may have guessed, I refuse to give you a specific diet to follow because sooner or later you have to go off it. The only chance is to learn how to eat. Throw out all your diet books. Do the basic things that dieticians have been telling you to do for years. Focus on some simple truths that are your only chance, and assume you have a svelte-friendly metabolism.

But because you insist and make me feel guilty, I'm going to give you the diet you've been begging for. Ready?

Eat whatever you damned well want, but eat less.

You've heard it before? Check the end of Chapter 2. There I showed you how this strategy could lengthen your life, thus enabling you to buy my future books. Now you discover that this is the yellow brick road to weight loss as well. This has got to be the easiest diet plan ever offered to the American public. Call it the Dr. Dean Shut-Your-Mouth Diet.

Finally, if you're not going to stick to any of this, then just give up trying and enjoy life. But do get some exercise.

4

EXERCISE IS NO FUN
IF IT KILLS YOU

Disclaimer: Call this "Confessions of a Sports-o-phobe." Now in my late fifties, I'm a guy still in search of his physical activity. Throughout my life I've had a very mixed relationship with exercise and athletics. I passed through the asphalt games of an urban youth, on to the organized sports of mainstream America—baseball, swimming, track (I still have a drawer full of my old track medals).

Yet my reaction to certain sports has always been the same: borrrring! Back and forth, back and forth, or round and round, round and round. I never learned to relish that burning in my chest and the rubbery pain in my thighs as I pounded or stroked my way to finish lines. It's the same reaction I have today when I look in a health club at all those people on treadmills to nowhere. Different strokes, I know, but I can't help feeling that too often they just don't look like they're having fun.

In school I ran in the Penn Relays, a major East Coast track and field tournament. I remember the sign over the gym entrance: "To win the game is great; to play the game, greater; and to love the game, the greatest." That was it. I've never loved the game, at least the round-and-round, back-and-forth kind.

At six feet four and 185 pounds, I'm genetically blessed with a body that should play. When I was a youngster, it didn't quite seem that way—remember the kid in the Charles Atlas ads? My grandmother called me a "skinny-merink." Whatever a merink was, I knew it meant scrawny.

I've played or tried innumerable sports over the years, but all of them pose problems I just can't get past—too much time, too much gear, too far to travel. I admit to a lazy streak.

The genetic blessing handed to me by my parents has probably made it tougher for me to fashion a consistent exercise program. I'm encouraged in this excuse by the occasional trek up a hill with friends who work out and are in much better shape than I am yet huff and puff more and produce higher heart rates than I do. We'll talk about why later.

That said, the best shape I have ever been in came about without my even noticing it. Living in the country started the fitness ball rolling. After purchasing property in northern California's rural red-woods country, my family lived in our bus at first while we built a house. There was no end to the work to be done. You want to be warm, you need to cut, haul, and split wood. There are holes to be dug with shovels and post-hole diggers, dirt to be moved in wheelbarrows. Building the house taught me a lot about how the human body wants to be trained. One of my friends took a picture of me then. I look at that picture today and can't believe the rippled deltoids and wash-board stomach. There wasn't a muscle group not in use every day, and I accomplished something in the process, through a multitude of applications, all voluntary and fun. Sometimes I wish I could come up with a big project to build in my backyard. I could just build it and take it apart and build it all over again. I know—it sounds perilously close to round-and-round and back-and-forth.

My wistful musings here are aimed at the same point I made in past chapters: Whatever you do, if it isn't *fun*, you aren't going to stick with it. My iron-willed friends who run every morning tell me it's not easy for them either. Once into it, they say, it doesn't feel so bad. Not feeling bad is different from feeling good, though.

Perhaps you feel good on an exercise machine. It's a time in the day where you are in control. No boss, no kids, no one nagging you. It offers a sense of power and control not felt in other moments of the day. Generally you don't see people getting hooked on activities they don't enjoy, whether good for them or not.

More than fifty million Americans say they have purchased home exercise equipment of one kind or another, at an average cost of $473, or around $3.5 *billion* a year. In 1996 alone, almost three million people bought abdominal gadgets. It's all there, in living rooms and garages: free weights, stationary bikes, treadmills, rowing machines, cross-country machines, stair-climbers and ab-rollers. For the financially strapped, there are oversize rubber bands and tubing, or boxes to step on and off. All those substitutes for "real" exercise, as if there were nowhere to ride a bike or hike or walk or row or even climb stairs.

For the most part, exercise machine users don't stay motivated for long. The novelty wears off, it gets boring, and the equipment collects dust. In one survey, one-third of exercise machine owners said they never touch the machines. Of those, almost half said the machines were just too boring to use; the other half said they didn't have the time. Of all those polled, 88 percent claimed they would never again buy exercise equipment.

WHEN IT HELPS; WHEN IT DOESN'T

I can't tell you that the only exercise you need is changing channels on your remote control. But I'm also not going to tell you that you have to run 10 miles a day to be healthy. I think when we get done you'll realize that you need less exercise than you think to accrue most of the health benefits. You'll also see that exercise is not a magic cure for all that ails you and that it can even have some very negative consequences. Every orthopedist I know drives the latest car, thanks to business. Look at the explosion in sports-medicine specialists and clinics to handle overexuberant weekend warriors who are playing too hard and worsening their health.

I place almost the highest premium on having fun. Otherwise all that activity may not be worth it, and you'll stop on the first rainy day you can manufacture. Like yo-yo dieting, dabbling in exercise here and there can make matters worse. If you're miserable every day because you hate your exercise program, that could have negative consequences on your health via the mind-body effect. At the same time, over the years I've noted a growing belief that all mega-exercise is good for everyone. I want you to respect exercise as you would a prescription drug, to consider the benefits and the risks just as you would for any therapy. You have to know what exercise can do *to* you as well as *for* you.

For that, science is once again your friend. If you are typically sedentary—and most of you are—the goal is to figure out what kind of activity is not only best and most appropriate for you but enjoyable enough that you'll stick with it. For those decisions, you need the numbers. You need to know what science can tell us about the benefits you'll get from dragging yourself out of bed in the morning and putting on your tennies. Then *you* choose, rather than letting the health nags sell you unnecessarily painful exercise regimens.

There is only one way to get truly scientifically objective data. Here's the protocol: Put test subjects in exactly the same cages, feed them exactly the same diets, exercise some and not others. Wait eighty years and see who does better. Short of that impossible standard, though, we can look at the biggest and best of the major studies conducted over the past few years and see what they found. I think you'll be pleasantly surprised.

In 1986 Stanford assembled a study of 17,000 Harvard alumni, men who had entered the university between 1916 and 1950. The men completed questionnaires in the early 1960s about their personal and lifestyle habits. They were then followed until 1978. Since the first questionnaire, 1,413 had died: nearly half from heart disease, 32 percent from cancer, 10 percent from trauma, and 13 percent from other natural causes. The researchers were very sensitive to criticism that these studies were distorted because only healthy people who feel fine engage in exercise. To counter this assumption, they looked at people with high blood pressure who smoked. Those people did better with exercise, but of course, skeptics would argue that the healthiest smokers might choose to exercise more than the unhealthiest.

There was a clear benefit to exercise. Death rates were one-quarter to one-third less among alumni expending at least 2,000 calories per week (that's 20 miles of brisk walking a week) compared with less active men. But when they expended more than 3,500 calories a week, the death rate started going up. By age eighty, the researchers estimated, the subjects who had exercised at 2,000 or more calories a week had added between one and two years to their lives.

That's pretty impressive, isn't it? But let's think about it for a second. Heard the one about Sadie and Sam meeting Saint Peter in heaven? He shows them their new five-bedroom house and 5-acre yard, right next to the twelfth tee, and hands them the keys to their matching shiny Jaguars. "See," Sam mutters to Sadie, "if we hadn't exercised, we could have gotten here sooner." Better still was a cartoon I once saw in a newspaper: a group of very old, decrepit patients sit in their wheelchairs in a nursing home. "Sure glad I exercised every day," one of the geezers says to another. "I wouldn't have wanted to miss all this."

The Stanford study provoked a flood of letters to the *New England Journal of Medicine*. Dr. David Jacoby of the Cardiovascular Research Institute at the University of California at San Francisco offered the following analysis: 2,000 calories a week for fifty-two weeks a year over sixty years would total between 1.18 and 2.37 years spent exercising. "Thus, the bad news is that although you may live an extra two years," Jacoby concludes, "those two years will be spent jogging." Of course, if you enjoy jogging—and I know that many people do—those are two years well spent.

Not to be outdone, several Johns Hopkins researchers took the Stanford study and performed some stair-climbing calculations: Climb five thousand stairs a week, use up 2,000 calories. At the Johns Hopkins hospital, with twenty-two stairs between floors, that means two hundred twenty-eight flights of stairs per week, or thirty-eight floors per day over a six-day work week. They actually recruited volunteers to try it out. The final calculation that may prove useful to you, especially if you're an urban reader who lives in a walk-up: every story climbed will add one and a half minutes to your life, or four seconds per step.

ALL RIGHT, FOLKS, ONE, TWO, LET'S BRING THOSE DEATH RATES *DOWN*

It's time for more encouraging news about exercise. In 1989 the Institute for Aerobics Research compiled the results of a massive and impressive project. I told you a little about their diet results in the last chapter. Between 1970 and 1981 they gave over 10,000 men and 3,000 women complete medical exams, took full histories, ran blood tests, executed electrocardiograms, and administered a full treadmill test for fitness. They then followed all of the subjects for eight years. Over that time, 240 men and 43 women died—most of them older, less fit, and with less promising health profiles. If all the unfit folks had taken appropriate measures to get in shape, the death rates would have dropped by 9 percent in men and 15 percent in women.

Impressive numbers, no doubt. Let's take it a step further. Out of 10,000 men, 240 deaths equals 2.4 deaths per 100. A reduction of 9 percent with fitness means, then, 2.2 deaths per 100. Doesn't sound so impressive anymore, does it? Hang on to the idea that they were measuring fitness here, not how much people exercised. As you will see, some people are fit without a lot of exercise.

The real good news is that if you decide to get in shape, you don't have to go for a 5-mile run every morning. Listen to this, from the institute:

> The greatest reduction in relative risk occurs between the lowest level of fitness and the next-lowest level of fitness. . . . Even a modest improvement in fitness level among the most unfit confers a substantial health benefit. This finding makes our health promotion task considerably easier. Inactive individuals are likely to find lower-intensity activities such as walking more acceptable than higher-intensity ones such as running. Lower-intensity activities are likely to be more comfortable, more convenient, more affordable, safer, and, thus, more likely to be done. We suggest choosing an activity that is pleasurable, or at least not abhorrent for the patient . . . .

Now we're getting somewhere. The very fit in this study did not show as high a degree of health gain as did the more moderately fit.

The next step in your reindoctrination is this: accept that if you *force* yourself to exercise, you may well diminish your results. Personally, this is my favorite excuse. Dr. Monika Fleshner at the University of Colorado says that if you exercise by choice, you "are going to get the full health benefit" from physical activity. Granted, her conclusions are drawn from rat studies, but people are all just big rats anyway. Essentially, assigning rats to the treadmill versus letting 'em get on and off at will made a big difference in their immune systems. In short, voluntary exercise was good; forced exercise was bad.

Fleshner also quotes studies on military recruits. Require them to exercise and march, and their immune systems start kicking up. She extends this notion to explain why physiologically stressed elite athletes may have immune problems. She is also concerned about heart attack victims who may be unwillingly placed in exercise programs and don't do so well. You don't have to be giddy with enthusiasm every time you start to exercise. But you may find that pushing yourself off the sofa and into the exercise of your choice may later leave you feeling glad you did.

We can say that focusing on the positives of exercise rather than the negatives seems to make you more likely to enjoy it and therefore stick to it. At Washington University in St. Louis, researchers studied 364 exercising women. If the women believed in the psychological and physical benefits of the exercise and focused less on the unpleasant stuff—sweating, discomfort, soreness, shortness of breath—they were more likely to exercise for longer periods and with greater intensity. In other words, think about the upside of exercise as you do it. Instead of dwelling on how much you hate that muscle ache, think of it as a sign that you are accomplishing something good. And as you get more fit, you should feel less discomfort.

Let's catch up with the Harvard alumni in the Stanford study. Now it's five years later—1993—and yes, the benefit of lifelong major exercise is still showing up. But there are new twists in the statistics. After twelve years, 476 more deaths had been registered among the 10,269 men remaining. Moderately vigorous sports activity was associated with a death rate now reduced by one-quarter. But put it in perspective. Quitting smoking produced a 41 percent decrease in the risk of death. Exercise, on average, added nine months to life. Frankly, the authors were disappointed by the findings; they had hoped for more from exercise. It's difficult to extend the human life span. "Some may be discouraged over the fact that you don't gain a lot of years," they said.

A Honolulu heart study begun in 1965 investigated the health of 8,000 Japanese-American men living in Hawaii. The more detailed part of the study honed in on a twelve-year period and 707 older, retired nonsmokers between the ages of sixty-one and eighty-one. The study found that it doesn't take much exercise to do some good. By walking 2 miles a day, they cut the risk of death from cancer and heart disease *in half*. This was just plain walking, not running. Really, a couple of miles a day loping around the mall isn't that much and could even be fun. Just don't stop off too often at Baskin-Robbins.

IT'S YOUR GENES . . . AGAIN

As with obesity, fitness may have strong genetic components. But in this area, the pendulum seems to be moving a little farther from heredity and back toward environment.

Return for a moment to our friends at the Institute for Aerobics Research. Only fitness, not exercise, was measured. Many of the fit folks doing well on the institute's treadmill are not that way because of exercise but because of genetics. That group will live longer because of their genes, not because of their hours spent working out. That said, of course you can improve physical fitness with exercise training. "It is well established that exercise training improves physical fitness typically by 15 percent to 20 percent in middle-aged men and women," the institute researchers advise. "Earlier reports suggested in 1971 that approximately 90 percent of the inter-individual variation in maximal aerobic power could be explained by heredity, but more recent studies place the genetic component at approximately 30 percent . . . . Athletes presumably have genetic advantages in terms of physical fitness." As far as I'm concerned, that explains why I'm not wheezing next to my friend, who huffs and puffs as we climb that hill together.

That doesn't mean you can count on your genes. Although this research found a strong genetic component to fitness and strength, like all such research this can only predict trends, not what's going on in any one individual. You cannot be sure your kids will be like you—genetics offers only an indication of a likely relationship. I mentioned that I'm in possession of all the excuses and am in search of the right activity for me. I hope one day to slow down a bit and spend more time in the country, where the lifestyle automatically dictates fitness. But the truth is that I'm lucky in my genes and am probably more active than I admit. At eighty-six, my dad weighs what I do—which is what I weighed in high school, although he walks and swims for fitness.

The best place to look for answers about genetics is again among twins. Researchers in Belgium looked at athletic test scores of 105 pairs and their parents. Some of the twins were identical and therefore had identical genes. Others were fraternal, which means that genetically they were no different from any pair of siblings. If identical twins are more alike in any characteristic compared with fraternal twins, then the explanation is in the genes.

The parents and their kids were remarkably alike. The identical twins were more alike than the fraternal twins. From that comparison, researchers were able to estimate how much of our athletic prowess is inherited. For instance:

- Heredity accounted for almost all aerobic capacity in girls and only two-thirds of that capacity for boys.
- Heredity accounted for most upper body strength. If one identical twin could do ten pull-ups, the twin averaged nine. But among the fraternal twins, if one could do ten pull-ups, the sibling averaged closer to five—which approaches the average of the population. The same held true for the ability to jump vertically.

David Allison at Columbia University said that the research "suggests we are not all created equal; we need to take these inequalities into account so everyone can experience some level of success."

Another study of twins in Finland looked specifically at weight loss in relation to exercise. The shocker from this study: researchers found a direct genetic influence on how much weight you will lose with each mile you run, and the influence was much stronger for men than women. In its authors' view, the study shows that "genetic factors may modify the effects of physical activity on weight change and suggests that a sedentary lifestyle may have an obesity-promoting effect in men with a genetic predisposition." In other words, some men can sit on their butts and stay thin. Other men sit on their butts and get fat. Some men can exercise and fat will come off easily. Some men can exercise and the fat will fight them. In women, it seems that changes in weight were independent of how much exercise they got. For them, exercise alone may not make a difference. There is other research—we'll talk about it later—indicating that exercise alone, without dieting, is not an effective weight-loss tool for women. It should be said that the women in this study did not get much exercise.

Strap on your gear and let's climb Mount Everest. Some mountain climbers may be genetically able to handle those kinds of elevations without oxygen. Scientists looked at fifteen male British mountaineers at 26,000 feet and measured certain angiotensin-converting enzyme (ACE) genes that confer fitness and regulate everything from blood pressure to muscle building. Six of the climbers had at least one copy of this special gene, while the rest had two copies. At sea level, the same researchers measured the length of time army recruits could do arm curls while holding a 33-pound weight. Those with two copies of the super ACE genes flexed their biceps for eighty seconds longer than those without.

Don't get depressed; this should remind you of another of my running themes: Unfortunately, you cannot know which group you fall into or, with certainty, whether or not you will get help from any particular strategy. The science doesn't exist yet to allow us to determine which genetic group you're in or to predict the real final outcome in terms of life span. While researchers can predict the average life span for a large group of people, for one person—you—in the end it all comes down to guesswork. Some people will do better with exercise, some will get no benefit, and some will be harmed. Although you don't know which group is yours, if you find yourself gasping with every effort, if getting out of the car is an aerobic exercise, it's a pretty safe bet that you should jump on the fitness bandwagon.

On the other hand, if you're a couch potato who seems to have the blessing of relative fitness without trying, you may be able to get away with a little less than the aforementioned individual.

Studies have shown that people who exercise are more likely to eat better diets, have more income, and get better medical care, all of which improve health. A piece in the *New England Journal of Medicine* concludes with the following: "Men who reported participating in sports may have adopted other kinds of health-promoting behavior, such as following a cholesterol-lowering diet that may have reduced their risk of cardiovascular disease or other illnesses."

MYTHOLOGY OF THE EXERCISE GODS

Every time I turn the corner, I hear another absolute untruth about exercise that just won't go away. Let's look at these myths one by one so that you can judge for yourself what makes sense and what doesn't.

Exercise Helps You Reduce Weight from Specific Parts of Your Body

Millions of dollars are made on abdominal exerciser infomercials promising a washboard stomach. If you let me rummage through your closet, I may well find one hidden under your old argyles. The reason these devices will never work is that there is no such thing as spot reducing. Most people figure—mistakenly—that the body part doing the exercise is the part that will slim down. For instance, if you just did leg lifts or squats, your legs would become thinner.

In one project, nineteen men did a total of 5,004 sit-ups over twenty-seven days. Makes me double over just to think of it. Then doctors took fat biopsies from their abdomens, shoulder blades, and buttocks. They measured the fat cells themselves for size and found a decrease in the cell diameters in all three sites but with no differences between sites. The fat in their bellies did not reduce any more than the fat in their butts. In fact, depending on the genetic programming of your body shape, the fat in your butt could decrease more than the fat in your belly. If you exercise and therefore use more calories than you are eating, the fat will be drawn from everywhere, depending on your physiology. You can, of course, tone or firm up the muscles in certain areas, but you only lose weight by burning more calories than you take in. Sorry. All the squats in the world will not shrink your thighs. Sit-ups will not shrink your potbelly. If spot reducing *were* possible, then right-handed tennis players would have less fat on their right arms. They don't. Fat deposition is programmed by your genes.

Jogging Will Bounce That Beer Belly Away

Now I'm warmed up, so let's take a second look at that potbelly. If you count on running to take off the spare tire that bugs your wife, a recent discussion in the *Journal of the American Medical Association* may surprise you. Running could make it worse. Runners get potbellies for a couple of reasons. The action itself will cause a change in posture over time. It is hard to hold in your stomach when you're hoofing it. If you're not accompanying that exercise with back and abdominal exercises, the abdominal muscles will wilt and weaken over time. The result even has its own names: "runner's swayback" or—surprise, surprise—"potbelly."

Upper-body strength helps your posture, and that can fight your belly. Aerobic exercises like running may not do that much for upper-body strength. Regular aerobic exercise may not counteract the normal loss of muscle mass that comes with age. One study of master athletes running more than 31 miles a week found that as they aged, there was still a loss in muscle mass and a gain in fat mass. To maintain muscle mass, researchers recommend adding strength training. So you can't beg off the sit-ups just because you're running. Here's a bonus tip on that belly of yours: Don't eat a lot late in the evening. Sleeping on a full stomach stretches abdominal muscles.

If You Build Up Your Muscles and Then Stop Exercising, Those Muscles Will Turn to Fat

This is just plain wrong. Muscle cells are muscle cells; fat cells are fat cells. They cannot turn into one another. With time muscles do get weaker and smaller, but they don't turn to fat. Those big-talking beer-bellied ex-athletes have simply done what we all do—taken in more calories than they used. The calories turn into fat deposits.

No Pain, No Gain

This myth is more than just a nuisance because many athletes put themselves in danger by believing it. It is one thing to be tough and another to be stupid. Experienced professional athletes can often identify the source of their discomfort. Their body is their work equipment, so it makes sense that they know their machinery better than the average bear. They know the difference between the routine discomfort of high exertion and the pain of true injury.

If you do not know the source of your pain, don't just ignore it. You might be making something worse that will give you trouble down the road. Pain needs to be heeded. Tendonitis, stress fractures, shin splints, and inflamed joints, tendons, and ligaments can more than slam you to the sidelines. All these conditions can permanently affect your joint and extremity function, even when you're not exercising. They can be tough to heal and can turn into worse injuries. Stress fractures are very common and are often missed by inexperienced physicians. Think of a stress fracture as a teacup that is cracked but not broken. You can keep using it, but sooner or later the cup will break. Many injuries accrue not suddenly but gradually through microtrauma to muscles and tendons and ligaments. Listen to your body, and do not exercise through pain. Check with a professional.

You'll Get Cramps If You Drink Too Many Liquids

Dehydration is the more likely explanation for true cramping of muscles. It is true, though, that if you gulp down a quart, that much liquid sloshing around your stomach will yank on the ligaments that hold it. That will make you uncomfortable for a few minutes until the liquid flows into the intestines and bloodstream. In general, drink ahead of your thirst when you exercise. Also, steer clear of carbonated beverages because they fill you up with gas, not water.

Sweat a Lot, Lose a Lot of Weight

Sorry, *schvitzers* (that's Yiddish for someone who usually sweats by the gallon). It would be nice if it were true. You could just go stand in the sun on a hot summer day and slim down to the real you. Sweat does have weight, about 8 pounds to the gallon. But as soon as you drink liquids for the thirst that accompanies the sweat, your body replenishes any fluid loss, as well as any weight that went with it.

If I Exercise, My Appetite Will Increase, Then I'll Eat More and Gain Weight

It sounds so logical. As counterintuitive as it seems, though, overweight women on a treadmill in one test did not increase their intake of food. It is true, according to studies, that the appetites of naturally thin women on an exercise program naturally increase to prevent their bodies from losing weight and to make up for the calories burned by the exercise. However, they may have a different metabolism compared with the naturally fat. No, the extra calories you might eat will be more than burned off by the exercise.

FEELING BLUE? EXERCISE AND *Maybe* FEEL BETTER

General wisdom holds that when you're feeling down, exercise will help you feel better. The public, the media, and many professionals have long professed that exercise will improve psychological health, well-being, and self-esteem. It's tough to prove. One experiment gave it a credible shot. It's worth taking a look.

Remember the placebo? It's a fake pill that makes you feel better because someone has told you it will and you believe it. The equivalent in exercise would be the belief that activity makes you feel better, so it does. Canadian researchers found an exercise placebo effect. They recruited forty-eight young, healthy adults to participate in a study of health and fitness. The subjects, split into two groups, trained three times a week for ninety minutes, including jogging, aerobic dancing, pool games, and soccer.

The researchers told one group that the project was designed to assess aerobic capacity *and* psychological well-being linked to exercise. The other group was told that they were being studied only for physical aerobic capacity. At the end, psychological health, well-being, and self-esteem were assessed among all the participants. You guessed yet? The first group soared in well-being; the second registered no change at all. This could well mean that at least some of the psychological benefits of exercise are due to the placebo effect. Personally, I'm now working to convince myself that coffee in bed in the morning brings me well-being.

The evidence is not clear about whether the mental benefits are truly there or not. A study conducted by researchers at Stanford University and the University of California at San Francisco found no improvement in mental health among two hundred formerly sedentary men and women between fifty and sixty-five who exercised for a year. At least one other major study confirms this conclusion.

Evidence has shown that exercise can help mood and anxiety levels by distracting you from your troubles. Endorphins, neurochemicals that have gotten a lot of press, may induce the "runner's high" but only in maximum endurance athletes. Even if there is no magic hormone or reflex at work, so what? If it makes you feel better and you're not ripping your body apart in the process, be my guest.

MORE MIND FOR YOUR BODY

That's not to say that mind and muscle are not connected in wonderful ways. A remarkable piece of research appeared in the 1940s, later confirmed in other studies, that looked at students who mentally practiced darts and basketball free throws. These students improved their games almost as much as those actually practicing the skills.

But can mental exercise actually improve strength? In another experiment, scientists measured the strength in the quadriceps and thighs of female volunteers. Then they divided the subjects into two groups. One group met in a room and mentally practiced contracting their thigh muscles. They were wired to an electromyograph to ensure that they really were not contracting the muscle. They increased strength by 13 percent compared with the women who didn't practice at all.

Under most circumstances, untrained individuals do not fully activate their muscles. Although this was a small study with admittedly amazing findings, the researchers speculated that the subjects may learn to move their muscles more efficiently, which in turn improves performance. By the way, none of this leads to an increase in the size of muscles. So you can't fantasize your way to tremendous triceps. Hypnosis, too, has been found to increase strength. Another project documented that when you imagine doing a task you actually turn on 80 percent of the brain circuits used in the task itself. If true, this confirms claims of pianists, violinists, and tennis players, for example, who practice their specialties in their brains.

EXERCISING YOUR WAY TO TROUBLE

You haven't forgotten why you bought this book, have you? It's about enjoying life. I want you to enjoy life, and if that includes exercise, I want you to do it in a way that will not create problems. Exercise is a potentially constructive activity, but there are loads of ways it can get you into trouble physically and mentally.

We've all known exercise nuts, people who swear that their day isn't complete if they don't hit the gym, run for miles, or grab that bike and head for the hills every chance they get. At some point, being nuts about anything subtly crosses the line into obsession. Dr. Morris Mellion of the University of Nebraska Medical Center has made a strong case that exercise addiction is every bit as real and serious as drug addiction and eating disorders and is very much like them in the way it works.

The generic definition of addiction specifies that it produces pleasurable feelings, requires increasingly greater amounts of the stimulus to produce the effect, and induces symptoms if it is withdrawn. In his experience with exercise addicts, Mellion says, all three criteria are met. Among long-distance runners, 70 percent experience "runner's high," a sensation characterized by a feeling of harmony with their surroundings and a sense of invincibility. In the beginning, it is triggered after forty-five minutes of activity for those who run an average of 23 miles a week. In classic addiction fashion, more and more exercise is needed to get the same high. Eventually athletes need that high to prevent depression and anxiety. Without it, they report sleep problems, nervousness, muscle twitching, restlessness, irritability, and even bloating. The condition affects relationships with family, friends, and work. Addicted runners ritualize exercise and minimize the pain and injury that can accompany the sport. Dr. Mellion treats his exercise-addicted patients in an anorexia treatment center. Unfortunately, the success rate is poor, but fortunately, the number of true exercise addicts seems to be pretty small. Yet we don't know how many people—even if they are not "addicts"—use exercise to avoid other issues in their lives.

Many addicts deny addiction because they insist that exercise is supposed to be good for you. So these addicts are seen by themselves and others as "having a healthy craving and demonstrating a positive commitment to well-being." How can that be bad?

Short of addiction, you can still overdo it. There's even a name: overtraining syndrome. Too much exercise can negatively affect your achievement in the sport and can even hurt your immune system. When amateur athletes who were already training ten to twelve hours a week increased their regimen by 30 percent over four weeks, they showed signs of decreased athletic performance. There were also decreases in immune system measures, including certain white blood cells that fight infection. Overtraining has also been tied to fatigue, increased heart rate, insomnia, and other sleep problems. Treatment, which athletes tend to resist, means cutting back training to the aerobically necessary—usually defined as exercise that allows you to talk at the same time—and forced rest at least one day a week for the rest of your exercising life.

If you suspect you might be overdoing it, you should ask yourself why you exercise. Everyone has his or her own reasons, from the beauty and grace of the sport to the delight in just getting outside and away from the grind. If the real reason you're trudging 10 miles a day on your treadmill is that your life is boring, out of control, or frustrating, well, you're missing the point. I think the world would be a better place if a little of the attention we pay to our abs went toward our cerebrums. Think about it.

But we all know weekend athletes who seem as driven to perform in sport or exercise as they do in their daily jobs. There may be some clues to this behavior in research from the University of California at Los Angeles that uncovered some disturbing trends among college athletes compared with their nonathletic peers. The athletes consumed more alcohol, were more likely to drive while intoxicated or under the influence of drugs, to drive with someone who was intoxicated, and to ignore seatbelts or motorcycle helmets. They were also less likely to use contraception and more likely to have greater numbers of sexual partners and sexually transmitted diseases. One theory behind this is that athletes are more likely to have a "type T personality." They are thrill seekers looking for excitement and stimulation.

Type T personalities are more attracted to sports than people without this trait, according to the work at UCLA. A fascinating follow-up study found differences among practitioners of particular sports. Football players are more likely to drive under the influence and not to strap on their seatbelts. Water polo players share those problems, plus more unsafe sex practices. Women in gymnastics, tennis, swimming, and diving have a higher incidence of unhealthy methods of weight loss, like diet pills and purging, and also suffer more from cessation of menstruation. Tennis players have more suicidal thoughts. Basketball players report more multiple sex partners and register more sexual diseases.

These problematic tendencies also show up in younger kids. I guess we shouldn't be so surprised by that in a culture that glorifies winning at all costs. If you don't believe me, saunter on down to the Saturday morning Little League game and listen to those supportive fathers for a couple of innings. Or ref a kids' soccer league season and enjoy the running commentary of their moms. Is winning no matter what the lesson we want our kids to take from sports? We talk endlessly about drugs in our schools. Have you heard that steroids among middle-school athletes is a huge and growing problem? It's been shown that these same kids are the most likely to be misinformed about the risks and supposed benefits of using steroids. So pay attention to *all* the kinds of drugs they may be using.

The University of Pittsburgh and the National Institutes of Health teamed up for a study of kids between seventh and ninth grades. This ongoing study will follow these twelve- to sixteen-year-olds for a few years. After the first year, when bad habits such as alcohol and marijuana use and cigarette smoking began appearing, there was no difference in rates between athletes and nonathletes. But boys in team sports reported three times the use of alcohol. Worse still, the more teams the boys were on, the more booze. Male players of soccer, street hockey, and baseball reported the highest alcohol use. Among girls, softball players and cheerleaders were the worst drinkers. Recently the *Journal of American College Health* reported a survey of fifty-two thousand students that corroborated the higher rates of alcohol use among athletes, especially among team leaders. Disturbingly, team leaders also reported more hangovers, impaired academic work, trouble with police, drunken driving, violence, and sexual misconduct resulting from use of alcohol and drugs.

Without concluding that sports are necessarily bad for our kids' behavior, clearly something is going on here. Parents, school administrators, and coaches need to get a grip on it.

THE RUNNERS' LAMENT

You'll find that many studies looking at the benefits and risks of exercise tend to focus on runners. Few other popular physical activities are as easy to measure. That, in turn, enables us to look at the effects of different levels of exercise on our lives.

For instance, some people let exercise get in the way of their family relationships. Several years ago, researchers at the University of Iowa Department of Family decided to study the relationship between running and family conflict. After all, we've all heard of golf widows. They wanted to know if there can be jogging widows. This was a straightforward approach with a questionnaire. The answers of more than seven hundred running club members were revealing. Of those men and women who lived with a partner, 5.5 percent admitted to high conflict in the relationship. These runners were found to have a lower commitment to the family and to feel they had less support from their partners for their running. But then one of the researchers figured maybe they should talk to the partners. Of these, 14 percent—nearly three times as many—reported the highest category of family conflict. So one in seven partners complained of high conflict within the family. These partners said they thought the runner was more committed to running than to the family.

YOU'RE NO RUBBER BAND

Should we take a break here and have a stretch? Whoa there, maybe not. Please reconsider everything you were taught about stretching and physical activity. Those masters of physical prowess, the Greeks and the Romans, couldn't be bothered stretching. Stretching is a purely modern phenomenon, its origins long lost.

The common belief is that stretching lengthens your muscles, increases their range of motion, boosts blood flow and therefore oxygen, and prevents soreness and injuries.

But the experts aren't so sure anymore. Consider several heresy-spouting athletes on this point: "I've run seven hundred and fifty thousand miles and I can say unequivocally, I'm not a poorer athlete for not stretching," says Stu Mittleman, the American record-holder for 1,000-mile runs (eleven days straight on two hours' sleep). Octogenarian Johnny Kelley, who has run more Boston Marathons than anyone, prepares for a run with "coffee, and stepping outside to check the weather." Most are coming around to the idea that just jogging the first half mile or so of a run is enough. Remember when you were supposed to start your car in the morning and let it idle a while to warm it up before pulling out on the road? Now just heading out and going easy on the gas warms up the oil faster and is better overall for the engine.

Still stretching? University of Texas researchers assembled three groups of stair climbers. One group stretched both legs; one group stretched one leg only; one group stretched neither leg. There was no difference in muscle soreness among the three groups. Among marathon runners at the University of Hawaii, those who stretched had no more demonstrable resistance to injuries. In a project in Ontario, Canada, the injury rate was identical between those who always stretched and those who never stretched, while the highest rate was registered among those who sometimes stretched.

In case you just don't trust me on this one, let me help you with three main methods. The ballistic stretch is the most time-honored and is used in activities as diverse as ballet, karate, and football. You bounce a little to stretch and push joints into greater range of motion. That said, it is also condemned by most trainers, mainly because it can cause microscopic muscle tears and actually shortens muscles. The second stretch, static, is in vogue at the moment. It's featured in yoga, where you allow muscles to elongate on their own while you help them along by breathing carefully. While it may help with yoga pretzel-bending, it has increased injury rates in some sports.

Then there's the latest stretch, proprioceptive neuromuscular facilitation, or PNF. This is 40 percent more efficient than static yoga-type stretching for elongating muscle fibers. Here is more or less how you do it: You contract a muscle hard for five seconds and then relax it. The muscle will be more relaxed then than if you tried to relax it right off the bat.

Let's try it out on the hamstrings, the muscle group in back of your thigh, about which stretchers obsess. To stretch it, you need a friend and some guidance or you can hurt yourself. Lie on your back and bring your leg up straight as far as you can. Loop a towel around your ankle and try to push the leg, still straight, down toward the floor, contracting your hamstring as hard as you can for five seconds. Then relax those hamstrings and the towel, and contract your thigh muscles by bringing the leg up higher. You'll get the leg up a few inches with several tries.

OTHER MILEAGE MALADIES

Other parts of your body, aside from your heart, muscles, and bones, can be affected by exercise. Your gastrointestinal system, for example. Many runners complain of diarrhea and cramps before, during, and immediately after they run. Although not talked about much, it is so common that some doctors recommend running as an effective and natural laxative (although one recent clinical trial did not find that running helped constipation. In this, fiber may be more effective than your tennies).

It doesn't end there. Serious runners also complain of rectal bleeding. In one study, a number of runners reported fecal incontinence. Sounds like a great sport to me, but then I'm probably the wrong guy to endorse it. The current theory as to why these problems occur is that running triggers increased blood flow to muscles and that the intestines react to the resulting lack of blood with increased activity.

Exercise may have a negative effect on immunity, colds, and other infections. Studies have shown that more training can lead to more colds, flus, and sore throats. Those training for the Los Angeles Marathon by running sixty miles a week had twice the colds and flus as those who ran twenty miles a week. Others trained for the race and then, because of an injury or conflict, could not compete. They were only one-sixth as likely to get sick as those who completed the race.

All this raises several possibilities. Either the all-out effort of the race depleted the immune system, or being crammed together with all those other people in the race increased the transmission of illness. There are no hard answers, especially with upper respiratory infections. Yet in the South Africa Marathon, faster runners got more upper respiratory infections than slower runners. In laboratory measurements, there are negative changes in the immune systems of exercisers. Such changes are extremely complex and include alterations in the levels of certain white blood cells at different times and in different levels of conditioning. Antibodies rise and fall unpredictably.

As if you needed another wrinkle, a runny nose doesn't necessarily mean an upper respiratory infection. In fact, it's normal with running because the nose wants to increase humidification. As you run, more air flows into your lungs. It needs to be humidified first, so your honker—clever organ—secretes more moisture in the form of mucus. This is called athlete's nose. (In case you were wondering, Dr. C. F. Stanford at the Royal Victoria Hospital in Belfast figured this out by inducing medical students to blow their noses into tissues. Then he weighed the tissues. Hey, science isn't always glamorous. Nor is it always about Nobel Prizes.)

Frankly, you should worry less about the air inside your nose and more about the air outside. Exercising in polluted air is worse for your lungs than not exercising at all. According to the Los Alamos National Lab, lung abnormalities caused by pollution, especially exposure to nitrogen dioxide, are made worse by exercise. It's been confirmed through studies of occupational exposure to pollutants among steel-workers and firefighters, as well as cigarette smokers.

The research parallels studies of silo fillers' disease. A silo filler is a worker who fills agricultural silos. One day, one of the fillers went out and performed other vigorous chores straight after leaving the silo. Within a day he landed in the hospital with respiratory problems. The current thinking is that people who regularly breathe oxidant gases (which are found in silos, among other places) should rest and avoid exercise. Because oxidant gases are an integral part of most urban air-borne pollution, it's got to make you think about where you're pumping your legs and your lungs.

Your nose has other problems. When you exercise, you breathe heavily, which can irritate your nose. That, in turn, inhibits the nose's ability to flush particles in the air through it, which can lead to grit nose syndrome. You didn't know your nose had so many complexes, did you? A Swedish doctor came up with this one. He found that it took exercisers' noses twice as long as nonexercisers' to flush particles through. This raises concern that the nose can build up quantities of toxic materials. Your busy nose has little hairs that keep mucus and embedded particles moving along to the throat, which dumps them into your stomach for disposal. We really don't know how all this relates to more polluted cities, but many runners say the running is rougher on high-pollution days. The advice here is to run in the morning when pollution is less and to run as far away from roads and highways as possible.

THE BEST EXCUSE WITH THE WORST CONSEQUENCE

Some lucky folks can claim a truly legitimate reason not to exercise: allergy. The name is exercise-induced anaphylaxis. The first signs can be unpredictable, occurring during physical activity, and they are classically allergic—warmth, hives, itching, swelling of hands, feet, and face. They can lead to serious, life-threatening symptoms such as lower blood pressure and obstruction of the airway. This is true anaphylaxis, like allergy to bee stings, and can end in death. The condition for some people can be worsened by unsuspected food allergies, which act as a warning bell. High on the suspect list are wheat, peanuts, tree nuts, soy, apples, pears, milk, and celery. It can help to avoid the offending food before sports or exercise. With serious allergies, you should never run or exercise alone and should consider carrying certain antihistamines or even a shot of epinephrine, which constricts the blood vessels and prevents swelling that can choke you. If you feel any weird itching when you exercise, that could be a sign, and you should see an allergist.

The sudden fatal collapse in 1984 of fifty-two-year-old fitness guru Jim Fixx reminded us that there can be serious side effects to whatever we do to help ourselves. Fortunately, a Fixx-like demise is not common, but its likelihood can rise in certain situations. Top among those: ignoring symptoms. That was Fixx's mistake. An autopsy revealed he had clogging of three coronary blood vessels and symptoms of heart disease that he ignored. The signals can be subtle, to be sure. Heart pain or angina is obvious, but did you know that nausea and abdominal discomfort during exertion, dizziness, and plain general fatigue could also mean heart disease?

Fixx was *the* statistic. A recent Harvard study found that one out of every twenty surviving heart attack victims reported heavy exertion within an hour of the episode. That may not sound like many, but it adds up to seventy-five thousand heart attacks every year—which result in twenty-five thousand deaths.

Other research has found more blood clotting in some men after strenuous exercise. While the risk of a heart attack was six times higher in the hour after strenuous physical exertion, this risk was directly related to the physical condition of the victim. Think of your system as a rain-swollen river tearing at its banks. Rapidly moving blood during exercise can break off pieces of cholesterol plaque from the artery walls, which can flow downstream and block arteries.

All bets are off if you have heart disease and don't know it. In other words, if you are not in shape, don't be an idiot by launching a strenuous exercise program for which you are not prepared. Build up to it gradually. If you're over thirty-five, get a physical before investing in Lycra shorts. Otherwise, it's far healthier to stay in your recliner and watch professional wrestling on TV.

THE DIFFERENCE BETWEEN THE SEXES

Our bodies are different.

All right, you knew that already. But exercise raises different issues for men and women. Let's start with women, whose problems range from the simply irritating to the serious.

Easy ones first. Runner's nipple is a pain in the you-know-where, especially for women who don't wear bras. Band-Aids can take care of the problem. If they fall off, try Dr. Scholl's corn cushions. It's not exactly what he had in mind for them, but who cares. I doubt you'll start sprouting corns in strange places if you use them.

On a more serious note, doctors are seeing more of a condition called benign galactorrhea—milk production—among nonlactating exercising women whose breasts bounce during activity. Overall, as many as 20 percent of nonlactating women find themselves producing milk either from exercise or sex play. In the case of exercise, Dr. Lois O'Grady at the University of California at Davis medical school believes it is caused by friction on the nipples and breasts from poor-fitting bras, or no bra, or from hormone secretion stimulated by the exercise itself. It is important to take a symptom like this seriously because it could result from other abnormalities of breast tissue.

If exercise is the cause, the solution is a piece of cake: a proper jogging bra. Thanks to the consumer-minded researchers at Utah State University, I can even tell you what to look for. They put volunteers on a treadmill at 6 miles an hour and used sophisticated equipment to measure the vertical motion of their breasts. They even rated the jogging bras on the market. There are no free advertisements in this book, but the general advice is that large-breasted women need more rigid construction. Smaller-breasted women can use the stretchy kind.

Exercising women can suffer in a more important and ominous way. The standard recommendation by the American College of Obstetrics and Gynecology is that a woman should exercise aerobically between three and five times a week, for fifteen to sixty minutes each time. The same recommendation says that you should exercise at between 70 and 85 percent of your maximum heart rate. To calculate that maximum, subtract your age from 220, then figure the range between 70 and 85 percent of that number.

In fact, that could be too much, but not because of implications for your heart. Some type of menstrual problem plagues an astonishing 80 percent of competitive athletes and 10 to 20 percent of recreational exercisers. Their most common problem is the cessation of menses, or amenorrhea. Some women look at this as risk-free and reliable birth control. It's not. A woman can still get pregnant. The bigger issue here is that amenorrhea can lead to thinning bones and osteoporosis.

It's thought that amenorrhea is caused by a damaging combination of low body fat; low-calorie, low-fat diets; and stress. Athletes with high body fat, like swimmers, usually do not have the problem. When body weight drops from exercise, the body, unaware of the fitness craze, figures starvation and does the right thing by turning off ovulation. Exercise combined with fad diets accelerates this effect.

This is no joke. A delay of the first period in a young woman is cause for concern. Bone mass reaches its peak in the early twenties in young women, earlier than we once believed. Bone mineral density in young female athletes without their periods was equal to that of fifty-one-year-old women. When young, women can lose 4.5 percent of total bone mass every year that passes without a period. If you are not menstruating, cut back on the workouts. If reducing exercise and gaining weight still doesn't work, you may need to go on hormones. The bone loss may remain as a permanent deficit, exposing you to increased risk of fracture. One study simply compared athletes with periods to athletes without them. The amenorrheic athletes had lower bone mineral densities in their spine, femur, and tibia.

For some women who are not having problems with their periods, exercise can help strengthen bones, but the risk of a fall and fracture goes up, so be careful. According to the latest studies, varied stress on bones is best, not doing the same thing over and over again. Swimming is not a good choice for increasing bone strength because it does not utilize gravity. Walking, jogging, and climbing stairs are better. While weight lifting and rowing increased bone density in wrist, spine, and overall body in women from sixty to seventy-four, it did nothing for the hip bone, a critical site for harm in older women. Yet simple walking can prevent bone loss in this sensitive area. Hip fracture can be a very dangerous injury among this group, leading to a high death rate from complications secondary to the actual injury. Just going through hip surgery and being in a hospital bed with increased risk of pneumonia and bladder infections make this an injury to avoid.

For women thinking weight loss, swimming may be the enemy. In an experiment where no diets were allowed, walkers hoofing it for sixty minutes a day lost 10 percent of their weight, bicyclers lost 12 percent, and swimmers gained 3 percent. Why? Water cools the body more efficiently, and the body wants to keep its fat insulation.

While we're on the subject of weight, another study tried to figure out how much exercise a woman needs to maintain a reduced weight. If she loses the weight by diet, exercise, or both, she will need eighty minutes a day of moderate activity, or thirty-five minutes a day of vigorous activity, to maintain the loss. As always, if you don't work hard to keep that weight off, it will come back. Unfortunately, in general, exercise without dieting is a difficult way for women to lose weight.

Some moms have said that their newborns did not nurse as effectively—they fussed or refused to drink—after the women exercised. So researchers at Indiana State University asked lactating volunteers to express milk before and after exercising. Then they analyzed the milk for lactic acid, a metabolite produced by the body with exercise. Then the moms, in double-blind fashion, bottle-fed the pre- and post-exercise milk to the babies and recorded the reaction. The researchers found increased lactic acid in postexercise milk, and the babies accepted the postexercise milk less enthusiastically. Who can blame them—new moms' breast milk tastes worse after exercise and apparently has lowered immune proteins. The lesson: nurse first, run later.

Why should girls have all the problems? Guys have plenty of their own, thank you. We can have runners' nipple, too. Of course, guys with chest hair have less of a problem. Also, men should avoid T-shirts with silk-screened designs, which, strangely enough, increase friction, especially when they get peely and rough with repeated washings.

Ah, yes, then there's sex. There has been scads of press relating to exercise and sex. I don't want to get you down, so let's talk about the positives. At the University of California at San Diego, researchers assembled two groups of middle-aged, sedentary men with an average age of forty-eight. One group performed aerobics three days a week for an hour. The second, the control group, walked four days a week for an hour. Then they all fessed up.

The aerobics fiends all reported some increase in intercourse frequency, orgasm, erection, and kissing. It must be better blood flow to the jewels, say the researchers. *But,* before you run to read this paragraph to your missus, the walkers stayed monogamous, while the aerobics dudes had more sex outside their primary relationship. Hard science is not easy with a subject like this, yet that's the best we have. The same lab offers some caveats. Training more than two hundred fifty minutes per week caused a reduction in libido and reduced testosterone levels while increasing prostate irritation and fatigue. Another study found heavy training—one hour or more, six or seven days a week—caused fatigue and very significant declines in testosterone, sperm counts, sex drive, and sexual activity. So, ladies, you can hide his running shoes altogether, or if you let him have them, either make sure he stays out for more than an hour or follow him. After you've nursed, of course.

One specific interaction to a guy's sex life could be an unfriendly bicycle seat and the nerves to a man's genitals. Urologists heard complaints from male cyclists about everything from numbness to erectile failure and found the cause to be ill-fitting seats and long hours in the saddle, which can impinge on critical nerves in the pelvic region. Fortunately, seat manufacturers now offer a range of options.

Now the negatives, although I really hate to depress you. For men who have decided to use exercise to take off some pounds, some facts first. Is running your slimming thing? A study by Dr. Paul Williams, an epidemiologist at the Lawrence Berkeley National Laboratory, found weight gain was inevitable even among habitual runners. Yes, runners were leaner than nonrunners. But even runners will find it an increasingly tough challenge to fight the march of time and the loss of their younger, thinner selves. After age fifty, the men did manage to lose muscle mass and some overall weight, but their waistlines . . . not a pretty picture, I'm afraid. The average six-foot-tall man gains 3.3 pounds per decade and 3/4 inch of waistline *regardless of the number of miles he runs every week.*

To compensate every year for that natural weight hike, men would have to increase their weekly running distance by 1.4 miles. So if a thirty-year-old averages 10 miles a week, by forty he should be doing 24 miles a week. Otherwise, at age fifty, a physically active man can expect to weigh 10 pounds more and have 2 inches more on his waist than at age twenty. Did you catch the word *active?* Yet the waistlines will *still* increase, depending on those genetics or testosterone, we just don't know.

Some researchers are raising the specter of male menopause. Remember that women tend to be pears, gaining weight in the butt and thighs, and men generally are apples, putting it on around the belly. We think abdominal fat is riskier to health. So this waistline gain of men is worth our consideration. And if you're hoping to lose that waist, get to work. The *New York Times* reports that you would have to do "half a million sit-ups to lose one pound of fat." You are not going to see those washboards without losing the fat. At the end of this chapter, I'll tell you the best way.

To cut his risk for heart attack, is a man better off exercising or losing weight? Researchers at the University of Maryland medical school gathered a group of sedentary men and put some on a diet to lose 10 percent of their body weight and others on an exercise regimen without losing weight. After nine months, the slimming group showed more improvement than the exercisers. Personally, I'd rather turn away the second helping of mashed potatoes than pound the pavement at the crack of dawn.

If you insist on eating poorly *and* exercising, just shovel down the burger and shake and then spend the next five hours walking or, if you're short of time, running for only three hours. So think twice about lunch, or you may as well just wear your running gear into the local Burger Meister. That way you don't waste time changing and you'll make it home in time for dinner. Come on, now, doesn't it seem a lot easier to learn to make better food choices and exercise moderately? Look at everything on your plate as its exercise equivalent, and I think you'll get the point.

DR. DEAN'S GUIDE TO TORTURE

All right, everybody is not like me, which probably makes the world a more interesting place. You want exercise? We should look at how much you should get. From a scientific point of view, it isn't easy to know how much you should get. We are all different, and no study can take that into account enough to tell for sure what works for you. At best, you can put together some general formulas and adapt them as closely as possible to your body and lifestyle.

There is no end to fitness tests. We love to compare ourselves to others, using real and not-so-real standards. The bottom line, though, is this: How efficient are your heart and lungs at supplying your muscles with enough oxygen to do the job?

First, what kind of shape are you in? There are some guidelines, but they can be dangerous because to test your fitness, you have to push yourself a bit. If you are over thirty-five and don't already exercise, first get cleared by your doctor. If you are out of shape, sudden exercise is asking for big-time trouble. One fitness standard, developed by Dr. Kenneth Cooper, an aerobic fitness expert in Dallas, is of the do-it-yourself variety and therefore not as accurate as a professionally administered treadmill test. But it's simple—all you need is a track or an accurate odometer on your car to measure how far you can run in twelve minutes. Stop if you notice any chest discomfort or shortness of breath that feels out of control, or pain in the calves, a sign of arterial insufficiency in the legs. Now, I'm not sure why you would try this if you're not fit, since you already know how much activity you get. Maybe, like me, you want to show off a little if you think you've got the magic genes.

In general, how far you can run in twelve minutes varies with age. To earn a good rating—and most of you won't—a man should reach 1.2 miles and a woman 1 mile. Get over 1.5 miles, gentlemen, or 1.2 miles, ladies, and you're in superior shape. On the other hand, covering less than a mile in the twelve minutes would earn a poor to very poor.

If you do well, you now have more reason never to get off the sofa except for bathroom breaks during commercials. If you do poorly, you confirmed what you already knew, that it's time for you to get moving. Maybe this will help you feel better—according to Cooper, 80 percent of Americans will fall in the fair to very poor range on this test.

EXERCISE LITE

OK, here are the rules. Try for thirty minutes a day of formal activity. I figure that three ten-minute sessions should do it. You can go shorter, to twenty minutes, and not lose anything in terms of calories burned by dividing into two sessions. But it will cost you in the aerobic department because it takes a little time to get that heart pumping and lungs chugging.

Pick a routine you can stick with. If you really hate people *schvitzing* around you and you're a gadget kind of person, get yourself a home exercise machine. But don't use it as a planter, or a closet dust-collector. These machines are not necessarily a bad way to go, especially because some evidence suggests that people have more success at home than at the gym. One survey found that 78 percent stuck with a program at home while only 48 percent did with group sessions. But which machine gives the best workout?

I'm glad you asked. Researchers compared a cross-country ski simulator, a stationary cycle, a rowing machine, a stair-stepper, and a treadmill. They checked calories burned among people using the different methods and measured the difference in exertion the exercisers said they expended. Their conclusion was that you will feel less pooped out per calorie burned on a treadmill. Some of the machines seemed easy, but participants did not get a full aerobic workout. By the way, the Air Glider, a top-selling infomercial product, was less effective than a quick walk or slow jog, according to the American Council on Exercise.

Our goal is to work off 2,000 calories a week, or 300 calories a day, which is so easy that it's almost no sweat at all. You can even do it around the house, which sure appeals to me more than staring at the wall of a gym. Consider these figures for a 180-pound man, in calories burned per hour, from Tuft's Lifetime Health Letter. In parentheses, you'll find the equivalent for a 130-pound woman.

> Gardening: 576 (416)
> Mow lawn: 486 (351)
> Rake leaves: 270 (195)
> Paint house: 378 (273)
> Wash and polish car: 270 (195)
> Dance with partner: 288 (208)
> Scrub floor: 522 (377)
> Clean windows: 288 (208)
> Chop wood: 414 (299)

Can you believe it? It's all comparable to "real" exercise. The health nags had us going, didn't they? I think they wound up discouraging lots of folks because they made getting in shape look so damned hard and unappetizing.

Here's an example of the exercise backlash. Doctors warned in the *American Journal of Cardiology* that mowing the lawn could be too strenuous for men with heart disease or recovering from angioplasty or bypass surgery. They gave them a lawnmower or a treadmill test and found that despite the subjects' perception that mowing was "light exertion," they exceeded maximum peak values obtained on the treadmill. The doctors concluded that "in some patients, the aerobic and myocardial demand of lawn mowing can be excessive."

You can look for easy ways to help yourself. Be creative. Park the car farther from your destination and walk. The meter's probably cheaper anyway. Take the stairs instead of the elevator, unless you live in a Fifth Avenue penthouse. Play table tennis instead of watching football on TV. Learn an instrument. It's not only good for your mental health, it burns 160 calories an hour. I'm working out right now: Typing uses 120 calories an hour.

Gee, I feel better already.

5

WOULD YOU FLY IN A PLANE
WITHOUT WINGS?

(The Wrong Kind of Medicine Can Hurt You)

I'm about to turn on my past.

Most of you who hear or see me through the media know me as a pretty conventional doctor, exhorting you to believe in what can be logically explained and proved and turn it to your medical advantage. It wasn't always so. I was, for a time, a full-fledged card-carrying member of a generation that rebelled against everything, from a distant and meaningless war to the seemingly hollow values of our parents. We rejected the modern world itself along with all the wrongs we perceived it did to people and the environment. I don't know if younger folks today can appreciate the impact of this period, but it was earthshaking.

By the time I was finishing my surgical residency in 1971 in California, I was champing for change. Bach now interested me less than the Beatles and rock 'n' roll. Marijuana and psychedelics flowed freely in those days. I grew my white man's afro longer and longer. Something happened back then that hit me over the head like a hammer. I still struggle today in search of the roots of what was to be one of the major turning points in my life. They go back even earlier, to when I was still a pup in New York.

I hated my Ivy League institution in New York City but nevertheless still played it kind of straight. I bugged the dean repeatedly, announcing that I was quitting medicine. Each time, he and my family and friends convinced me to get my M.D. and then decide what to do with my life. Plus, Vietnam loomed large, and all graduating physicians were drafted. The only out, even temporarily, was to stay in school.

I was tired of the striated and structured atmosphere of New York Hospital, one of the most revered and traditional medical centers in America. I wanted something different, and took a rotation at Bellevue. These were the front-line trenches. The facility was grungy and primitive. The patients fit the locale. This was a unique medical experience.

But I'd had enough of New York. By chance, I stumbled on a group of like-minded residents and interns who were putting together a deal. The University of California at San Diego had just finished building a new medical school and medical center. They needed personnel: interns, residents, nurses, the whole shebang. Presented with an all-or-nothing deal, medical students headed for internship and residents already in postgraduate training, they said yes to us all.

It was 1967, and I had no idea what was going on in the world around me. I was typical of the genre, a straight shot through boarding school to college to medical school and soon on to internship and residency. I was also a city boy, born and raised. I loved museums and symphonies and antiques. I didn't know from California. But I was heading west.

San Diego was intended to be a one-year sojourn, a change of scene, nothing more. My then-wife had trouble seeing it that way, crying as we drove to our new home through the bleak outer suburbs of Southern California. It looked so sparse. So boring. So *ordinary*. It turned out to be anything but.

You know all the obvious clichés. Allow me another: You had to be there. Anything that could change was changing. The sexual revolution. Peace and love. Outrageous dress and hairstyles and lingo swept from the streets to the boardrooms. Movements steamrolled across our consciousness—environmental, animal rights, woman's rights, civil rights. We protested the edicts of the system, then disobeyed them.

Roles changed. Men took care of kids, greeted each other with special handshakes, and hugged each other. Women changed the oil in their cars and delivered their babies at home. Cults and cooperatives and new utopian groups flourished. Communes formed overnight, enabling people to band together to get what they wanted. Food habits changed radically. Co-ops and bulk purchasing opened access to new foods like sprouts, tofu, and granola. Concepts were born: Processed was out, organic and natural were in. Vegetarianism carved out a place in the landscape.

Our minds and bodies and health were altered. Spirituality from oriental philosophy and new religions brought us meditation, massage therapies, yoga, gurus, and macrobiotics. A maniacal obsession with things psychic and metaphysical and astrological wafted through every conversation. Talk was incessant about tarot readings, vibrations, energy fields, reincarnation, herbs, mind-body therapies, laying on of hands, touch therapy, faith healings, all kinds of diets, acupuncture, accupressure, and homeopathy. Straight society went out with the bathwater, along with alcohol and cigarettes. Mood-altering chemicals like marijuana, LSD, and mescaline moved in. It all fit so well with our gypsy clothes, our beads and crystals and swirling colors. Whatever was "in" had to be entirely unknown to our parents' generation. Peace, man.

We were weird, and our parents worried about our judgment, not to mention our sanity. Despite what we thought at the time, very little of what we were into was invented then. Most of it had been lying dormant for much of the century until rediscovered by a restless generation. It exploded when we came along.

I embraced it all wholeheartedly, leaving conventional medicine behind to join in the revolution. I was insatiable, reading all the books I could get my hands on, many originally published before World War II. The Mucusless Diet System, Iridology, herb books, pre-war herbal pharmacology texts, Eastern philosophy, magic, cosmic conscious-ness, soma, and sacred mushrooms all had their turn. I took an organic farming course at the University of California extension. I joined a yoga and meditation group, became a vegetarian, delivered my third child, Caleb, at home, blissed out. I went back to the land, built a house, and heated it with wood. I longed for a simpler, lower-tech existence.

Of course, I knew where medicine should travel. It was time to overthrow the old ways. The Age of Aquarius was here. Nontoxic and natural healing therapies would topple the treacherous tyranny of the cold-hearted, mechanistic, inhumane, mainstream medical machine. We would bring down the arrogant, pompous, know-it-all professors and scientists who had driven me nuts during my previous twelve years of professional schooling.

It felt great. I was at the forefront of the brave new world. In spite of 120-hour work weeks as an intern, then as a resident, it was all romantic and intoxicating. I wanted to join "the movement" but couldn't walk away from medicine just yet. Uncle Sam was relentless. By lottery, I won the chance to forestall induction into the military by taking a residency. I opted for a surgical one. I liked working with my hands and hated night calls and blood. The most innocuous specialty seemed to be eye surgery. I was the first resident in this field at the University of California at San Diego medical school. It was perfect. I got to do everything myself and also had the freedom and ability to drift and explore the world professionally and personally.

My point in dragging you through my sordid past is to set the stage a bit, to give you a sense of how medicine, health, and health care have changed so radically over the past three decades. This period gave birth to wholistic health—or as the w quickly disappeared, holistic health.

NONMEDICAL MEDICINE

Many of my nonmedically trained friends were becoming healers of different sorts. Some became naturopaths after two months of instruc-tion. Others got into various types of touch and massage therapies. Some became plain old "healers." It was soon obvious that none of these people really knew what they were talking about.

I was amazed by the ignorance regarding diagnosis. For instance, a member of our hippie tribe came down with a stomachache one evening. That was due to a misalignment of vertebrae, said the naive massage therapist with a two-day course in spinal manipulation under her belt. Nope, said the astrologer after doing the patient's chart, the stars were wrong. The past-life regression expert in my circle of New Age friends thought this was just a simple negative experience from a past life that needed to be resolved. The herbalist, meanwhile, was going to fix it with mint and chamomile tea. The colon therapist wanted to flush away the toxins. The therapeutic touch team laid crystals on the tummy to reorient the energy field. At 4 A.M., when the surgeon removed her grossly infected appendix, I realized the level of danger here.

Shortly after that, a holistic doctor I knew, this one a dropout M.D., saw a baby with a fever and what seemed to be an upper respiratory infection. The baby's breathing was labored, and the kid was pretty lethargic. Conventionally this warrants a pretty careful listen to the chest and at least an X ray. But X rays were not holistic. He prescribed a fruit-juice fast. The child died in three days from a bacterial pneumonia, which would have easily responded to antibiotics. I was getting scared of holistic medicine.

As deeply as I immersed myself in the alternatives, I rejected the idea of opening a practice of alternative—holistic—medicine. By now I realized that no other system on earth was going to usurp the ability of Western medicine at least to diagnose illness. I also realized that a medical education was a necessary prerequisite to practice holistic medicine. You had to know the basics first before going on to the esoteric, theoretical stuff. To do it right and with some ethics, you had to be good at both. As a responsible practitioner, you had to diagnose the patient, assess conventional Western treatments, then know with certainty that the holistic remedy was the better of the choices. To say the least, there was not a lot of research available then on what worked and what didn't. That wasn't stopping loads of practitioners from doing their harm.

After all, the body of knowledge that we call science is the outcome of countless struggles, the sweat and blood of incredible individuals who little by little nudged us out of the darkness and accomplished extraordinary things. Afro hairdo aside, I found myself being cast as the counterrevolutionary when I started voicing my doubts. Disagree with any of these holistic folks and you got a quick reminder of how easily they became dogmatic and closed-minded. I had gone full circle. Now *they*, not my med school professors, were the pompous, holier-than-thou types.

I wanted so badly to believe. Yet nobody around me was willing to question anything. I thought we questioned all authority. When I challenged this garbage, I was quickly accused of narrow vision. Had I read the latest book on the latest healing fad? If not, how could I know about the treatment? "Have you read the latest textbook on internal medicine?" I would fire back. "How can you claim to know the newest stuff if you don't know what existed before?" Nobody rejected anything. Every scheme that came along was given equal weight. People would take pills, potions, and herbs, and try treatments indiscriminately. Any source was credible as long as it was alternative.

Just because something is alternative doesn't mean it should escape the scrutiny of science. Although most of these practices actually lend themselves well to the scientific method, mainstream scientists figured they had already proved many of these techniques worthless over past centuries. Yet public demand and pressure forced us to take a new look at alternative techniques, using established scientific means when possible. I've kept track over the years and will present to you the best evidence we have on these subjects.

First, though, you must recognize that there are folks who have no interest in the truth. They would rather the facts not get in their way, especially when they're selling you something. I still balk at authority and love it when the big-time experts are proved wrong. I want to stand by my hippie roots and the good things I still believe we brought to the world. But that sentiment takes a backseat to my interpretation of the facts as they emerge.

THE TIMES THEY ARE/AREN'T A-CHANGING

While the hippies grew up, got jobs, and had families, the wave of change they'd started rippled through the mainstream to be absorbed, repackaged, and perverted. Weirder stuff started creeping in. Drug abuse and sexually transmitted diseases told us we weren't right about everything. Meanwhile, strange people squeezed in under the holistic umbrella. Cancer quacks with bizarre cures of apricot pits and coffee enemas. Chains of clinics in Mexico changed their names to holistic this and holistic that. Since *holistic* really meant nothing, it was replaced by *alternative* medicine, then *complementary* medicine, *New Age* medicine, and most recently, *integrative* medicine. Once considered a matter of principle, belief, or conviction, it now began to carry a price tag.

Alternative medicine was ready for prime time.

Suddenly there were multilevel organizations and infomercials peddling cures for every disease known to man. Health food stores, filled with expensive organic veggies, and vitamin shops popped up in shopping malls across America. Herbal tea companies went public. New Age health fairs peddled crystals for big bucks. Travel agents sold weekend retreats to guru-fests. The food supplement industry came up with new cures du jour and had gross sales in the billions. Psychic phone lines ripped off the multitudes at $3.99 a minute. American marketing meets the New Age.

Take a look at who is buying this stuff. The typical customer of a suburban health food store, according to a *Los Angeles Times* story in 1998, is "a well-educated white woman with medical insurance who takes six different dietary supplements and doesn't discuss any of them with her doctor." There was nobody like that among us when I was a hippie.

Of course, neither did we have Hollywood medical authorities like Kelly LeBrock, actress and ex-wife of action-figure hero Steven Seagal. In 1998 Ms. LeBrock repaired to the halls of Congress to talk about her very own homeopathic product—Kelly LeBrock's Natural Medicine for Kids—with the nation's legislators. "Everything is against the body," she pouted. "*Anti*biotics, *anti*inflammatories, *anti*depressants. In order to create balance you need to create harmony. People will say that's hippie talk, but it's not." How would she know? She was barely born when hippies roamed the earth. Four years ago she "got into alternative medicine for her kids and for herself" after she had spent thirty thousand dollars on tests that did nothing to help her with "panic attacks." It still tickles this old tie-dyed hippie to see how big this has all gotten. Sorry, Kelly, it *is* almost all hippie talk.

Barry Beyerstrein at the Brain Behavior Laboratory of Simon Fraser University in British Columbia asks the following question: If an alternative therapy is implausible because it disobeys and contradicts well-established laws of physics and chemistry, lacks a scientific rationale of its own, has no supporting evidence from controlled, randomized studies or has failed to work in such studies, and appears improbable just through common sense, then why would so many well-educated folks continue to sell and purchase such a treatment?

He places a lot of blame on heavy marketing and promotion by the purveyors of such treatments to a public with marginal scientific literacy and a very strong desire to believe. But there is something else, he says:

The appeal of nonscientific medicine is largely a holdover from popular counterculture sentiments of the 1960s and 1970s. Remnants of the rebellious "back to nature" leanings of that era survive as nostalgic yearnings for a return to nineteenth century-style, democratized health care and a dislike of bureaucratic, technologic, and specialized treatment of disease. Likewise the allure . . . is a descendant of the fascination with eastern mysticism that emerged in the sixties and seventies. . . . They retain a strong appeal for those committed to belief in mind-over-matter cures, a systemic rather than localized view of pathology, and the all-powerful ability of nutrition to restore health.

As an ex-hippie, I have mixed feelings here. The antiauthority rebel in me is proud to have participated in a movement that rocked the world. The classically trained doctor in me is ashamed of what much of it has become.

Many people have grown distrustful of science in general because its mistakes have been exaggerated by the media and its triumphs either misunderstood or taken for granted. Neither conventional nor alternative medicine can guarantee a disease-free life or a cure for all your illness. That inability breeds frustration, especially in an era of unprecedented technological power, when people live longer and healthier lives than ever before.

Health anxieties have a voracious appetite. In our search for knowledge, we turn back the clock. For pre–twentieth century medicine, there was only the anecdote. If the patient got better, whatever the doctor did was assumed to work. Then, little by little, something started to change. During the age of reason, logic, and great exploration, early medical pioneers discovered germs and vaccines. The triumphs and failures of these visionaries are forgotten now. The struggle to be freed from the tyranny of superstition and ignorance resulted in nothing less than the greatest accomplishments of our species. People dissected corpses and examined their own anatomy. They peered through lenses and realized that they shared the planet with creatures they could not see but that made them sick. They extracted medicines from plants and herbs and created new ones from chemicals. They found true cures.

They also found that old ideas did not die so easily. One by one, existing beliefs succumbed to scientific medicine, but not without a fight. That's not hard to understand. It's not easy to turn away from thousands of years of human struggle and on a whim discard what took so long to build. While many want all the goodies and technology handed down by these giants of the past, few want to take the time to understand the methodology and thinking that got them here. Despite all the wonderful advances of science, people are ready to trash it in a heartbeat in exchange for a magic cure based on superstition.

WHY YOU DO THAT THING THAT YOU DO

Who uses alternative medicine?

It's difficult to get accurate figures. In 1993 a report in the *New England Journal of Medicine* found that 34 percent of the public had used some form of AM. The main (unproved) theory to explain the popularity of alternative medicine assumes that its adherents are all science morons unable to tell a molecule from a meatball. Yet that groundbreaking 1993 report found that AM users were more educated than nonusers. Other theories: Those who turn to AM are dissatisfied with regular doctors because they haven't helped or there were side effects from their treatment; that mainstream medical care today is too technological and impersonal; that users want personal control; that AM is less authoritarian and more empowering and offers more autonomy and control; that AM is more compatible with many spiritual and philosophical world views.

But what are patients really looking for? In fact, not everybody is running to their local naturopath, homeopath, and acupuncturist. In surveys, respondents identify chiropractic, lifestyle and dietary changes, exercise and movement, and relaxation as the most popular alternative practices. Not very weird. The most frequently cited health problems treated with AM were chronic pain, anxiety, chronic fatigue syndrome, sprains and muscle strains, addictive problems, arthritis, and headaches. The poorer the patients' self-perceived health status, the more likely they were to be an AM user.

What draws those with poorer health to AM? One explanation: They are sicker because they failed to take care of their health problem, then sought out alternative treatments. The front-running theory, though, is that many people who report poor health, more pain, and more symptoms may be "somatizers," displaying "the propensity to experience and report somatic symptoms that have no pathophysiological explanation, to misattribute them to disease and to seek medical attention for them," according to Harvard psychiatrist Arthur Barsky. Somatizers get more tests, are more frequent users of medical care services, shop around more, and experiment more with different types of providers. It is reasonable to expect that more of them will gravitate toward the alternative.

In 1998 Stanford researchers identified even more important factors that predicted use of alternative medicine. These related more to personal philosophy. People with a holistic philosophy of life ("the health of my body, mind, and spirit are related, and whoever cares for my health should take that into account") tend toward use of AM. While the media label some of these folks as New Agers, marketing experts use the more carefully defined term *cultural creatives*. "These people have stated a commitment to environmentalism, commitment to feminism, involvement with esoteric forms of spirituality and personal growth psychology, self-actualization, and self-expression, and love of the foreign and exotic," according to the Stanford researchers. More than half of them use alternative medicine. According to demographer P. H. Ray, this group has been steadily growing since the late 1960s and now accounts for an amazing forty-four million Americans, or nearly 24 percent of the adult population. Not only are they better educated and complaining of worse health, they are drawn to AM because they find it more in line with their philosophy of both health and life. In other words, they are not simply dissatisfied with mainstream care.

FOLLOW THAT DUCKY

With demand growing, enter the quacks to feed this hunger for alternatives. They dig deeper and deeper to dredge up forgotten rip-offs of the past, entering the realm of long-dead superstition that science thought it had buried forever. Health practices dating back to the Middle Ages and even the ancient Greeks and Romans have come roaring back. Nonsense of the seventeenth through nineteenth centuries seems fresh to this new audience as forgotten gimmicks reemerge in new guises.

Older therapies were adapted to fit modern ills. Acupuncture became a treatment to help smokers and dieters. Entirely new therapies were created, like channelers bringing back the dead from thousands of years ago to counsel today's psychically needy. You think I'm exaggerating? Board a United Airlines flight and pull out a High Street Emporium catalog for in-flight shopping. As many as 1.4 million copies per month fly around the world. Inside you can find such musthaves as a metal bracelet that "although it looks like a piece of fashion jewelry," claim its makers, "is a concentrated, polarized multi-metallic bracelet. Based on the same principles of acupuncture [it] regulates a person's bio energy frequency and ion levels. When your energy levels are unbalanced, the body's function is thought to be altered, which can be very annoying and debilitating. This bracelet will balance your body the natural way to help promote health in body, mind and spirit." The price for bio balance? Between $109 and $169.

Have you ever heard such baloney? Metal cannot be "polarized," and this has nothing to do with the principles on which acupuncture is based. There is no such thing as "bio energy." Even if there were, it would not have a frequency. Ions are simply charged atoms that are found throughout your body. Sodium and potassium are two examples. Pardon me, but what the hell are "unbalanced energy levels"? I'm particularly intrigued by the notion that all this can be "annoying and debilitating." My favorite part is that when you get your magic bracelet, you will now be "in balance."

This has all the lingo, and all of it is utterly meaningless. Clearly it works with some patsies. A relative of mine once described to me a holistic book that was "really scientific." How did she know, I asked? Because she didn't understand it, she answered. The only thing "annoying" here is that an airline that passengers trust with their lives is willing to double as a storefront for this garbage. Do United's jets fly via concentrated, polarized bio energy frequencies and ion levels, the natural way? If airline ads said they did, would you board their planes? Then why would you put something in, or on, your body that was not proved safe or effective?

DEFINING THE ALTERNATIVES

I don't have to tell you that seeing is not believing. The earth outside your window looks flat, but you know it's not. Yet people can easily be duped into believing the most preposterous things. Magicians are wonderful conveyers of wisdom on such matters, and the team of Penn and Teller are no exception. In their 1992 book, *How to Play with Your Food*, they offer insights worth hearing. Their key point is that we should live as open-minded, polite skeptics. When facts contradict your beliefs, they astutely hold, change your beliefs: "We should all gather together on the shoulders of the giants that have gone before us, look around, and use our heads." Simple truths, but too easily ignored. Consider a list of their lovely bromides that *can never be overstated:*

Extraordinary claims require extraordinary evidence.

I don't have to prove there's no chance it doesn't exist. Believers have to prove it does exist. You can't prove a negative.

I understand that it seemed to work for your headache, but who was your control group?

Just because you, Geraldo, and the *National Enquirer* can't explain it, doesn't mean it's unexplainable.

Real scientific breakthroughs are rarely first announced on TV chat shows by washed-up dancers.

Every malady does one of three things if left untreated:

1. It gets better.
2. It stays the same.
3. It gets worse.

After trying any bogus treatment:

1. It'll get better.
2. It'll stay the same.
3. It'll get worse.

To be a healer that some people will believe in, simply have your comments ready in each situation:

1. See, I told you so.
2. We arrested it.
3. I guess we need more of it.

If the person died you can say "We got to him too late."

What *is* alternative, anyway? Arnold Relman, retired editor-in-chief of the *New England Journal of Medicine*, has this to offer: "There really is no such thing as alternative medicine, only medicine that has been proved to work and medicine that has not. Many standard treatments have not yet passed that test, but many have. Unfortunately most of the methods advocated ... simply have not been proved. Undocumented anecdotes and testimonials don't count." Don't be fooled by marketers and promoters.

You see, if something "alternative" turns out to work, it is then embraced by the mainstream and is no longer alternative. This, in fact, has been the history of medicine: Sorting through everything out there, checking it out, and figuring out what's worth keeping and what's not. Science can easily answer these questions if it chooses. There is no need to guess. There is no need to hope. And most of all there is no need to change the rules.

The failure of AM believers to remember that last point makes me angriest. I often get the impression that because something is labeled alternative, we are expected to abandon long-established standards of proof and simply change the rules.

Science can give answers only if you demand them. If you are seeking the truth about a particular alternative remedy and truly have an open mind, there is much to discover. I have a wonderful example in snake oil, the quintessential symbol of quackery and charlatanism. Recently a doctor sought the truth about snake oil. First he considered fish oils, which contain bioactive fatty acids that have been found to have anti-inflammatory and anticlotting properties, among others. Could snake oils carry similar fatty acids and therefore actually have therapeutic potential? He studied three snake species—Chinese, black rattlesnakes, and red rattlesnakes—and discovered that the Chinese snake may well be endowed with bioactive oils. Check those supermarket shelves soon for the return of snake oil.

RESPECT THE P-WORD

Western medicine is committed to selling you treatments that have been proved to work. It's far from perfect, mistakes are made, and patients slip through the cracks. Medicine can't cure all diseases, but you should get a reasonable answer when you ask your doctor for the evidence on which a given treatment is based.

At the end of the day, as they say, there are only three kinds of treatments: those that work (proved), those that don't (ineffective), and those we don't know about yet but could if we invested the time and money to check (unproved). The *don't knows* are a big category.

Nothing would be simpler to determine than whether or not an herb really works. Just assemble subjects, give them the herb and a placebo, then determine whether the herb outperforms the placebo. Yet even when this kind of evidence is amassed, some of the biggest AM gurus reveal their bias against science.

In my experience over the years, AM practitioners are far more myopic than conventional doctors. Western medicine is committed to a method that rests on a simple foundation: If new evidence emerges, we change what we do. You do the tests, you find out what works. Take biofeedback. It's easy to measure that bodily functions can be altered, to a certain degree, by the mind. This is not breakthrough science. Blood pressure, for example, can be altered through biofeedback. Normally there is no way to "feel" blood pressure. So the early biofeedback machines offered a pressure reading of blood flow through a finger. By making a characteristic sound to accompany an altered status, a patient could associate certain internal feelings with the sound and thus learn to regulate these body functions. Biofeedback works and is a standard therapy today.

Therein lies the beauty of science. You *can* change your mind about something when the facts warrant it. You don't have to cling to some outdated or outrageous idea. That's why I laugh during my inevitable arguments with health gurus who accuse me of being close-minded. I've never found one who can conceive of any evidence that would prove him wrong—or even admit the possibility. I can easily explain the kind of evidence it would take for me to be a believer in any alternative therapy. An herb? Show me a simple double-blind study. You're psychic? Tell me the winning lottery number before the drawing. Laetrile, a scam treatment made from peach pits, cures cancer? Give it to a hundred patients and show me the results.

Too many alternative types, though, refuse to alter anything they do based on evidence, and by that they admit to all of us that they don't give a damn about the truth. Their egos have become enlarged by public adulation. They view as defeat any change in practice based on new evidence. They behave as if a treatment has to be controversial and revolutionary to have pizzazz.

This attitude has a name: the Galileo Effect. Because Galileo took the alternative view against the authorities of his time and was right, we figure that anyone who takes the iconoclastic view must be right. Early on, I was a proponent of this approach, using it to bolster my own views. I could justify it historically, too, having studied plenty of pioneers in medicine who challenged the status quo, were rejected and laughed at by their peers, and in the end were proved correct. But they proved themselves right by demonstrating their ideas logically and objectively—not by yelling louder, making bold self-proclamations, or going on talk shows.

Don't expect science to waste precious research funds on every preposterous claim. There are too many of them. Alternatives that make no sense, that defy the basic tenets of physics or chemistry, are just not worthy of our attention. Remember our bio energy bracelet? Believe me, the fundamental laws of physics are not going to be toppled by the salesclerk at your health food store or multilevel marketers or media personalities.

Unfortunately, public pressure based on nothing more than airy assumptions does force scientists to spend research time just proving zealots wrong. But please—*please*—when we do put up the money that finds something worthless, let it go. Don't make us go back and repeat the entire nineteenth century. It's a terrible waste of time and money to study something that has already been researched and shown to be bogus.

Too many people just don't want facts to get in the way of their self-indulgence. AM vendors accumulate a lot of weak information and figure that it somehow adds up to strong information. Soft facts do not petrify into hard facts given enough time. Think of your body as a courtroom with a given health practice on trial. Courtroom protocol is carefully constructed so that only real evidence is allowed. It generally keeps the system from falsely convicting the innocent or setting free wrongdoers. You should always demand the highest standards of proof, not the lowest, before accepting any treatment into your body. Don't be a health slut.

The New Age promoters peddle products one year that they warned you against the previous season. This year's anti-aging supplement is last year's food preservative. Weren't magnetic fields supposed to make us sick? Now sleep with magnets on your body to cure what ails you. Ozone is a component of air pollution. It's bad for you and its levels are regulated by government air quality standards. Yet health food stores sell ozone generators to "purify" your air. The California Department of Health Services became so concerned that it issued a formal warning that these devices could *make* you sick by damaging your immune system and lungs, irritating your eyes, ears, nose, and throat, and aggravating asthma.

HOW THEY KEEP 'EM COMING

Why do people seek out the hucksters? The National Council Against Health Fraud considers the following to be the central ongoing myths about alternative medicine.

Alternative Doctors Are Holistic and Look at the Whole Person

You hear this one a lot. Although I was taught in medical school to do the same thing, actually it is impossible for any practitioner. Do you expect your gynecologist to check your bunions, or your orthopedist to do a Pap smear? Yet alternative practitioners often ignore even the simplest technologies available to treat the broadest aspects of your whole body. Acupuncturists do not check your whole person; they are too busy obsessing over the needles they stick in imaginary points. Chiropractors check your spine. Naturopaths sell you supplements. Colon therapists focus on, well, you know.

Alternative Doctors Spend More Time with You and Care More for You

Many of us are upset with what has happened to our medical care system. Doctors are often rushed, care is expensive and confusing, and specialists seem distant in manner. This hippie-at-heart understands the longing for a simpler, lower-tech, more humane era. Some alternative practitioners *do* spend more time with patients, and that translates into patients feeling more coddled. Doctors sometimes are surrogates for mommy, and many of us need the TLC the alternative docs have the time to give.

Alternative Practitioners Are More into Prevention

Frankly, this is a joke. Just because they prescribe vitamins does not mean they are preventing anything other than smart health care. Many alternative practitioners horribly undermine our attempts at prevention. In attacking some of the best preventive efforts—vaccination, fluoride, pasteurization, water chlorination, and food irradiation—they dissuade people from using the most effective preventive options in human history.

Alternative Practices Are More Natural

One of my favorites—if it's natural, it must be better. Tobacco, poison oak, botulism, hemlock, arsenic, and digitalis are all natural. I've got news for you: Acupuncture needles are not natural. Swallowing bizarre concoctions of supplements is not natural. In many parts of the world, fluoridation, which many AM adherents oppose, occurs naturally. Immunization occurs naturally every time you get an infection. Gargantuan gigadoses of vitamins are not natural. Even when something says "natural" on the label, it's often not. Natural vitamin C from rosehips? A 500-milligram vitamin C pill, made entirely from natural rosehips, would be the size of your head. The pill you buy is actually just ascorbic acid, made in a lab, with a dusting of rosehips. Everyone wants simple, benign treatments that are not worse than the disease itself and don't induce side effects. Unfortunately, responsible, proved medicine cannot always offer benign treatments and still give you the care you need.

THE FACES BEHIND THE SHINGLE

There are three kinds of practitioners of unconventional medicine. Let's stop by for an office visit, one by one.

You know what happens when the door is open to anyone who claims he can heal, yet no standards, regulation, or proof are required? The worst slime crawls in. These characters trash any serious efforts at legitimacy by ethical alternative practitioners. Rip-off artists and con men of the worst kind, they are neither deluded nor are they believers. Taking advantage of your naiveté, they peddle bogus treatments without care. They often hide behind P.O. boxes and fake organizations. Their catalogs belong on a *Saturday Night Live* skit. They are usually so slippery that the law has trouble catching them. These cons are pros, and they *love* alternative medicine. They know the lingo, and they know what you want to hear. They return over and over to the same themes—weight loss, sexual potency, anti-aging, and cancer cures among them. I am dying to name their names here—you know many of them—but I have no interest in meeting their lawyers. A little later, though, I will arm you with the weapons you need to recognize them and the skepticism you should have to counter them.

The second kind of practitioner also deals in bogus cures but truly believes they are on to something. Their charisma sells the product, and what they lack in evidence they make up in caring and charm. They are equally dangerous but simply misled and innocent of purposefully ripping you off. Recently a well-meaning, grandfatherly, eighty-five-year-old doctor in Italy, Luigi Di Bella, turned Europe and Canada upside-down when he claimed to have found a cure for cancer made of vitamins and hormones. Thousands of Italians took to the streets to force their government to approve the treatment. But government studies quickly found the cure to be worthless.

Last are those on the cutting edge who struggle to develop new therapies that work and are safe. Some are smart enough and care enough to try to prove their case to the scientific community. That's important to me. If they have no interest in keeping data and bringing in others to learn of their efforts, they drop a notch on my list. Those who refuse to keep data on their patients do so for a single reason: They are afraid their pet therapy will be proved wrong. If it's proved right, the world will beat a wider path to their door. Traditionally this is the downfall of the cancer-cure vendors. When I ask them for records on their patients, I get the weirdest excuses. Anyone who truly cares so much about patients should surely care about sharing their therapeutic breakthroughs with the rest of the world, shouldn't they?

It's a curious thing, though. All that said, you still find a movement within mainstream medicine toward the alternative. Some of the reasons are admirable. Some are not.

Times are tough in medicine, believe it or not. Doctors are feeling the squeeze from increased malpractice claims, a growing glut of specialists, and the demands of managed health care. Many articles in medical magazines counsel doctors to practice alternative medicine for financial gain. "Integrated medicine could boost your income," reads one such piece. "It's in demand. Here's what it takes to turn that demand into dollars." The offer is appealing: no HMOs and insurance companies to hassle you, and what the heck, you're giving the patients what they want. Because you're a physician, at least you won't hurt people the way many untrained alternative practitioners have by missing the diagnosis and delaying the patient's access to an easy and definitive cure.

Every health plan is likely to offer these services soon, and not because the CEO is cosmically conscious. The interest is in marketing and profit. If it's good for you and for business, then it's a win-win for the company. The HMOs recognize the huge demand for these services. Remember the somatizers? They are major overusers of medical services. Western managed care just does not do well with patients suffering from anxiety and other chronic problems that send them to their doctors frequently. Many M.D.s would love to recommend greater personalized care, which might help these patients more than prescriptions. Increased accessibility addresses the greatest secret in all of medicine: That most people coming into a doctor's office don't really need to be there. Their problems will go away by themselves (and those patients will credit the cure to the HMO and its alternative techniques), or the problem is psychosomatic or the result of somatization. If meditation and biofeedback can do a better and cheaper job on your blood pressure than mainstream treatment, that's just fine by me.

One reliable estimate sets the alternative care market at a whopping fourteen billion dollars a year. Health care plans need to be competitive in the marketplace and will respond. So far those HMOs that have offered a full range of alternative services have failed financially. Since alternative therapies don't easily lend themselves to objective evaluation, the normal scrutiny that HMOs exercise over treatment outcomes has also been problematic. HMOs have complained as well that acupuncturists, for example, are not really interested in having their results evaluated. They prefer to remain as "outsiders" and claim their practices should not be subjected to Western standards. Still, I believe that sooner or later the HMO folks will find a way to make money from AM.

WHEN ALTERNATIVE MEANS CULT

My hate mail drips with vitriol when I take on alternative practices. Many people just prefer to believe in magic, even when confronted by the facts.

I'll present one bizarre case. I once did some stories about psychic surgery, which is practiced mostly in the Philippines and in some Latin American countries. At the time, it was spreading here. This AM is a great spectacle. The "surgeon" plunges his hands into the patient, splashes a lot of blood around, plucks the offending organ or a bit of it, and—voilà—patient cured. Best of all, no unsightly scars or aftereffects.

In 1989 there was just such a scene in Colville, Washington, a town of 4,500 people where an itinerant psychic surgeon had opened a practice. An estimated *one thousand* people had flown to this hamlet for treatment. There were plenty of testimonials. A forty-four-year-old waitress had suffered pain and fatigue for more than a year. Doctors couldn't cure her, she said. Hooray for psychic surgery. "He took some tumors out of my stomach," she claimed, "and removed a tumor from my heart. Out of my ears he took something. He shows it to you and throws it away. My problem has been healed. My husband wants me to go again because I've now got a lot of energy to clean house."

That same day, county and state authorities raided the surgeon's house, where he was "operating." His schedule book noted 130 appointments at seventy-five dollars per patient. Do the math. When police broke in, thirty-five people were standing around in their robes. A bucket of organs, allegedly removed from the hapless victims, lay next to the operating table. The organs were bovine, police said later.

Immediately, the community split into skeptics and believers, the latter group containing some of the town's more prominent citizens. Those "healed" and "cured" claimed they were consenting adults and had a right to their beliefs. The customers insisted it was their constitutional right to worship, as prayer sometimes accompanied the surgery. The authorities countered with their duty to protect the vulnerable and sick.

So, intrepid medical reporter that I am, I decided to have psychic surgery done on myself, live on camera during one of my television shows. Bob Steiner, a local magician and psychic-buster, played doctor. There was a lot of blood and bits and pieces of organs were plucked right from my insides. Although different techniques are used by various psychic surgeons, Steiner used a phony thumb to hide the ghoulish goodies.

Then we showed a film from the Philippines of "real" psychic surgeons in action. We ran it in slow motion, then backward, to expose the sham. Sometimes the surgeon stretched a small piece of plastic wrap between his fingers against the blood-soaked skin. This looks uncannily like peritoneum, the last layer surgeons cut as they enter the abdominal cavity. One retired surgeon observing this procedure proclaimed it to be real.

The lesson? Experts can sometimes be fooled more easily than laymen because they think they have special knowledge that makes them less likely to be fooled. Then again, some people still don't get it even after you tell them. Shortly after that segment, I got a letter from a viewer. "My sister needs gallbladder surgery," the viewer wrote. "Where can I get ahold of that psychic surgeon you featured on your show?" Of course, the angry letters poured in as well. Challenging someone's belief in the paranormal is like criticizing their religion. Most people pasted me for not using a real psychic surgeon, arguing that I had proved nothing. They also argued that my "negative energy" influenced the result.

Excuse me, what kind of energy was that again?

WE WON'T BE FOOLED AGAIN

Before we go into various types of alternative medicine, you need to learn several basic concepts. I promise that if you really get them down, you'll never be fooled again. Underlying them all is this fundamental rule: There is usually an explanation for everything.

To grasp the first, the placebo effect, you must understand the incredible healing power of the human brain. *Placebo*, Latin for "I shall please," separates modern medicine from all that went before. It is this simple: Give a patient a pill with nothing in it. Tell the patient it will heal him. Depending on his condition, he will get better. Placebos work via brain-secreting endorphins. Administer an endorphin-blocker and the placebo effect is decreased.

We all believe we are not susceptible to this reaction. Yet there are remarkable tales of its power. Pull a patient's eyeteeth and the pain responds to a placebo. Fully half of all migraine patients get significant pain relief from placebos. This is not to say that the pain isn't real, just that the brain can fight pain on its own.

Baldness has been lessened by placebo remedies. Placebo creams help varicose veins. Breast enlargement has occurred with placebos. Even surgery—not the psychic kind—can act as a placebo. Before we had coronary bypass surgery, there was an operation called internal mammary artery ligation. Between 65 and 75 percent of patients with angina heart pain reported considerable improvement after this surgery. So doctors did an amazing thing that they could never get away with today. They did placebo surgery. That's right, in some patients, they just performed a minor skin incision, though the patients thought it was the real thing. You guessed it. They got better between 65 and 75 percent of the time, too. There are all sorts of quirks to the placebo effect. Red placebos, for instance, work better than green.

When testing a new drug, medicine insists on controlled studies that compare the new medication against a placebo. If a drug makes it onto the market, it means it has outperformed the placebo. Of course the system isn't perfect, and some drugs do slip through. The bigger question, though, is when you feel better after a real treatment, even surgery, how do you know that you're not improving because of the placebo effect? The answer: You cannot.

But a real placebo test is only effective when it's been conducted in a double-blind fashion, meaning that nobody—not the doctors involved or the subjects—knows which are the placebos and which are real. If the doctors know which pills are real, their speech patterns, subtle levels of enthusiasm, and body language could influence the patient.

For instance, in one study, students put their arms in a bucket of ice water to see how long they could stand it. They were split into two groups, one told that this activity could enhance circulation and tighten pores, the other given a negative spin, told that this activity risked triggering a decrease in circulation and discoloration of their fingernails. Students who heard the optimistic account kept their arms in for forty-five seconds longer, a remarkable feat. If you don't believe me, I'll wait while you go try it yourself.

So does all this mean that if an alternative treatment is a placebo and the doctor knows, it is OK? This is an ethical dilemma. Dr. David Spiegel, a psychiatry and behavioral science professor at Stanford University, thinks it is all right. "Even if an alternative remedy is just a placebo," he told the *New York Times* in 1998, "if patients get better and there are no side effects, what's the harm in trying it?" This is a defensible position in the hands of well-trained medical doctors who know that serious illness is not being missed and that other treatments are not available. But in the hands of a quasi-licensed practitioner, it is a prescription for disaster.

The next concept for your notebook is called the *natural history of illness*. A doctor who does not know the natural course of a disease cannot know whether patients are responding to treatment or just getting better on their own. Consider this one: Treatment A for a cold and the patient gets better in a week, treatment B for a cold and the patient gets better in seven days. Makes no difference. You can't affect the course of a cold.

Some diseases come and go. They're called relapsing, and they are treacherous because patients attribute any improvement to whatever they were taking or doing at the time. Multiple sclerosis may attack a patient for a few months and then disappear for years. The remission of this disease is often used by alternative medicine practitioners as evidence of their magical powers. Brain cancer is similar. The tumor causes swelling and edema (water retention) around itself, greatly incapacitating the patient. Off to the Mexican cancer clinic for the coffee enemas. Coincidentally the edema spontaneously resolves, the patient improves temporarily, and the enemas get the credit. Some diseases, even awful ones, have a certain spontaneous remission rate. While we are very interested to learn from these cases—twelve out of every six thousand cases of normally fatal cancer, for instance—they are part of the natural course of the illness.

With these warnings in mind, let's take on some of the more popular alternatives, the good, the bad, and the ugly.

LEARN TO DISCERN

When I originally envisioned this chapter, I planned to discuss in
detail each of the more popular alternative therapies out there. After
all, I've been waiting a long time for this, saving articles and stuffing
file cabinets for over twenty years. Such an endeavor, though, would
fill this book, or warrant one of its own. More important, these therapies arise so fast that if I did manage to convince you of the efficacy, or
lack of efficacy, of a particular therapy, it would not help you as you
faced the new crop next year. Instead, I offer you the Chinese proverb:
If you give a starving man a fish, he will still be hungry the next day; if
you teach him how to fish, he will never be hungry again. I would
much rather tell you how to evaluate new ideas on your own than just
tell you what works and what doesn't.

Use this process any time you feel tempted to use an AM treatment:

- Develop and demand a certain standard of proof.
- Understand the placebo effect and why scientists insist on controlled studies.
- Know that a major claim running counter to the basic laws of
  nature needs major proof before you should believe it.
- Any claim that contradicts the way we know the body works
  requires major proof as well.
- Claims cannot be sustained by a single study conducted by par-
  tisan investigators or rest solely on anecdotal evidence. Rather,
  they must have the weight of many studies from a variety of
  research sources.

Establishing definitive proof is not easy or fast. Look how difficult
it's been to come up with definitive recommendations even when a
therapy has been studied thousands of times over the years. Whether
it is estrogen and menopause, margarine in your diet, or second-hand
smoke in your living room, we're still not sure. Beware of absolutes
about vague health issues and therapies. Steer clear of the persecuted
iconoclast who claims to be right but unrecognized because other

scientists are jealous or feel threatened. He knows how much we yearn for heroes. Science eventually proves who is right and who is wrong. If it sounds too good to be true, it usually is. No one needs an alternative when there are proved, effective treatments available. There are no alternative dentists claiming that with meditation or herbs you can treat tooth decay. There are no holistic muffler repair shops. You know the noise of a faulty muffler, so it makes rip-off a tough sell.

Be aware that you may not need a lot of help from anybody to stay healthy. I find it inconsistent that the folks peddling you the notion that things natural are superior are also peddling you all kinds of products aimed at improving on your natural body. They seem to think that God or nature screwed up in the design phase. Somehow I trust the design of the human body and think we all meddle too much. The mainstream medical doctor is as guilty of that as the alternative practitioner. For the most part, the human body is perfectly capable of taking care of itself without a health food store full of useless and sometimes dangerous pills, potions, and nostrums.

I have no stake in any alternative therapy, so don't worry about my bias. You can try any of them—as long as you are aware of the variables. If you know what condition or illness needs treatment, and you are not foregoing effective, safe, mainstream therapies; if the alternative is proved safe and you are not being financially ripped off, go ahead and give it a whirl.

Indulge me for one more word of advice: Get your diagnosis nailed down first. No one does that better than your mainstream doctor. You do not want to delay rational conventional therapy until it is too late. Sure, we all want to be cured with the painless, nontoxic, simple, natural, cheap treatment. But it's unwise to allow your disease to become untreatable by any method while you pursue alternatives that may be useless.

In just one year, three of my friends were being treated for back pain by alternative therapists. None had gotten diagnoses from their M.D.s. Two of the cases turned out to be breast and colon cancer that had spread to the spine; the other was kidney stones. Only the friend with kidney stones survived.

You have to learn what normal medicine can do first. It kills me to see lymphoma or other cancer patients running to Mexican cancer quacks. Treated early, most cancers are curable. Treated late, they may not be. Once you have the diagnosis for your problem, evaluate the treatments and success rates—the real numbers—of whatever options your doctor can offer. That is *your* responsibility. Then decide on the next step.

It's your prerogative to try something nonscientific. But be intelligent about it. Ask for the proof of any particular treatment you consider. What are the cure rates? What is the basis for the treatment? Ask to see the best evidence. If you get a blank stare or a load of double-talk and you still want to proceed, then be honest with yourself and admit that you don't care about evidence and probably never did.

Now let's look at some of the goods.

Mind-Body Techniques

I have no doubt that meditation, biofeedback, and hypnosis can be helpful, as long as you know what's wrong with you. You should not attempt to treat serious diseases on your own with these methods, but most doctors would agree that these have a place in medicine. If you suffer from insomnia and pain, for instance, I see nothing to lose and a lot to gain from mind-body aids. The simple relaxation that can ensue helps these problems.

You may not need a mantra or a complex technique. Just taking the time to learn to imagine a pleasant scene—a beach, a mountain, listening to classical music—has helped patients on chemotherapy to control their nausea and vomiting.

But do beware of a certain genre of New Age character, emblematic of the kinds of voices that hit the circuit and develop an extraordinary following. One biggie casts illnesses as a set of spiritual symptoms and herself as the "medical intuitive" to cure them. Who could doubt her and her ability to read your "energetic dysfunctions"? I'm amazed that people fall for this tripe, but hundreds of thousands pay $155 for her seminars. What really burns me is the damage she does with attitudes that blame people for their disease. She speaks of one "friend" who died of lupus, a potentially nasty autoimmune disease, because she had a "fear of letting go." These people rob you of your self-reliance and individuality and give a bad name to a wing of treatment that could actually help you. You don't need them, but they sure need you.

Chiropractic Medicine

In the 1880s, D. D. Palmer, a grocery store clerk enthralled by contemporary psychic and healing cults, set up a "magnetic healing studio" and performed—what else?—magnetism healings. Like others of his ilk, he was looking for the one cause of all disease. In 1895 revelation struck: "Ninety-five percent of diseases are caused by displaced vertebrate; the remainder by luxations of other joints." Unfortunately, too many chiropractors still believe this.

What do we do with this field? It is among the most popular alternative practices. To their credit, chiropractors are allowing extensive scientific investigation of their practices. Yet a recent flurry of controlled, peer-reviewed studies by chiropractors and physicians found that chiropractic treatment offered no more relief from back pain and tension headaches than physical therapy. More studies are pending.

My advice, and that of many modern chiropractors I know, is straightforward. Stay away from any chiropractor who believes the Palmer edict that all disease is caused by pinched nerves and who wants to treat illness with spinal manipulation. It's now one hundred years later. We know what pinched nerves do—they hurt, but they do not cause disease.

Look for the promotional posters in chiropractors' offices that show the poor shriveled pinched nerves running to your organs and creating disease. Watch out for pamphlets that make outrageous claims. I have them in my files, sent to me by consumers in recent years. The titles alone tell you everything: "Chiropractic and Appendicitis," "Chiropractic and Ulcers," "Chiropractic and Asthma." One claims that "nerves control all body functions." Listen up, please. The nerves that do connect to your inner organs are not affected by spinal mechanics—they don't run through the spine. You can disconnect those nerves, then transplant a kidney, a liver, even a heart, and they all work fine.

Be afraid—be very afraid—of chiropractors who tell you that your children need regular adjustments of the spine to be healthy, or who ask you to fill out a health profile on said children. Many chiropractors claim they can treat asthma, despite a recent controlled study that found it worthless. Wrongly treated, asthma can be fatal, so be careful. And, of course, run the other way from chiropractors who tell you not to vaccinate your children. There are loads of chiropractors out there who believe this. Such practices are *not* endorsed by the American Chiropractic Association, the professional licensing body.

Sadly, surveys show that many chiropractors endorse these danger-ous and irresponsible practices. Other chiropractors complain that these eggs are the most vocal of their profession and make them all look bad. There are plenty of modern chiropractors who would love to treat your aching back and are equipped to do so as well as M.D.s. They want to treat backs, not your kid's asthma. Back pain is difficult to treat, and no one yet has a cure. Some M.D.s are suggesting that chi-ropractors act as the gatekeepers for back problems in the managed care environment. But within this field, they are a mixed breed.

Herbal Medicine

Herbs? A no-brainer. What could be simpler and easier to evaluate? Nothing could be less alternative. Modern pharmacology began as herbal medicine and still scours the herbal kingdom for herbs that work. Many of today's prescription drugs have their origins in herbs. Digitalis, used for heart failure, comes from foxglove; ephedrine, for respiratory and other problems, from the Chinese herb Ma huang; morphine, for pain, from the poppy; vincristine, an anti-cancer drug, from periwinkle; Taxol, for ovarian cancer, from the Pacific yew tree; aspirin, for every-thing, from willow. The list stretches on.

Are these mainstream Western pharmaceuticals alternative? Of course not. The difference is that these have been proved to work.

There's the p-word again. There is so much new interest in herbs. Fortunately, double-blind, controlled studies can easily tell which herb treatments work and which do not. Reliable studies have recently shown, for instance, that ginger works for motion sickness, feverfew works for migraines, ginkgo increases cerebral circulation, possibly easing the risk of strokes (but does nothing for memory), elderberry shortens the duration of flu, red-pepper creams help nerve-related pain and are now available by prescription, marijuana eases nausea, a cock-tail of twenty traditional Chinese herbs calms spastic colons, and saw palmetto may shrink swollen prostates, to name a few. See what a little scientific method can do?

Of course, it's not always supportive of our herbal beliefs. For instance, the biggest-selling herb right now is echinacea. In spite of some European studies, which found that it helped certain immune cells, it failed in a recent double-blind study to prevent the common cold—which is the reason most people take it.

The problem, though, is that the herbal industry remains wholly unregulated. You have no way to determine either the potency or the quality of a specific herb. When scientists discover and extract the active ingredient, at least we know how much of it does what. That process takes time. Right now, we don't know for sure if Saint-John's-wort is a cure-all for depression despite what Larry King barks in those ads. We don't know whether kava-kava is an antidote for a stressed-out life. Many people swear by these nostrums, but I'm just honestly warning you that high-quality research isn't in yet. Sorry.

Just like drugs, many herbs can be dangerous. The medical literature is full of cases. You must be careful. If an herb has not been tested—and plenty have not—you could be taking a chance. Pennyroyal causes miscarriages. Chaparral and comfrey cause liver damage. I love Chinese culture, but on my own I would never take herbal pills from China. I have a thick file of cases of horrible complications from toxic Chinese herbs. Unscrupulous Chinese companies have allowed their products—mostly capsules and powders—to be contaminated with mercury, codeine, steroids, fenfluramine (remember fen phen?), powerful anti-inflammatories, even Valium.

It is maddening that some herbs have such undeserved good reputations that hard research cannot challenge their standing. Take aloe vera, for example. In one study, gynecological surgery wounds that were slow to heal were treated with aloe or a placebo. The aloe-treated wounds healed in eighty-three days compared with *fifty-three* days for the placebo wounds. Aloe slowed healing for these women. Yet is aloe any less popular as a treatment for cuts and scrapes? There is, however, the possibility that aloe can help mild burns, so aloe does not yet go down in flames.

Even when we do prove with a good double-blind, controlled study that an herb does not help, the herb gurus will not let go. Dong quai has been definitively discarded as a treatment for menopause symptoms, especially hot flashes. Yet the biggest alternative and herb guru going still insists on pushing it because "I've seen good results in patients who take my standard recommendation for hot flashes, a combination of dong quai, chaste tree, and damiana." Do I need to tell you, again, that this is not science? Unless, of course, you just dropped in from the nineteenth century and are used to doing things this way.

Food Supplements

Obviously this is a biggie. Like herbs, supplements are easy to evaluate, scientifically speaking, because any one of them can be subjected to objective study simply by giving some folks the real thing and others a placebo. Given that, I wish I could point you to more studies on these substances. But it seems that the manufacturers have no interest in proving that their products work. Why should they? Health food stores sell supplements by the bucketful without studies because neither the government nor you, the consumer, demand it. Just call anything a food supplement and you can put it on the market, from hormones such as melatonin, DHEA, and androstenedione to bizarre and toxic drugs like GHB. In addition, you have no guarantee about the contents of these pills. A recent survey of sixteen brands of DHEA found that only seven came close to the amount of the hormone claimed on the label, and three contained absolutely no DHEA at all.

Want to have some fun? Give your kids a summer project replicating a Food and Drug Administration investigation. The FDA sent undercover agents into health food stores to ask simple questions such as "What do you sell to help high blood pressure?" Left untreated or treated ineffectively, high blood pressure is a killer disease. The clerks in the stores were practicing medicine without a license, plain and simple. They recommended bizarre products, some of which I had never heard of, and I keep up on these things.

Another of their questions: "I'm feeling kind of weak. Do you have anything to help fight infection or help my immune system?" That elicited prescriptions such as Immunaid, 155 Shou Wu Chi, echinacea, licorice, burdock root, and astragalus. Here was the question that frightened me the most: "Do you have anything that works on cancer?" One clerk in Pearl City, Hawaii, handed the customer a colon and blood cleaner. He promised that it would cleanse the vital organs, liver, kidney, and colon. Better still, this was one-stop shopping at its best—the product prevents *and* cures cancer. How do you know it's working? Why, your feces will float.

In a store in Springfield, Illinois, a store employee recommended germanium to cure lung cancer. The same illness prompted a sale of antioxidants and bee propolis in Albuquerque; shark cartilage, reishi mushrooms, Pau D'Arco Taheebo Tea, red clover, and LBS II Vegitabs in Oklahoma City; and CO Enzyme Q in Puerto Rico.

Sex supplements, in all their glory, have recently enjoyed a boomlet within the industry. Libido boosters and erection pills have long been a staple crop of the rip-off artists. In the age of Viagra, though, these products find their niche dangerously crowded by the real thing. The same week that Viagra was approved by the FDA, a federal district judge issued a restraining order against companies that were marketing two bogus supplements with names nearly identical to Viagra.

Vitamins

This subject is near and dear to me, especially since vitamins put me through college and medical school. My father and his brothers were among the first successful marketers of a multiple vitamin in the United States. By 1952 Rybutol was eating up the competition. They advertised on national television, rare in those days, and controlled 18 percent of all vitamin and mineral sales in the country. I'm sure if they could have divined that the vitamin business would one day reach six billion dollars in annual sales, they would not have sold the company in 1953.

I started most of my days with a fistful of vitamins. To this day I can swallow ten pills without water. Later my father worked for a company associated with Dr. Carlton Fredericks, a very well-known health and vitamin guru in the early days. Fredericks got a Ph.D. in education and then started writing advertising copy for a vitamin outfit in 1937. In 1945 he was fined five hundred dollars for illegally practicing medicine. He had a radio program on which he would read letters from listeners. He recommended vitamins for every listener's problem. He died prematurely from a heart attack. He was a chain smoker. His vitamins could not help with that.

In those days, scientists paid little attention to vitamins. Because the industry has become so large and its claims so extravagant, science has finally taken an interest. The results so far are mixed. First, most vitamin research in humans presents a major problem. People who take vitamins are generally not "average." They have more money, which dramatically affects their health, eat better diets, get more exercise, and overall, pay more attention to their health. Trying to control for that in a study is a nightmare, so you cannot take too seriously studies that compare vitamin-takers to nonvitamin-takers.

We are surrounded by vitamins, yet generally, the large controlled studies have been disappointing. Critics charge that the doses have been too small. Researchers have observed that vitamins have positive impacts on substances in the blood thought to determine risk for heart attack. But that kind of evidence is hard to translate into rates of disease and death. Folic acid has emerged as the latest star, helping to prevent birth defects like spina bifida and as a modifier of some risk factors for heart disease.

The best research gives some subjects vitamins and others placebos. The subjects must be followed for years in order to see what happens. This has been done for a few major vitamins, and the results are strange. Beta carotene, the form of vitamin A in almost all multivitamins, appears to increase the rate of cancer in high-risk groups. It seems that natural foods contain a lot of different forms of vitamin A that are more beneficial. Another prospective study found beta carotene of little use in decreasing symptoms of heart disease. Lycopene, a phytochemical in foods like tomatoes (especially cooked and canned), not vitamins, seems to be reasonably effective in preventing prostate cancer. Many other micronutrients and antioxidants in vegetables and fruits, but not in vitamin pills, have been proved to be helpful as well. But Ohio State University has found that thiamine, vitamin B-1, may in fact increase the growth of cancer cells.

Vitamin E has had better press and was found in one study to decrease prostate cancer rates. It seems to decrease the risk of cardiovascular problems, but we must wait a few more years for results from long-term controlled trials.

Vitamin C, meanwhile, has been a big disappointment, especially since it has a longer history of scrutiny than any other vitamin. In 1747 British naval surgeon Dr. James Lind confronted the horrors of scurvy among sailors. He selected twelve sailors with scurvy and fed them identical diets but added six additional items (hard cider, elixir of vitriol, vinegar, sea water, oranges or lemons, and barley water or cream of tartar), then divided them among the men. The citrus fruits cured the scurvy. But vitamin C wasn't discovered until the twentieth century. It is strange that people in the eighteenth century recognized the value of a controlled clinical study, yet only now are we doing the same types of studies on vitamins.

In the end, I do not view the vitamin issue as a tough call. You get a more complete variety of vitamins directly from food. Nature intended it that way. Don't buy the idea that food is less nutritious today. Of course, if you live on junk food, it is. But there seems to be no harm in taking a good cheap commercial multiple vitamin. I take one in the morning, but don't forget that I'm an offspring of the industry. There is one great danger, though, in assuming that vitamins make up for a crummy diet. If that's the choice, drop the vitamins and eat right. Or take your vitamins, but still eat those damned fruits and veggies.

Acupuncture

Oh boy, I know I'm going to get lots of mail on this one. First, remember that I am an enduring fan of things Asian. Yet I am underwhelmed by the evidence for the efficacy of acupuncture. Of course, if I stick needles in you, you will notice an effect. That's the placebo effect. The only way to draw an objective bead here is to perform sham acupuncture as a control. That means sticking the needles anywhere other than on the classical Chinese meridians. That in itself is a problem. This cannot be double-blind, because the acupuncturist knows when he is using the right points and when he is using the sham points. His subliminal reactions and expectations can influence the outcome.

Nevertheless, many studies have found that the location of the needle makes no difference in the patient's improvement. I also have studies in my file that found more of an effect with the real acupuncture. Yet when you separate out the studies by the quality of the methodology, the better and higher the quality, the less the effect of acupuncture. All this will change in the future because a German researcher has come up with an ingenious placebo acupuncture needle that retracts into itself like the toy knives of old. Finally we will have a good shot at some scientific proof in this area. Nevertheless, a few recent studies have already found no difference in results between fake acupuncture and real acupuncture in the treatment of asthma. The same held true for treatment of patients with back pain and pain due to HIV-related nerve damage.

A few decades ago, the Chinese began to apply electricity to acupuncture needles and noticed a big increase in efficacy. A top American acupuncture researcher believes the electricity accounts for most of the pain-relieving effect attributed to acupuncture. Electricity applied to skin is known to decrease pain.

In fact, irritation of the skin from any cause—including needles—also could explain some of the effects. The application of burning skin creams like capsaicin pepper creams or Ben Gay, vibrations, or ice can all induce a sort of physiological distraction that may block the flow of impulses to pain nerves.

And be skeptical when Western acupuncturists want to cure your tobacco addiction or help you lose weight. The Chinese never use acupuncture that way. The most recent study on electroacupuncture for smoking found it to be worthless, which should come as no surprise. The Chinese didn't start smoking tobacco until thousands of years after acupuncture's invention.

The acupuncture points themselves are problematic and fall in different places on different charts. If you show the same ear to two acupuncturists, they will differ as to the exact acupuncture point because all ears are different.

I'm afraid that I agree with the position paper by the National Council Against Health Fraud, which emphatically declares that "after 20 years in the court of scientific opinion, acupuncture has not been demonstrated effective for any condition." In all fairness, a recent consensus panel of acupuncturists and other interested parties issued a statement concluding that acupuncture was effective for mild to moderate pain and nausea and a couple of other minor problems. These were advocates, though, not independent researchers.

Again, if it helps you with pain, I have no problem. But I do draw a line. First, acupuncture is not known to cure any disease. Run from any acupuncturist who tells you it can. Even the consensus panel of acupuncture enthusiasts would agree. Second, and most important: Get your diagnosis first. In many states, anyone can obtain an acupuncture license without any real medical training. How would that untrained practitioner know if your headache is a migraine or a brain tumor? If you're not going to obey that rule, at least find an acupuncturist who has a legitimate medical degree.

In the right hands, acupuncture is a nontoxic, safe therapy, and if you respond to it without Demerol, well, I'll concede it as a win-win. But I will never concede that your health problem is caused by blockages in the flow of energy along a mythical road map on your body.

Homeopathy

Homeopathy was the invention of Samuel Hahnemann, a German physician. He theorized that if a drug or herb caused a symptom like nausea in a healthy person, then it could treat nausea in a sick person. The theory went like this: If a patient had runny eyes from allergies, then onions—which cause the normal eye to tear—would ease the allergic eye symptoms. He tried it. Of course it made allergic patients worse, so he started to dilute his doses, concluding that the smaller the dose, the more powerfully it would treat the problem. In the end, not a molecule of the original substance remained. That, according to Hahnemann, was the most powerful medicine of all.

I can think of little else that more defies the laws of chemistry and physics—as well as logic. Its popularity today is bizarre. Hahnemann lived in the eighteenth century, a time in medicine when all doctors could do was to drain your blood, thus purging illness and probably making more patients worse than better. Perhaps some adherents of homeopathy view the dangers of our prescription drugs and surgeries in the way that Hahnemann viewed bleeding in his day, and this perhaps could explain why homeopathy has made such a comeback. To be sure, it is a nontoxic therapy, but put it in the bin marked Major Claims Need Major Proof.

Homeopaths will offer up studies showing that it works. To be fair, there are some. But I also have another file full of studies that show it to be nothing more than a placebo. The weight of the evidence is certainly not there. To their credit, homeopaths keep trying to amass it. But let me put it this way: I don't plan on investing in homeopathic-product stock.

Therapeutic Touch

In case you're wondering how such an offbeat practice made the cut into this chapter, consider these numbers: It is taught in more than eighty nursing schools nationwide (some of which even offer graduate credit). Its promoters have scammed—pardon me, been awarded—hundreds of thousands of dollars in federal and university grants. At last count, there were a hundred thousand practitioners, forty thousand of them health professionals. One California hospital even allows a TT practitioner in the operating room to wave her hands over the patients. I'm not sure I'd trust that hospital to care for someone I love, but then again, it *is* in Marin County, the land of alternative medicine.

What is it exactly? It first appeared on the scene in 1975. Its practitioners simply wave their hands a few inches from the patient. In that wave, the healer first detects the human energy field and its "disturbances"—disease—and then alters the field for various health benefits. The therapeutic claims range from the simple relief of tension and anxiety to preventing rejection of transplanted organs.

The fundamental skill of the TT practitioner is to sense that energy field. Or it was, until a nine-year-old schoolgirl in Colorado named Emily Rosa indisputably proved it nonsense. In 1996 she decided to test the accuracy of the TT claim for a school science project. The TT practitioners trusted her. What's to fear from a nine-year-old girl?

The experiment was scientifically unassailable. Emily simply sat the TT healer behind a shield, both hands facing out, palms upward. Emily put her hand above either the left or right hand of the TT subject, who had to feel Emily's energy field above the correct hand. Of course, the healers did no better than by chance. At age eleven, Emily became the youngest person ever to publish an article in the *Journal of the American Medical Association.*

You can imagine the response by the TT community to this simple and elegant experiment. Predictably, they attacked the American Medical Association for using a "specious" methodology to try to debunk them. Good science is hardly specious, whether practiced by an eleven-year-old or a forty-four-year-old. Much upset was registered in letters to the editor of the *New York Times,* which ran a front-page story about Emily and her study.

Of course, none of this stops the promoters. That same month, I got a pitch to invite a "doctor" on my show who claimed he could cure patients of cancer and other major diseases by healing them with his hands. His press release, meant for more gullible radio producers and hosts, had an appalling line: "He has dramatic live-case examples and medical documentation to back up his claims." Dead case examples are not convincing. "He can teach these amazing and mysterious, magic-like techniques to almost anyone. Right on the air, he will reveal the secrets that will enable your audience to try it for themselves. Alternative medicine is one of today's red-hot topics."

I wonder how many shows booked him? I guess it doesn't much matter. If you want to believe this voodoo doo-doo, if you don't want to trust in your own common sense, then go ahead. There will always be hucksters out there waiting to grab at your gullibility as they grab at your wallet. I hope you won't let them get either. Then there are the well-meaning but misled enthusiasts, who may be just as dangerous.

Remember that if you look behind the bright lights that flash "alternative medicine," you'll find a dim 15-watt bulb blinking "unproved medicine." Science is finally dealing with many of these therapies. Eventually, we'll know which ones have merit and which should be sent back to storage. In the meantime, be patient, and be careful.

6

TAKE THE ABUSE OUT OF SOME SUBSTANCES AND THEY CAN BE GOOD FOR YOU

W e had traveled by small ship halfway around the world, to Sumba, a dot of an island in the Indonesian archipelago. Among the first Western visitors to this remote village, Sharon and I could not have been more anxious and excited, nor farther off the beaten tourist track. The night prior to our visit the local village chief augured a chicken to see if the visit was auspicious. Apparently it was. Yet, as a physician and usually willing adventurer, I was surprised at my trepidation over what we were about to do.

This was a "when-in-Rome" situation. We were going to ingest a narcotic that, by most accounts, is among the most widely used and abused drugs in the world. It was, we were warned by our guide, the only way we would be allowed to crash the boundary between their way of life and ours. Throughout Sumba, Indonesia, and all Southeast

Asia, much of the population is addicted. It is not tobacco or alcohol, marijuana or heroin. It is betel.

Betel is a nut from the *Areca catechu* palm tree and contains the drug arecoline, consumed by hundreds of millions of Southeast Asians. Like many drugs when traced to their ethnic origins, it is an integral and essential feature of the culture.

"The craving of the betel nut chewer for his drug is hardly less strong than that of other drug addicts for their respective intoxicants," writes Lois Lewin in *Narcotic and Stimulating Drugs: Their Use and Abuse*, a 1931 textbook. "With regard to the daily frequency and persistence with which betel is chewed, it even surpasses all other substances of the same kind. Aficionados would rather give up rice, the main support of their lives, than betel, which exercises a more imperative power on its habitués than does tobacco on smokers. To cease to chew betel is, for the betel chewer, the same thing as dying."

I thought I had seen most everything when it came to mood-altering drugs. Certainly, in an earlier era of self-discovery, I had experienced some of them first-hand. But betel was beyond this ex-hippie's ken. I was feeling a little intimidated. A quick look at our hosts was warning enough, for betel country is a periodontist's paradise. The locals' eroded gums and stubby brown teeth attest to the vigor of their habit. Blood-red drool coats their mouths and lips. Our guide counseled us that chewing "a little" and spitting it out after a polite interlude would satisfy local custom. We didn't have to go "all the way."

When we got to the village, we were ushered to benches in a clearing beneath towering trees. I noticed the fabrics with which the villagers swathed themselves. The colors and patterns were extraordinary, and repeated on banners hanging everywhere from trees and ropes and sticks. They call this unique type of weaving *ikat*. Unlike conventional fabric work, where plain colors are printed with a design, or colored threads woven into a pattern, the Sumba women employ an intricate, seemingly impossible technique. They take a bundle of individual plain threads and tie-dye them so that each one becomes a rainbow of random colors. Other bundles are tie-dyed differently.

Then they get creative. Sitting around the village, chatting, chewing betel, and occasionally spitting on the ground, the women weave these seemingly random threads into whole cloth. Remarkable patterns emerge. Horses and human figures dance across the fabric. This beauty is accomplished with magnitude and complexity, without preplanned patterns or mathematical formulas. One cannot help but invoke the contribution of betel in their artistic achievement.

At the moment, I wasn't thinking about fabrics. Trays had been passed, lined with slivers of betel, burnt lime, and leaves of a special gum-and-pepper tree. We followed the villagers, taking some of each and wadding them together. We started chewing. Stimulated by the tart concoction, saliva flooded my mouth, which was rapidly turning red. It felt as if a sheepdog were rolling around in there. I immediately wanted to spit. And spit and spit, even as the buzz now was coming on strong. After an acceptable interval had passed, I finally achieved salivary relief. The tiny amount of drug by now in our bloodstreams felt like strong coffee, minus the jitteriness. Others, in fact, have described the sensation as a combination of caffeine, coca leaf, and tobacco.

"The greatest privations and sufferings of human life—insufficient or bad nourishment, hard work, rough weather and illness—lose their disagreeable character before the comforting action of betel," writes Lewin. "The betel-chewer experiences a feeling of well-being. He is in good humor and gay, he is very little, if at all, bored, and is . . . inspired to self reflection and to work if he has the disposition thereto. . . . It has a soothing effect and gives rise to an excellent humor on account of its slightly inebriating action on the brain. . . . The feeling of thirst and hunger is said to be appeased and the sexual impulses augmented by the chewing of betel."

I'm still sorry I chickened out so early.

Forgive me the length of the story. I tell it because it is typical of civilization. Mood-altering chemicals have played a part in all cultures throughout human history. One can infer that evolution favored this symbiosis. Learning that an herb enabled its people to work harder, with less hunger and thirst, would certainly give a culture a survival advantage. This same scenario applies throughout the world, whether to betel in Asia or kava in the South Seas, khat in East Africa, mescaline in the New World, cannabis and opium in Asia Minor and Africa, coca leaf in South America, and alcohol and tobacco everywhere.

Much human behavior involves a search for pleasure and ecstasy in the myriad ways available to us. Religion, art, music, food, and sex come to mind. Ever watch children spinning around to make themelves dizzy, laughing delightedly in the process? What of our hunger for amusement park rides that take us in heart-stopping loops? At a party I once watched a band of whirling dervishes do their thing. They spun and spun until it made me dizzy. The induced dizziness is the desired aspect of altered consciousness that was originally part of the religious ecstasy sought by the Sufis. The rituals of other ethnic groups involve centrifugal dances that induce dizzying highs.

In a more natural setting than our modern one, drugs seem not to wreak the havoc they do here. Chemicals in other worlds have helped with the integration of culture and family. That makes them worthy of our respect and investigation. Obviously, in our Western cultures, we have blown it. With technology we have been able to extract and concentrate the psychoactive chemicals from native products and boost potency to such a degree that we can use them to destroy, rather than to enhance, our lives.

Humans learned early, around the eleventh century, to distill and transform low alcohol levels in naturally fermented beer and wine into 150-proof liquor. Potent white powders extracted from opium poppy and coca leaf provide a high till you die. Caffeine concentrated into pills and sodas push the buzz. Nicotine and the delivery vehicle of tobacco are manipulated to addict millions. And now, scientifically created molecules make an alphabet soup of mood enhancers like LSD, PCP, MDMA, and GHB.

Dr. Ronald Siegel, a psychopharmacologist at the University of California at Los Angeles, proposes recognizing that this penchant of man and animal to alter feelings with chemicals is the fourth drive. Hunger, sex, thirst . . . and altering one's consciousness?

"In every age, in every part of this planet, people have pursued intoxication with plant drugs, alcohol, and other mind altering substances," Siegel insists. "This 'fourth drive' is a natural part of our biology, creating the irrepressible demand for drugs. In a sense the war on drugs is a war against ourselves, a denial of our very nature."

I will discuss a number of mood-altering substances in this chapter. You may not use all of them, but I'll bet you use at least one of them. People enhance consciousness with all sorts of things, from the bottle of 100-proof hidden in the lower desk drawer to the eye-opening shot of java in the morning to the bong sneaked out after the kids go night-night.

EVEN THE BIRDIES IN THE TREES . . .

Fall in downtown Iowa City. An early snow knocks the leaves off a tree, exposing its berries. The sight is not lost to a flock of migrating cedar waxwings. It is the time of year when the berries start to ferment. Called to the scene, the local animal control officer confronted a rowdy situation. In the berry tree, thirty birds barely clung to the branches. Another forty were passed out on the ground. Fifty had flown into the window of a convenience store next to the tree. "They are eating wine," one animal expert concluded. Officials decided to close the bar, wrapping the tree in a blue tarp.

Clearly, humans are not the only creatures who crave drugs. Siegel has documented the desire to get high in almost every animal group he has examined. His book, *Intoxication*, is an eye-opener. A tireless and indefatigable researcher, he has collected an astounding array of examples, from insects to birds to mammals. Robins loaded on pyracantha berries will dive-bomb cats. Cattle eat loco weed. Water buffalo nibble opium poppies. A mongoose upset over the loss of a mate or the destruction of a burrow will seek out and eat a plant with psychedelic qualities.

Fermented and semirotten fruit is a big draw. An odd, rugby-ball-sized durian fruit covered in spikes grows in Southeast Asia, its odor somewhere between garlic and digestive gases. The taste, however, is creamy, fruity, and delicious. Many native animals have cultivated a taste for the durian drunk, available after the fermented fruit falls to the ground. Civet cats, squirrels, pigs, deer, tapirs, rhinoceroses, and tigers have all been caught in the act. Elephants, observes Siegel, start listing in a torpor. Monkeys find that their motor coordination disappears, have trouble climbing, and develop a head tremor. Flying foxes, night feeders that actually are the largest bats in the world, lose their navigational ability as the alcohol cripples their sonar. "The bats," writes Siegel, "keep falling down and waddling on the ground."

With strong alcoholic proclivities, elephants, especially, are lushes. They prefer a drink with 7 percent alcoholic content, the equivalent of strong ale. They will vocalize, growl, sway, stagger, and inappropriately wrap their trunks around themselves. They become aggressive with one another and will chase the Jeep carrying the drum of booze, desperate to keep the bar open.

People aren't so different. Once intoxication has been experienced, individuals—entire cultures—will persevere to repeat the pleasure. Wars on drugs notwithstanding, nothing can stop this quest. Not even regular war, horrifying poverty, or starvation gets in the way. Remember the mayhem in 1991 as millions of people faced starvation in Somalia during warfare among competing local war lords? While the West struggled to deliver food to starving refugees, correspondents were amazed that planeloads of khat, the national drug of Somalia, made it to the local markets each day. All the warring factions, which couldn't agree on food supplies, easily agreed to let the khat through. Said one participant: "Khat is a part of our life, and it helps us forget the hunger."

WHO GETS ADDICTED—AND WHY

If all nature's creatures are driven toward chemical stimulation, why is it that some people are able to handle it better than others? Recent studies have found a genetic link with narcotic troubles. As you might expect, there appear to be certain inherited personality and psychiatric patterns that connect to drug abuse. This has been reflected in a study of adoptees separated from their biological parents at birth. First a relationship was found between genes and antisocial personality. If the biological parents had such a personality, the child was more likely to share it, and the child who had that antisocial personality was more likely to have a drug problem. Kids whose biological parents had an alcohol problem, themselves had greater rates of drug abuse, even if they did not have antisocial personalities. Nurture played a role as well. Divorce and psychiatric problems in the adopted family led to more drug abuse among the kids.

Does this mean you can use, and not abuse, drugs if you do not carry the genes for a drug-abusing personality? No one knows for sure yet. Obviously there are strong environmental influences as well. When patients in pain take opiates, they do not get addicted as easily as folks who try these narcotics recreationally. As a matter of fact, an exaggerated fear of addiction is why so many people are undermedicated for pain. Some heroin addicts can even sustain low use patterns.

On the street, the expression is *chipper* for people who can maintain an occasional, low level of use. Such users tend to be able to control their desire so that it doesn't disrupt their lives and jobs.

Chipping as a phenomenon is worth a good look to see who gets addicted and the role of environment in the cure. The war in Vietnam offers arguably the best example that once an addict is not always an addict. Many GIs got hooked. In a world of cheap heroin, often smoked rather than injected, fully one-third of America's soldiers in Vietnam tried it; half of those became addicted. Psychologist Lee N. Robbins of Washington University in St. Louis followed addicted soldiers after their return home. Of those who were addicted overseas, half tried heroin here in the states; only 12 percent became readdicted.

Chipping takes lots of forms. One of the most addicting drugs is tobacco. Yet there are folks out there who can smoke cigarettes without getting hooked. Saul Shiffman, a psychologist at the University of Pittsburgh, has studied these rare birds and their ability to resist addiction. He found that chippers are different from other people. They cope well with stress and seem to have less of it in their lives. While the addict smokes to sustain that blood level of nicotine, chippers appear to smoke in response to specific external cues, sometimes in relation to other habits—drinking coffee, for example. Shiffman asked his chippers to record their behavior and moods throughout the day. It made no difference whether they were alone or in social situations with other smokers, they could go days without lighting up. You can imagine the effect of that deprivation on a real smoker.

Chippers do not suffer the full withdrawal syndrome when they don't smoke. Everyone has seen the tremendous variability in people's ability to quit smoking, and this, of course, raises that gene thing again. The chippers in the study also had fewer relatives who smoked, and those relatives were more successful at quitting when they tried.

THE DEPENDENCE CHAIN

Whatever the damage, the drive toward some chemical pleasure is not without its internal chemical reason. Opiates are innate to our body. Our brains secrete opiatelike chemicals to help us with pain and modulate our moods. When they are used, and *not* abused, the cost is less. If alcohol, the cause of so much mayhem in our country, can be tolerated and used for pleasure without causing harm for many people, why can't we do the same with other substances? Are you ready to take a truly objective look, free of emotion and politics? Evaluating drugs is a tricky business; expect some surprises.

Dr. Jack Henningfield of the National Institute on Drug Abuse and Dr. Neal Benowitz of the University of California at San Francisco tackled the problem independently, but using the same system. They put together a list of abusable drugs and narrowed in on the six biggies: nicotine, heroin, cocaine, alcohol, caffeine, and marijuana. Then they established a rating system using the most important characteristics of abusable drugs. These criteria included the severity of withdrawal symptoms, the need for increasing amounts, dependence on the substance, intoxication level, and personal and social damage.

They found that nicotine seems to be the hardest drug to quit, marijuana the easiest. (Cigarettes, ironically, also seem to give the least pleasure of any drug.) Alcohol, which produces the greatest intoxication of any of them, also trips the worst withdrawal symptoms. I worked in alcohol rehabilitation centers years ago and have no trouble believing that one. Watching someone in delirium tremens—DTs—is a horrible sight. Cocaine is the drug that makes its user most want more immediately.

I took it a step further and added up all their scores for all the drugs. This total score gives equal weight to all the qualities of a drug, which is not an accurate picture of how they affect your life when you use them. But this is the most objective analysis available at the moment, from least damaging to worst for you: marijuana, caffeine, nicotine, cocaine, alcohol, and heroin.

Consider one notable user: In 1884 one of the most famous surgeons in American history, William Halstead, who invented surgical techniques like the mastectomy, became fascinated by the anesthetic effects of cocaine, applied locally. You can imagine how amazing it must have been, a drug that not only reduced bleeding but also rendered tissue numb when applied directly. His fascination got a little out of hand and he wound up becoming addicted. In those days the prevailing treatment for cocaine addiction was to readdict the patient to morphine. Believe it or not, Halstead remained addicted to morphine for the next thirty years. Could he function? Absolutely. He headed the department of surgery at Johns Hopkins Medical Center and was acknowledged as the country's leading academic surgeon throughout that period. This is not the usual image of the morphine addict.

The dose range of morphine for a patient in cancer pain can vary by a remarkable thousandfold, from 15 milligrams to 15 grams a day, or even more. Most patients hover around 200 milligrams a day. The most common side effect of that dose is constipation. At high doses, opiates can cause a dulling of consciousness. But it seems that at a stable dose the drug is unique in its lack of effect on psychomotor tasks. If I gave you a walloping dose of morphine, you definitely would know it because your body is not used to it. But as a chronic user, your reaction would be different.

Researchers in Finland studied two groups of cancer patients, one group on a daily dose of morphine averaging over 200 milligrams, the other not. On a standard battery of tests, there were no significant differences between the morphine group and the nonmorphine group in intelligence, vigilance, concentration, fluency of motor reactions, and attention. Both groups also scored equally on neurological, auditory, and visual tests, reaction times, and body sway with the eyes open. Those on morphine were even able to drive fine. Only when their eyes were closed did the morphine group perform slightly more poorly.

A nonmedical approach reveals some interesting conundrums. Robert Kaestner, a labor economist at the National Bureau of Economic Research, decided to try population studies. His research turned on its head the notion that mind-altering drugs transform your brain into fried eggs.

It sounds logical that the inability to focus, pay attention, and stay motivated would have a profound effect on the capacity to hold a job or earn a living. Yet Kaestner found that men who used cocaine and/or marijuana were likely to earn *more* money. Those who had tried cocaine made 21 percent more money than abstainers. Those using drugs more heavily made even more money. The same held true for women. Still another study by other authors found a 37 percent wage differential in favor of hard-drug users.

At this point it might appear that people with greater income have more of it to blow on drugs. The economists thought of that and factored in possible influences such as race, education, and the fact that those with higher income might consume more drugs because they could afford it. This is similar to those studies that find college students who experiment with drugs get better grades. Because these are disturbing results, it's important to try to understand them, even if we do not like them.

One front-running theory is that people who are innately more curious about the world may command higher salaries and also be more likely to try drugs. To test this "natural inquisitiveness" theory, the researchers followed individual users. They figured that drug use would take its toll in both absenteeism and job loss. It did not, but the results were not conclusive. The question does arise, though, whether drug use actually improves performance in some workplaces. Could it make boring jobs more fun? I hope not and expect that over time researchers would chart a deterioration in job performance. But the evidence is not in yet.

CONTRADICTIONS GALORE

Few issues in life come in black-and-white, and this one is no exception. None of this means that the pursuit of a high is always good for you. Nor does it mean that at certain levels it is always bad for you. This is where I part company with conventional thinking. Can any of these substances actually be good for you? That may sound radical, but the answer is yes in some circumstances. Yes, when mind-altering chemicals are abused, it's pleasure at a high price. Yes, too much of most mood-altering chemicals does harm. Still, the consumption of certain compounds is illegal, while the consumption of others—alcohol and nicotine, for example—is legal and even abetted to great excess.

The dividing lines are cultural and historical, not physiological. One could argue that the most toxic and dangerous chemicals are exactly those that we glamorize and promote, while people are imprisoned for using those more friendly to the human body. You would not notice opiate addicts getting their fix if they did it with a prescription for morphine filled by their neighborhood drugstore. They could hold a job, drive a car, and function normally. I believe I do a balanced job on the air of reporting on alcohol and other drugs. Don't shoot the messenger because the truth upsets you.

Let's face it, as a society our attitude about drug use is all over the map. Alcohol is a legal mood-altering chemical, a drug that is abused by many and enjoyed by most people who use it. A recent poll of 1,500

Americans by *Wine Spectator* magazine found that 20 percent support a total ban on alcohol. The same survey found that 75 percent of wine consumption occurs in the drinker's home, almost always with dinner. As with most other abusable drugs, there are real and potential constructive uses for alcohol, as well as reasonable, moderate pleasures to be had.

Amphetamines such as speed are, of course, illegal. A truck driver could wind up in jail for using them to stay awake on the road. But somehow they are acceptable for the commander of a fighter jet to use. This is a well-known practice by the military. During the Gulf War, the air force confirmed that some of its pilots took amphetamines to stay awake during missions. "They were used only under careful circumstances, supervised by the flight surgeon," the air force surgeon general's office confirmed. "We have never had an aircraft accident because of this."

Does that mean speed is safe and compatible with good health? Why are amphetamines OK for a fighter pilot but not for a tired truck driver? Civilian pilots could never use these drugs, but they are available to any fat person who wants a diet pill. Like it or not, we have to admit it: Illegal drugs can have positive uses. The military currently is on a full-bore search for drugs "that can keep soldiers fighting after several days without sleep."

Even the term, *drugs,* is loaded. Publicly label alcohol or caffeine a drug and publicists from the appropriate trade group are all over you. I first did this on the air twenty years ago, when it was not yet socially acceptable. The reaction was vociferous, to say the least. Yet from a medical perspective, it seemed as clear to me then as now. There is a reason I refer to them as mood- or mind-altering chemicals. Pharmacologists look at them as molecules that affect the human animal, not as legal or illegal substances. The latter definitions are artificial, man-made distinctions based on culture and tradition, not biology. If a society is trying to decide which drugs are safe and which are less safe, the laws don't hold the answers. These answers lie in biology.

Pharmacologists don't expect any drug—legal, illegal, abusable, usable, prescribable, or over-the-counter—to have only good or only bad effects. If society could accept this basic fact, it might well extricate itself from this intellectual bind. How many times have politicians ranted that allowing patients access to medical marijuana sends the wrong message to our kids? It just doesn't wash. Does a cancer patient on morphine send the wrong message? Does giving amphetamines to the hyperactive kid or the fat person send the wrong message? What about cocaine used by eye, ear, nose, and throat surgery patients? The important point here is to separate abuse and medical use. Because a drug is abused by one segment of our society, it shouldn't mean that another segment is denied its benefits. Will those politicians be proud of their antidrug legislation when they cannot relieve their vomiting from cancer chemotherapy with one remarkable herb, cannabis?

It is generally accepted that alcohol leads to a hundred thousand American deaths a year. That includes auto accidents, fires, falls, drownings, liver disease, cancer, cardiomyopathy, and dementia. In addition, alcohol is implicated in most homicides, domestic violence, and homelessness. Yet alcohol is used responsibly by millions of folks and, as we'll see, can be an important factor in preventing illness. Does that mean illegal drugs can be used and not abused? Tobacco kills an extraordinary four hundred thousand Americans each year and disables thousands more. All illegal drugs *combined* account for nine thousand deaths.

People get upset, again, when I say this on the air, but it makes a very important point. If I could get a clean and uncontaminated supply, I would rather be a heroin addict than an alcoholic. Assume a lifetime addiction, which is not unreasonable since both are hard to quit and have similar recidivism rates; then compare someone drunk on alcohol to someone stoned on heroin. The drunk can neither walk well, speak coherently, nor drive a car. Alcohol is one of the few known drugs that can induce violence and aggression. When abused, it is very toxic to the body, rotting the liver, the brain, and the nerves. Opiates, on the other hand, allow one to function fairly normally and leave the organs generally unaffected.

Which of these two chemicals do we as a society advocate? I haven't seen ads for Absolut heroin lately.

THE WAGES OF FEAR

Drug abuse costs between $70 billion and $150 billion a year. Drug offenses account for nearly half of the inmates in crowded federal prisons. But the country pays still more for inconsistent attitudes about drugs.

Mood-altering substances are divided into good drugs (legal) and bad drugs (illegal). Right or wrong, this classification system extends to prescription medicine as well. Even though it is legal for me to prescribe morphine, Demerol, and other opiates for your pain, as a typical doctor I am reluctant to do so because of society's stigma. There are no painkillers on a par with this class of drugs, and yet they are underutilized. No one suffers more as a result than the patient in pain.

Our fear of opiates is unfounded. Chronic-pain patients rarely get addicted. As for terminal cancer patients, so what if they did? The point is to relieve human suffering. Misplaced attempts to control the flow of illegal narcotics mean that doctors in many states must fill out special forms each time they write a prescription for opiate analgesics. One medical journal after another decries this situation, yet nothing changes. The saddest articles describe children in pain who can find no relief because of our misplaced, distorted priorities. A child with leukemia may require up to twenty bone-marrow aspirations and spinal taps. These treatments are excruciatingly painful. They are routinely denied relief by the most effective opiate-based analgesics even though research finds that the pain becomes cumulative in later treatments.

Here's an example of how these attitudes augment pain. Stanford University developed a clever delivery system for a narcotic called fentanyl. They wanted to give it in a lollipop to kids about to undergo surgery. It was an elegant solution to an old problem. Children often become fussy before surgery, and the lollipop ended the need for presurgical shots or pills. No sooner had this study been announced when the Public Citizen Health Research Group fired off a well-publicized letter to the Food and Drug Administration complaining that the lollipop sent a "dangerous message" that drugs are candy. Dr. Lawrence Feld of Stanford responded angrily—and appropriately— that "kids don't become drug addicts because of anesthetic care they get in the hospital."

Adults in pain pay a higher price. Physicians play a defensive game, and I don't blame them. A hearing in the California state legislature elicited testimony from doctors that many refuse to prescribe certain drugs in adequate amounts because, as Senator Leroy Greene said, "they fear prosecution from state authorities for overprescribing a controlled substance. . . . Physicians also fear being sued for medical malpractice by patients who misuse the drugs." Responding to critics worried that patients might become dependent on such drugs, Greene, who sponsored a bill to make them more available to patients in severe pain, countered that "dependency is a matter to be desired if you are in endless pain."

This is a huge problem. Half of patients with advanced cancer still experience severe pain. Of cancer patients who die, 25 percent do so in great pain that, tragically, could have been prevented. An article in the *Journal of the National Cancer Institute* documented "a regulatory climate that is hostile to the distribution of all substances with the potential for abuse." Federal law prevents doctors from phoning in prescriptions for powerful pain medications, although we can for other medications. We can't give refills. Triplicate forms are required in most states, which makes doctors feel that they are doing something wrong. In fact, doctors end up prescribing less effective medications to avoid having state and federal governments looking over their shoulders. Research at Brandeis University found that in states where triplicate forms are required, doctors shy away from the best pain medications for broken bones, muscle and joint injuries, and other pain.

I'm not exaggerating this issue. Things have gotten so out of hand that major medical organizations are issuing their own guidelines. The American Geriatrics Society warns that the consequences of inadequately treated pain in older Americans are massive. These patients are likely to have more pain and to suffer depression, isolation, and decreased socialization. Less powerful drugs such as aspirin and ibuprofen have more side effects than more powerful drugs. "Fears of drug dependency and addiction do not justify the failure to relieve pain, especially for those near the end of life," the society concludes.

TURN ON THE LIGHT AND THE BOGEYMAN'S NOT SO SCARY

Alcohol is the most dangerous drug in the world, based just on its pharmacology. It is also a marvelous medical preventive when used appropriately. The only intellectually honest approach is to ban it or to allow folks in a supposedly free society to make up their own minds. As I've made clear, I fear disallowing a medicine because some abuse it.

I am wading into a quagmire and I know it. Ours is an alcoholic culture. There is little if any enlightenment from the media on the issue. Many of the pro-health messages we hear about alcohol are pushed and financed by the alcohol industry, which is girding for battles it does not want to lose as did big tobacco. There can be bad health consequences from alcohol abuse. And yes, there are other ways to relax and improve your health that do not expose you to the risk of addiction. Yet a cultural preoccupation with the negative effects of alcohol works against frank scientific discussions.

Who drinks? Slightly more than one-third of American adults abstain completely from alcohol, and there has been a steady decline in drinking overall. Surveys show vast differences based on region, ethnic group, and social class. Half those with less than a high school degree don't touch the stuff. Yet 80 percent of the college educated do. Those with more money and education are more likely to drink. Those within hyphenated American ethnic groupings—including Italians, Chinese, and Greeks—rarely abstain but rarely are alcoholic. Only 1 percent of American Jews are alcoholics. Irish-Americans have a higher abstinence rate than Italian-Americans but are seven times as likely to become alcoholics. Adolescents continue to increase consumption in new patterns like binge drinking. The majority of Americans continue to drink without problems. The minority have drinking problems.

So how do we develop policy with such a mixed bag? Black-and-white, just-say-no approaches will fail. In spite of extensive literature on the health benefits of moderate alcohol use, the official response has been nil. Listen to one government pamphlet on dietary guidelines: "Drinking alcoholic beverages has no net health benefit; is linked with many health problems; is the cause of many accidents; and can lead to addiction. Their consumption is not recommended." No major American medical organization recommends drinking as good for the health. Apparently there is some fear that if told alcohol could be beneficial, people would all go out and become alcoholics.

Which is unfortunate, because alcohol *is* beneficial if used correctly. I define moderate consumption as two drinks a day for a man and slightly less for a woman. Admittedly this is not very exact because everyone is different, with different weights and metabolisms. There are also differences of opinion about whether beer, wine, or liquor offers the quickest route to a longer life. Of ten major studies, one-third found this true for wine, one-third for beer, and one-third for liquor. Most researchers now believe that it is the alcohol in all of them that provides the magic, but they don't rule out other components of alcoholic beverages. Researchers at Cornell University endorse wine because of resveratrol, a substance in grape skins. Other research suggests that flavinoids in grape juice and other beverages, including dark beer, also help.

In any event, let's start with the heart. With a moderate intake of alcohol, there is a 20 to 40 percent drop in the risk of coronary disease. These reductions are comparable to those from vigorous exercise and low-fat diets. Combining the major studies on the subject from around the globe, these are conclusions drawn from half a million subjects and the results are surprisingly consistent.

In France, thirty-five thousand Frenchmen who drank two or three glasses of wine each day had a 35 percent reduction in heart deaths and up to a 25 percent reduction in cancer deaths. It seems that the French Paradox is at least partially, if not mostly, explained by wine. A study in Shanghai, China, of 18,244 men found a 36 percent reduction in heart deaths with light to moderate drinking. Other research suggests that those at highest risk, with high cholesterol levels, would benefit the most from wine.

It's still a mystery exactly how wine works its wonders on the heart. Does it thin the blood? Or does it reduce platelet stickiness and thus inhibit clotting? Could it change blood cholesterol and fats? Maybe it relaxes arteries or blood vessels? Or perhaps it's something more obvious, like stress relief. Stress, anxiety, and depression can affect your heart. Relaxation itself is positive for heart health.

How about wine as a digestive aid? It was just as effective as Pepto-Bismol, one of the old standards, in killing travelers' diarrhea germs. In fact, the wine outperformed its drugstore counterpart when both were diluted, which is what happens when you eat. Wine was also better than diluted tequila or diluted pure ethanol against E. coli, shigella, and salmonella, all nasty, food-born, disease-causing germs. So wine and travel make good companions.

Many folks use alcohol for relaxation. As a drug it still defies exact classification. Is it a sedative? It seems so sometimes. Is it a stimulant? It could be that as well. A study of moderate-drinking adults at the

University of California at Berkeley, all with similar levels of stress, found them less likely to get depressed compared with teetotalers or heavy drinkers. It worked the other way as well. Heavier drinkers (minimum four per sitting, several times a week)—along with abstainers—did far worse, especially when hit by stress and financial challenge in the same year.

No one from this study was willing to endorse alcohol as a means to handle stress, and I'm not advising it either. Moderate drinking could mean that these were moderate people who were moderate in all things. Some studies have found that teetotalers were often ex-alcoholics, and that explained their abstention. The Berkeley study documented that the teetotalers were in poorer health overall, potentially leading them to depression and making nondrinkers seem less healthy.

Alcohol may protect against colon and rectal cancer. It has shielded people from outbreaks of hepatitis A and seems to lessen macular degeneration—deteriorating eyesight—in the elderly. Alcohol increases blood estrogen levels in women already taking estrogen by a whopping 327 percent. However, it does not increase estrogen levels in women not taking estrogen. Therefore if you drink, you may be able to take a lower dose of estrogen. In one study, loss of memory and cognitive skills was less among elderly folks who consumed moderate amounts of alcohol. This was especially true for those already afflicted with heart disease. Researchers at Indiana University studied four thousand twins, all World War II veterans, over twenty years. They first eliminated abstainers and alcoholics, then measured reasoning and problem-solving. Scores were lowest among the heaviest and the lightest drinkers. Those who drank between eight and sixteen drinks a week showed the best brain work. The results were consistent among identical twins. The researchers were quick to add a politically correct admonition that lots of drinking can cause a serious decline in mental function, which of course is absolutely true.

Scientists have even played around with the effects of alcohol on creativity. Researchers gave creativity tests to moderate drinkers, then administered vodka and tonic or water and tonic. The test included questions like "What would happen if the earth was shrouded in a fog, so that only people's feet were visible?" Other questions asked about new uses for old objects. The results? Those low on creativity at the beginning of the experiment were helped by the vodka, but those who showed some creative spark at the beginning had their creativity dampened by booze. Unfortunately, looking at known alcoholic writers won't help if they were drinkers all their lives. You can't know whether their alcohol use shaved creativity because they were creative at the start or whether their drinking helped because they were originally dullards.

It seems that the scientific community is in a state of disbelief, or denial, about all this. How do we decide on recommendations to the public when we are caught between the growing evidence on one hand and our culture's puritan tradition on the other? Dr. Curtis Ellison, Chief of Preventive Medicine and Epidemiology at Boston University, got in a tangle over this at an American Heart Association meeting in 1994. The issue: How much should the public know about the benefits shown in alcohol research? Ellison suggested publicizing findings that five to six drinks a week cuts heart disease risk by 28 percent. That compares with 15 percent by rigorously lowering blood pressure or 23 percent with a low-fat diet. Only quitting smoking can compare.

A firestorm ensued. Dr. Michael Criqui of the University of California at San Diego came down hard, arguing that it is irresponsible for doctors to recommend even moderate alcohol consumption to prevent heart disease, because some people will drink too much. Criqui conceded that "if everybody could drink a glass of wine a day, period, that would be fine. But everybody can't drink a glass of wine a day, so I think it's dangerous."

Of course, Criqui is right, technically speaking. Not everybody *will* stick to the limits of the recommendation. But ethically, is it right to withhold information from people who could benefit because others might be harmed? Criqui studied the French Paradox, that people with extraordinarily high levels of fat in their diet and wine at their table have extremely low rates of heart attack. But they also have radically elevated rates of cirrhosis of the liver, a disease with a mortality rate in France twice that in the United States. Despite that, Ellison feels just as strongly that physicians are obliged to let their patients know the potential benefits of alcohol. "The best recommendation should be that if you choose to drink alcohol, it will reduce your risk of heart disease," he insists.

As with illegal drugs, the central question here is whether we allow historical, cultural, and religious attitudes, rather than science, to determine our decisions about public health. Some international comparisons might help.

"Temperance cultures," according to addiction expert Stanton Peele, are those acutely concerned with alcohol, mounting large-scale, consistent temperance movements over the past two hundred years. They also have four times the number of Alcoholics Anonymous groups per capita compared with nontemperance cultures. These turn out to be Protestant, English-speaking countries, as well as the northern Scandinavian nations. Compared with other countries, they drink less total alcohol per capita but consume a higher percentage of the alcohol they do drink as spirits, which leads to more loss of control and public drunkenness. Nontemperance cultures consume wine as part of family rituals and food traditions. Yet the rate of heart disease deaths is 90 percent *greater* in temperance countries.

TO IMBIBE OR NOT TO IMBIBE? THAT IS THE QUESTION

So, bottom-line time. Should you start to drink if you do not already? Obviously that's tricky. Many public health officials still resist giving counsel on that one. Yet as we've seen, the evidence is very suggestive. If you hate the taste but want to try it, cook with booze. The alcohol content varies with the cooking method, but some should remain in the food. Researchers found that a recipe of orange chicken simmered in burgundy retained up to 60 percent of the alcohol; pot roast Milano, simmered in wine, retained only between 4 and 6 percent of the alcohol; scalloped oysters baked with dry sherry held on to more than 40 percent of the alcohol. Some desserts do best of all—Brandy Alexander pie, cherries jubilee, and Grand Marnier sauce all saved from 70 to 85 percent of the alcohol.

None of this is particularly reliable, though, because we still don't know whether it is the alcohol or other elements in the wine that are healthy. If it is something else, then it doesn't matter that the alcohol is cooked out of the food.

If you already drink and do it moderately, no doctor is going to argue with you. If you drink too much, please get help because you need it. (By the way, most studies find that the negative effect of lots of booze is worse than that of teetotaling. Those who do not drink have higher rates of death but not as high as those who drink too much.)

Doctors just don't know what would happen if we put out the recommendation that you should drink a *little*. Would more people become alcoholic? Would the net effect on our nation's health thus be bad? Or would most of you who don't already drink turn into moderate drinkers? I think that is the more likely scenario. If you are not a drinker, how likely is it that you would become addicted to alcohol? While no one really knows the answer, I think we can draw some safe conclusions from studies of chronic-pain patients on opiates. It is a very addicting drug, yet the rate of addiction among those patients is very low.

Statistics show us that many other countries have much greater per-capita alcohol consumption than America yet do not suffer the violence and tragedy that we do. Most think it's because drinking, not getting drunk, is part of the family dinnertime ritual. This may be the secret to alcohol success among many Europeans. The French and Italians consume more alcohol than anyone in the world yet suffer less alcohol-associated mayhem because kids are familiar with alcohol from a young age and associate it with family and food, not drunkenness and violence. To be sloppy drunk is not encouraged and is considered a social faux pas. Alcohol is seen as an inappropriate means of resolving personal issues, depression, and stress.

Some specialists are touting the radical notion that we fail to teach our youngsters the appropriate uses of alcohol by expecting them to abstain until age twenty-one. First of all, they don't abstain anyway, they just do it behind their parents' backs. We are supposed to teach our kids about life, sex, and religion, yet we back away from crucial areas like drugs and alcohol. Those brave souls behind this new line of thinking, including academics, writers, and family doctors, regard drinking as a social skill, like table manners. If your Friday night tradition is pizza and beer, offer a touch of the beer to your teens. Take the mystique out of it. Use the opportunity to express your trust and confidence in them.

Critics of this approach insist that it's better to teach them to abstain. That would be fine, except it's not working. Why pretend it is? Take a shot at the experience of other countries. "Kids should learn how to drink responsibly under the guidance of someone who cares and won't let anything happen to them," says Dr. Patricia Roy, a family practitioner and advocate of the new thinking. She tells her teen patients that "the place to find out that your limit is three beers is at home, in your parents' presence. Not at your friend's party, or worse, when you're behind the wheel of a car." Radical and untested, true, but an option for you to consider.

JAVA, AND NOT THE COMPUTER KIND

My name is Dean, and I'm an addict.

Fortunately or not, I never feel lonely. I'm constantly juggling different grinds, roasts, methods of preparation, and gadgets, all in the elusive quest for that perfect cup of coffee. At home with my family and at work with my colleagues, it makes no difference. My assistant, Susan, has become a local legend in the neighborhood coffee shops—one named her employee-of-the-month—with her demand for the quadruple espresso added to a large cup of regular brew. We are hooked, plain and simple, on caffeine, the most widely consumed mood-altering chemical in the world. In North America, 80 percent of the adult population gets a daily dose through a variety of sources, including sodas.

Although caffeine shows up in more than fifty different plants and herbs, we like it as coffee, which is second only to oil in international commerce. It is a stimulant and an emotional pick-me-up. It may speed your ability to do math problems and it makes you talk faster. It also makes your bowels move faster, a not-so-secret reason many people start their day chugging it.

Even though coffee consumption has actually dropped from former years, we seem to be savoring it more. Clearly there is a coffee chic at the moment—witness the explosion in coffee bars and gourmet grinds in your neighborhood supermarket. Remember when it used to come in three main flavors: black, white, and/or with sugar? Now there are enough Italian names and profound nuances to confound a linguist. Numbers don't lie: 47.2 percent of the population drink coffee, consuming an average of three cups a day. Of course, if you don't like the taste of coffee, you can have your caffeine in a pill. One entrepreneur is pushing caffeinated water. Keep your eyes open for the caffeine patch.

Coffee drinkers come in three brews, according to a marketing survey: regular Joe, who will drink anything that passes for coffee (slightly more than half the drinkers); stylists, who prefer concoctions like the Girlie-Man Latté (16 percent); and the guru, who feasts on specialty gourmet bean coffees (30 percent).

Now I'm going to surprise you regarding this substance you devour. Which has more caffeine, a shot of espresso from Starbucks or a cuppa the regular from Dunkin Donuts? It's the DD brew, by a long shot. The espresso is far less in quantity—57 milligrams of caffeine—and the steam used in the process may actually destroy some of the caffeine. The 8 ounces of Dunkin coffee shoots you full of 104 milligrams.

Forget caffeinated water. One fad treatment for cancer among alternative medicine types is the coffee enema. Don't laugh. This has become big enough that the *Journal of the American Medical Association* devoted four full pages to criticizing the practice. After you read about it, I suspect you'll stay with the oral approach. It started with fifth-century healers and got picked up again at the turn of this century by German physicians who believed that this was a way to rid the body of "corrupt humors." I don't know about corrupt, but I certainly can believe it takes care of your humor. The buzzword today is *detoxifying*. Sooner or later, colon therapists will be pushing the iced frappuccino flush as a summer treat.

Is this elixir that attracts so many of us truly safe? Suspicions that coffee might be dangerous to our health began with a simple observation, later verified, of a condition called the coffee-withdrawal headache. It was detected in 1991 when postsurgical patients woke up with headaches blamed on an unfortunate anesthesiologist. Yet the doctor's gases and techniques all proved blameless.

Then it struck someone that these patients were not getting their usual dose of caffeine on the morning after surgery. In an ensuing study, it was found that each 100-milligram increase in daily caffeine consumption triggered a substantial decrease in the odds of a post-operative headache. The solution, better than colonic cappuccino, was intravenous caffeine. It worked like a charm: Only half of those who got their fix had a postop headache.

But the discovery raised an unpleasant question. If caffeine induces withdrawal symptoms, is it therefore—by definition—addictive? A study at Johns Hopkins University added more weight to such suspicions. In place of their average 2.5 cups a day, a group of coffee-drinking adults took either a caffeine capsule or a placebo. The placebo-takers had more depression, indecisiveness, fatigue, anxiety, confusion, unfriendliness, grumpiness, social withdrawal, muteness, foggy head, headaches, flulike feelings, and heaviness in the arms than their caffeinated cohorts.

The conclusion was indisputable. Caffeine is a drug. You can imagine how the media loved this, and a war of press releases ensued. The International Food Information Council, a trade group, included, in their defense, letters from the Office of National Drug Control in Washington, D.C., and a drug abuse prevention group. "To equate caffeine containing foods" with drugs, they insisted, "sends the wrong message to children. Linking the devastating problem of drug abuse to the addictive qualities of caffeine-containing foods and beverages is not only wrong, it is a disservice" to young people. The feds quickly insisted that "an effective anti-drug program should focus on illegal drugs." There's that science-versus-emotion thing again.

Psychiatrists came up with an interesting compromise. They decided that caffeine withdrawal, not caffeine abuse or dependence, should take its place in the official manual of mental illness. It appears under heading 305.90, "Caffeine Intoxication," in the prestigious *Diagnostic and Statistical Manual*, the standard reference for mental disorders. At 250 milligrams a day, you have your basic buzz—restlessness, nervousness, excitement, insomnia, diuresis (urination), and gastrointestinal complaints. Up the ante to 1 gram, or ten Dunkin Donuts coffees, and you now have twitching, rambling flow of thought and speech, cardiac arrhythmia, exhaustibility, psychomotor agitation, ringing in ears, and flashes of light. Hit 10 grams, or a hundred cups of coffee, and you're looking at seizures, respiratory failure, and death. Shhhh, that could send the wrong message to the children.

At average doses—moderation again—the health impact from caffeine addiction seems to be minimal. Studies showed that fears of caffeine-related heart problems were unfounded. Caffeine can raise blood pressure in unaccustomed drinkers, but once they adapt, their pressure returns to normal. However, if you are a middle-aged man with high blood pressure, there are indications that three cups or more a day could lead to stroke.

There are chemicals in coffee—cafestol and kahweol—that can raise cholesterol levels, but a paper filter in the coffee-making process removes them. Be warned that a French press, Scandinavian-type boiled coffee, and brews like Turkish (boiled powdered coffee with water) leave the chemicals in the drink because the grounds are unfiltered and come in direct contact with the water. Percolating is probably OK because the grounds are packed in tight and the bad substances are filtered out through multiple passes of the water.

Anything else you should worry about? Not much. Coffee can upset some people's stomachs. Higher levels of consumption have been thought to thin bones slightly, but the most recent study failed to confirm that concern. It's a draw for now. Coffee is not good for people with panic attacks and major anxiety. If you have frequent heart palpitations, think about switching to a noncaffeinated drink. And while coffee once was thought to be linked to pancreas, bladder, and breast cancer, the latest evidence finds no connection. Nor have low levels of caffeine consumption been found to affect pregnancy, fertility, or the rate of premature births among women.

Overall, in fact, coffee comes out of many studies with a clean bill of health, and maybe even with some benefits. It can act as a bronchodilator, which is good, especially for asthmatics. The most common asthma drug, theophylline, is related to caffeine. In a pinch, on a camping trip without medication handy, a cup of joe could be an asthmatic's best friend. It also helps hay fever sufferers, which explains why it appears in many over-the-counter allergy medicines. Studies have confirmed a sharp improvement in symptoms with 400 milligrams of caffeine. After marathon runners and bicyclists drank a double espresso—a relatively light dose—their hearts were found to use less oxygen and to pump more blood at lower blood pressures.

A Harvard study found 66 percent less suicide in female coffee drinkers, even though coffee drinkers were more likely to smoke, drink alcohol, and have higher levels of stress. A study of more than one hundred thousand Northern Californians confirmed a lowered suicide risk among coffee drinkers. Coffee drinkers reported decreased irritability and improvement in mood after a jolt. New coffee drinkers, oddly, reported that caffeine made them upset and lowered their mood. The lesson seems to be to stick with it. An English study found improved cognition, problem-solving, and delayed recall. There was a statistically significant "increase in clear-headedness, happiness, and calmness, and decreases in tenseness." Where's the wrong message to the children now?

Ever notice that caffeine is a common ingredient in many pain remedies? So did the Food and Drug Administration, which then challenged the drug companies to prove it worked. And work it did, better than expected. Add between 200 and 400 milligrams to ibuprofen, and not only does the combination fight pain better, but coffee alone outperformed ibuprofen for the first couple of hours after ingestion.

All that said, if you're still wondering how much you should drink, think about the following list, poached both from David Letterman and a book called *You Know You're Drinking Too Much Coffee When* . . . :

- Juan Valdez names his donkey after you.
- You grind your coffee in your mouth.
- You sleep with your eyes open.
- You go to AA meetings just for the coffee.
- Instant coffee takes too long.
- Your next-door neighbors often call to complain about the sound of your chattering teeth.
- On the way to work you get pulled over for speeding and you don't even have your car.

GONE TO POT

"Dr. Edell, I am a forty-two-year-old male in good health," the fax read. "My wife and I have a habit I wanted to ask you about. For the past fifteen years, we've smoked marijuana occasionally on weekends. We giggle and munch and make love (we love sex with marijuana) and play in our backyard like a couple of kids. Our two children are in college and we are enjoying our newfound freedom. It doesn't seem to affect us the rest of the time. I have my own company and earn over $200,000 a year. My wife has a little business at home. I am not happy that I am breaking the law, but am I harming my health?"

Walk with me into a minefield here. Let's first admit that some illegal drugs give pleasure to people who do not, as a result, suffer apparent horrible consequences from the practice.

There is no evidence that occasional marijuana use is harmful. Most studies, in fact, have found that marijuana users are better off. I suspect that is due to the demographics of the user.

This is not meant to send the wrong message to kids, for whom chronic abuse of marijuana is a bad thing. As we have discussed, abuse of *any* drug is bad, but healthy use is possible. It's the same problem again: Should adults in a free country be prohibited from using a substance responsibly because some people are unable to do so? However you may *feel* about it, making these substances illegal has not worked. I think the only choice is to educate your children and then talk—and listen—to them about their views and experiences on pot (as with all things). Repeatedly and often.

The real danger of marijuana is its subtlety. Kids use it, wake up without hangovers, feel fine, and assume that it poses no problems. Chronic abuse by youngsters is bad, but responsible use by adults is of no consequence. There is no proved short-term or long-term damage to health from occasional recreational use of marijuana by adults. Nor has there been a recorded death associated with its use, other than possible motor vehicle fatalities.

Should we allow sick people access to what has been proved to be a versatile and effective herb? Marijuana has unique pharmacological actions. It is a powerful antinauseant and stimulates appetite, which explains why it is so valuable in the treatment of cancer and HIV. The list of conditions that researchers believe can be alleviated by marijuana is lengthy, including multiple sclerosis, seizures, strokes, breast cancer, PMS, and headaches. The Food and Drug Administration has approved a pill form of the most active ingredient in marijuana, delta 9 THC. But nausea pills are not very user-friendly when the patient is throwing up. When marijuana is smoked, the active ingredient— THC—flows immediately into the bloodstream without passing through the stomach. And delta 9 THC is not the only active ingredient in marijuana. Research from Israel on kids with cancer found that another component—delta 8 THC—prevented vomiting altogether.

Of course, science is way behind in answering a lot of questions about the efficacy of pot because the government has made it nearly impossible for legitimate researchers to study the drug. You know the problem with this line of thinking. If we could have worked in this area over the past decades, by now there might be THC inhalers to eliminate the need to smoke marijuana. I just cannot understand the logic that would deny sick people—some of them terminally so—a drug that could ease their pain and suffering. Any one of us could face that situation one day.

Other "recreational" drugs are far more complex an issue. Cocaine is a very dangerous drug. Although many people have successfully chipped it without destroying themselves, many others have not been so lucky. Still, I must say that the location of cocaine consumption seems to affect its use and abuse. In native populations where it has a long tradition, the harm has been minimal. In South America, coca leaves are chewed and brewed as tea. The dose is low, and the herb is honored as a gift from the gods. Its pharmacology makes that understandable. When Westerners figured out how to extract the drug and concentrate it into pure white powder, trouble began. As a stimulant and antidepressant, cocaine knows no peer and hooked Sigmund Freud, among others. It eliminates hunger and thirst and increases work output. It also makes the user desperate for more, faster and more intensely than any other drug I know. Avoid it.

Psychedelic drugs are fascinating, but we know little about them because, as with marijuana, most research has been barred. This has deprived science of working with some incredible molecules. One known chemical, MDMA, has the ability to dissolve emotional barriers between people. I saw a teaching film of an actual couple on the verge of a bitter divorce. After the psychiatrist gave them both a dose of MDMA, their arguing gave way to healthy emotional communication and even affection. What might we learn, if legitimate psychopharmacologists could study drugs like MDMA, of the phenylethlyamine class of molecules, which seem to tap into human emotional centers with extraordinary effectiveness? We'll learn nothing if we don't look. In the meantime, its abuse on the streets is dangerous.

THE EVIL LEAF

I have another addiction, but not to a substance. I adore Chinese snuff bottles. Chinese artists applied all their power and artistry to these bottles. Every material known to the Chinese went into them—jade, quartz, porcelain, glass, metal, ivory, bamboo and wood, peach pits, coconut seeds, and an astonishing array of minerals. Some of the finest bottles that come to market today bear the emperor's seal. They all have a little spoon that the user employed to prepare a small pile of powdered tobacco and herbs for snorting. Smoking tobacco was discouraged; snuff was their habit.

Tobacco swept the world in the century after its discovery in the New World during Columbus's second visit. I have the first book in English by a physician talking about the new plant from America. *Joyful Newes Out of the New Found Worlde* (1596) treated tobacco like any other herb, extolling its use for a variety of health problems, including headache, worms, toothache, stomach upsets, sores, and hysteria. Occasionally there is still research on the medical aspects of nicotine. Studies have found it useful for colitis and neurological syndromes from Parkinson's disease to Alzheimer's. Of course, early complaints were registered, too. "Tobacco is a custom loathsome to the eye, hateful to the nose, harmful to the brain, and dangerous to the lungs," declared King James I of England in 1604, way ahead of the California state legislature. So what else is new?

Can you use tobacco safely? Can you extract its pleasure and still enjoy good health? There are exceptions to the smoke-and-die dictum. One of my early radio callers sought advice on his pack-a-day cigarette habit. I could hear from his voice that he was a senior listener. "How old are you, sir?" I asked. "A hundred and two," he rasped. And I'm going to tell this guy to give up his butts? You can't count on that, though, so I do not recommend smoking.

Looking at the death-and-illness statistics, and given the mysterious truth that smoking does not seem to make its users high or happy, one has to wonder what the draw is here. A kid's first cigarette tastes horrible and makes him cough, yet he goes on to the second and then he gets hooked. My mother, sensing my youthful interest in smoking when I was twelve, stuck a cigarette in my mouth and lit it. "Here's how you do it," she said as her lighter flicked hers. I followed her and sucked in a loud and full breath. I never forgot the searing pain in my chest, or the cough. It's got to be peer pressure and desire to fit in that drives youngsters to the second butt. It sure isn't the joy of inhaling.

Whatever you have heard, if there is such a thing as a "gateway drug," research confirms that it is tobacco. That fact is not publicized, for obvious reasons. The National Institute on Drug Abuse found that teens who smoked were much more likely to go on to other illicit drugs. "The vast majority of people who have ever used illicit drugs, such as marijuana and cocaine, had previously used cigarettes and alcohol," researchers concluded. "Conversely, people who have never smoked only rarely abuse illicit drugs or alcohol."

Teens and preteens who smoke, according to Senate Finance Committee testimony, are twelve times more likely to use heroin, fifty-one times more likely to use cocaine, and fifty-seven times more likely to use crack.

Do everything you can to keep your kids from smoking, but I'm afraid that the more illicit we make it, the more desirable it will become. You can't be sure your children will be among those lucky chippers able to keep their habits down to five cigarettes or fewer a day. They seemed to have unusual personalities.

Are there other ways of using tobacco that are healthier? Pipe smokers have higher rates of lip and mouth cancer, but I have not seen modern studies, because the habit has become relatively uncommon. The current cigar fad will give us fruitful data. Logic dictates that they should suffer fewer lung cancers than cigarette smokers since less smoke gets to their lungs.

What if people used nicotine without the smoke? The smoke seems important to users for reasons that are hard to explain. After all, if nicotine is the addicting drug, why does it matter how you get it? One surprising study using new delivery systems, including nicotine patches, sprays, and gums, found nicotine not harmful to the heart. As a matter of fact, when smokers switched to an alternate nicotine delivery system, their hearts became healthier and stronger.

Is it possible that something other than nicotine causes heart disease in smokers? We are only just learning about hundreds of other substances in cigarettes, some added by the manufacturers, others there naturally. Nicotine itself is an interesting drug. When it was given intravenously to experienced drug users who were not told what it was, most thought it was cocaine. When smokers switch to the nicotine patch or gum, will those alternatives become just as addicting as cigarettes? In Europe, patients routinely chew nicotine gum for five to ten years, and doctors are starting to think it might be wiser to let them have the drug indefinitely. Certainly this makes sense if the alternative is smoking.

A University of Alabama dental pathologist came up with an approach to help smokers that incited near riot among antitobacco warriors: smokeless tobacco. This is the most successful known way to quit smoking. It lets smokers have their drug but reduces most of the risks to their health. In the United States, smokeless tobacco has been associated with oral cancers because it contains a carcinogen called nitrosamine. But there is a form of smokeless oral tobacco available in Sweden that apparently does not cause any cancers of the head and neck. Sweden has the highest per capita consumption of moist oral tobacco in the world. It is placed on the gum inside the upper lip. A United Nations report concludes that there is "no evidence for any increased risk of cancer" from this form of the drug. Other incarnations of nicotine replacement will be forthcoming. They may be the final avenue for the heavily addicted person.

I worry that our current war against smoking will backfire on us. Smoking rates have plummeted among adults since World War II, but kids—who have been targeted by tobacco companies—are not hearing the antismoking message. The more we make smoking an illicit activity, the more they seem to be drawn to it. Bureaucracies have been built around this battle, and my fear is that after they finish with tobacco, they'll move on to other "bad" habits. Alcohol certainly looms as the next target. After all, why should alcohol be innocent if the tobacco industry is guilty of using cartoons to addict children? Alcoholism among children certainly causes more mayhem than smoking, yet clearly, even making these substances illegal doesn't work. We should be careful in deciding on our goals.

Humans like mood-altering substances for a reason. They make us feel good. Nature gives us a taste for them and provides a wide range from which to choose. As thinking creatures, we shouldn't be afraid of our desires. It is right to fear abuse, but we must learn to accept what we are and what we like to do to feel good, always within limits. In determining the limits, we need to use our heads, not our fears.

7

THERE *IS* A SANTA CLAUS

Great Sex Is Good for Your Health

————

The tables were turned, and I did not mind at all. With millions of people tuned in, *she* was lecturing *me*. This irritated caller was absolutely right, and I knew it.

"You're a doctor," she scolded. "Don't talk to us like children. It's OK to say *penis* on the air. Use the real word."

I felt properly ashamed for substituting "down there" in reference to the male generative organ. It is a sophomoric phrase for an important part of a man's body, one of the crucial centers of our culture. Yet talking on the radio about male and female genitalia—and the words related to them—generally gets me in trouble, no matter how gingerly I try to manage the issue. Many adults in this country still go apoplectic when I talk about these most natural of things. When I use anatomically correct terms, I get accused of pandering to our lesser instincts. Listeners blast furious letters to station managers, demanding that they silence my disgusting talk. If I try to be a little tactful by using euphemisms or more oblique references, I incur the wrath of folks like my caller that day. Listeners like her hearten me. They are far healthier, sexually speaking.

Thankfully, the design of the human body made its procreative proclivities sturdy enough to allow us to reproduce and persevere and even overcome prudery. Sex is the most powerful and critical instinct of the human body. Our survival depends on it. It is the act that led to our creation. Orgasm, that glorious release, is the highest state of ecstasy and altered consciousness most humans will ever experience. If there is any moment in life that stands in opposition to death, it surely must be the orgasm. This probably explains why our sexual nature is so extraordinarily strong. It must persevere through famine, disease, stress, war, and late-night television. Somehow, it does.

Of course, that driving impulse can overwhelm at times. Human sexual urges can cause great harm. People assault one another sexually. Sexually transmitted diseases kill people. Unwanted pregnancies create turmoil. At critical junctures, history has turned on the erotic draw between individuals. Kings have given up the throne. Presidents have destroyed their reputations. Doctors have lost their licenses. And many ordinary folks have ripped their families apart.

What *is* this thing called sexual health? Physicians have struggled with it for decades. Agendas of all kinds—personal, political, social, religious—work their way into the debate. In my view, the best definition to date finally came in 1995 from researchers published in the *British Medical Journal*. Their approach works in a wide range of social, religious, and sexual contexts. It is not based in sexual orientation and can be used to promote two of the safest options—masturbation and abstinence. This research defines sexual health as "the enjoyment of sexual activity of one's choice without causing or suffering physical or mental harm."

It's all there, isn't it? From that viewpoint, it makes complete sense when they go on to argue that sexual health is a basic human right. How elegant, how simple. What is more *basic*, more *human*, and more *right*? Why, then, does sex scare and obsess us, dominate our thinking and our culture, lend itself to such distortion and misrepresentation? Why do we simultaneously run toward it and flee from it? I can't think of any other area of human behavior weighted with such complexity.

Much of the confusion starts with what we think we are *supposed* to feel. Obligation seems to underlie a good deal of our notions about sex. Aren't men, for instance, always supposed to be thinking about sex, ready and able at a moment's notice? Women, of course, are never sup-posed to be thinking about sex and always have to be talked into it. We are supposed to work hard at both giving pleasure and taking pleasure. No wonder so many people worry that they're not feeling the way they think they should.

Confusion starts at a young age. Many people are unprepared for early sexual encounters, and the quality of those experiences reflects it. We are harsh judges of our sexual selves, and as we get older, we often add anxiety and guilt to the experience.

People are born with powerful sexual feelings. Society constantly struggles with sexual expression. Even an act as straightforward and natural as masturbation defies universal approval. It was not long ago that Jocelyn Elders, the surgeon general of the United States, had to resign after suggesting that masturbation was a normal part of sexual function.

It doesn't get much more basic than masturbation. The *American Journal of Obstetrics and Gynecology* recently ran a story about an extraor-dinary film made by ultrasonographers of a female fetus as she mas-turbated. It is common during second trimester ultrasonography examinations to see the fetus touch itself repeatedly and rhythmically on the genitalia, offering fairly compelling evidence that masturbation is rooted not in sin but in biology. Of course, newborns and toddlers will touch themselves and rub their pelvises against a variety of objects. Why does it all scare us so?

I do see hopeful signs of growing awareness. A recent survey by researchers at Cornell University asked 350 pediatricians, elementary school teachers, and psychotherapists for their views on appropriate sexual behavior by children. Most answered that many behaviors are acceptable among four-year-olds, including undressing together, show-ing genitalia, and fondling nongenital areas. Many people would find that conclusion surprising.

I mention masturbation to illustrate a point about communica-tion and sex. The inability to communicate to our children about masturbation, for example, can have tragic repercussions. Coroners are reluctant to release the information, but each year as many as three hundred adolescents die from autoerotic death—asphyxia while masturbating. Cutting off the blood supply to the brain can cause a light-headedness and euphoria that supposedly reinforce the sensations of orgasm. Evidently these youngsters hear or discover that tying something around their necks during masturbation will heighten the experience. We do not know how many youngsters are into this, but extrapolating from the number of lethal cases tells us this is a good reason to open a dialogue with your children about sex.

THE SHAME OF OUR SHAME

At their worst, discomfort and ambivalence about our sexual selves extend beyond issues of guilt, pleasure, and shame. One survey found 90 percent of physicians agreed that serious medical problems could be averted if patients were more willing to talk about such sensitive topics. A majority complained of difficulties treating patients who struggle to discuss "embarrassing" issues. Asked to rate their reluctance to talk to their doctors, one in four patients admits that embarrassment makes them more reticent than does their fear of bad news, fear of treatment options, or thinking the symptoms are unimportant. Take just one "embarrassing" condition. Half of those questioned said they would feel embarrassed if their doctor asked them about bladder control. Considering that seventeen million Americans suffer from bladder-control problems, this translates into many people sacrificing effective treatment.

People blanch at having their reproductive organs medically examined. Yet cancers of the reproductive system and lower gastrointestinal tract together represent the vast majority of cancer cases and deaths. After lung cancer, cancer of the colon is the most common cancer in both sexes. Nearly every man will be struck by prostate cancer by the time he is in his eighties. Add cancers of the breast, uterus, cervix, ovary, bladder, testicles, and vulva, and the cost of timidity becomes tragically clear.

This discomfort has captivated the interest of researchers. For instance, the Chinese-American community still deals with remnants of an ancient culture that often took modesty to extremes. The traditional Chinese physician would never directly examine a woman. At most he might examine her pulse or tongue, but he would never dare to look, touch, or directly observe the female body. Instead he used a small ivory doll. His patient would point to parts on the doll that corresponded to the areas of her body with symptoms. Recently I saw such a doll in a museum exhibit of Chinese art objects. The bottom half of its torso was covered with a tiny cloth. The museum director explained that many Chinese-American patrons, offended by the doll's disrobed state, had demanded that it be clothed.

Chinese-American women have relatively low rates of breast cancer. But studies have shown that this group is also less likely to examine their own breasts and that when cancer is found, it can be more advanced and deadly than in other women. Because of this discomfort with examining themselves or even talking about such issues with their doctors, these women often wait until it is too late to get definitive medical care.

Young people grow up with few blueprints except media and advertising images. Parents are uncomfortable approaching the subject of sex, and most school sex education classes barely go beyond the films featuring sperm in leisure suits. Too often children are on their own here. Young men think that sexy women are the air-brushed busty babes in the magazines and on *Baywatch* and are shocked by the reality of most bodies in the real world. Women, meanwhile, fret that for the most part they don't look like that.

All my life I have loved to draw. I remember my first life drawing class, as a college student, and the first live nude model I ever encountered. I flushed slightly when she dropped her robe, but within seconds my mind and eye were immersed in drawing her. For the next hour, I gazed intently at every shadow of this young woman's body. I had no erotic feelings and even recall wondering vaguely if something was wrong with me. Class ended and I was busily packing up my pad and drawing instruments when I happened to look up and catch a glimpse of the model getting dressed. She was partially behind a screen. She had put on her panties and was hooking her bra. I thought I would faint. Now *that* was sexy. I figured I must be weird. No one had taught me that erotic images are not necessarily the ones Madison Avenue shows us.

YOUR SHEEPISH DOCTOR

Never automatically assume that your doctor is any more comfortable with these issues than you are. As young medical students, we are presumed to make an instant transition from bashful naiveté to fully matured self-confidence. All this, of course, is supposed to happen the moment we approach our initial patient on an intimate level.

Actually, we first practiced on each other. We males, who made up almost the entire medical class in those days, were segregated into separate rooms and taught to do rectal exams on our fellow students. Trust me, nothing breaks down social hierarchies and barriers more quickly. Comrades were now subjected to each other's inexperience. We prodded, we poked, we learned. We assumed that our few female brethren did similar things, but we never asked. None of us ever talked about any of this again.

We had a pitiful smattering of lecture material on sexuality that never addressed anything useful or real. During the single hour-long lecture that covered our entire course material on human sexuality, a renowned sexologist taught us how to counsel patients on the correct way to thrust the pelvis during intercourse.

I hate to say this, but the situation has not improved noticeably. Study after study has found today's physician unprepared to deal with human sexuality. The AIDS epidemic has made this a critical issue. Even on a subject as basic and fundamental as birth control, doctors are not getting adequate training, as confirmed by a recent survey of 244 residents in family practice by the University of California at San Francisco. The majority said they had no clinical experience with fitting a diaphragm or with inserting and removing an intrauterine device (IUD). They said their education did not include reproductive health training. Learning to take an adequate sexual history is critical in today's medical environment. This is not just procedural. Sexual dysfunction, for example, can be the first sign of heart disease. Sexual attitudes can reveal risk for HIV and other sexually transmitted diseases. Pain during intercourse can be the first sign of certain cancers. Lowered libido can relate to depression and alcohol and drug abuse. Sexual medicine is complex, challenging, and vital.

Female and male physicians differ in their skill and comfort levels in dealing with screening exams of the breast, pelvis, rectum, and prostate. Studies show that female physicians are more comfortable with and rate their skills better at performing intimate exams and taking sexual histories of women patients. Male doctors feel more confident than their female colleagues performing prostate exams.

FROM RUSSIA, AND ELSEWHERE, WITH LOVE

Each day a hundred million acts of human intercourse occur on the planet, according to estimates by the World Health Organization. Those acts end in one million pregnancies and 350,000 cases of sexually transmitted diseases.

Surveys on sexual matters are notoriously unreliable, but what the heck, let's look at a few. In 1996 *Cosmopolitan* magazine questioned readers (not a scientific sampling) of twenty-nine international editions. Of all the readers, Russian women were the most likely to report having sex every day, and while they were least likely to call it fabulous, they were most likely to label it satisfactory. As for fabulous, Czech women were happiest with the sex in their lives, followed by American, French, and Italian women. Australian women were most likely to have sex on the first date. More Greek women preferred sex during the day than women in any other country. Japanese women had the least sex of all (three times a month or less). As for the exotic, Russian women (again!) were most likely to have had sex with other women, to have used sex toys, and to have cheated on their mates. French women—forget the movies—reported being the most faithful, followed by Taiwanese and Americans.

In another survey, this one by Durex, the British condom manufacturer, Americans claimed they spent an average of about 30 minutes making love. At 13.8 minutes, Italians—of all people—were not exactly there for the long haul. Hong Kong had the worst of both worlds—sex was the least frequent and the fastest—12.3 minutes from the first raised eyebrow to oops-gotta-go.

THE SEXIEST BEDROOM

I find an overwhelming bias in the media, from movies to television to novels to magazines, that the best sex is to be had with strangers or the first time you engage in it with a new partner or embark on an affair. When did you last watch *really* hot sex on the screen between a married couple? How often have you read in a popular novel of an adult couple having sex for the first time and fumbling all over themselves?

All this is counterintuitive. No human interaction that requires such a complex array of physical and emotional skills, sensitivity, daring, and trust can attain a high level of accomplishment without practice. Whether dancing or doubles tennis, team bridge or gourmet cooking, it takes time to develop the kind of mutual coordination and feedback, the give-and-take that makes for graduate-level sex. People invest years in improving their golf swing but cannot see the logic dictating that something as intricate as sex can take two people lots of practice to explore and perfect. Casual relationships, one-night stands, and short-term relationships cannot foster great sex. Ice-dancing partners perform better and better with the years. Do you remember the first time you made love to someone? It could not have been high quality. First times are usually filled with blunders, insecurities, and lots of worry. "Did she . . . ?" "What does he think?" "Was I too fast?" "Does she like when I . . . ?" "Am I good enough?"

For the best sex of all, look to your own bedroom. I have developed a fairly conservative attitude about the most important prerequisite to great sex: monogamy. People with multiple partners are admitting that no one partner gives them enough satisfaction to stick around and explore more deeply. This may seem obvious to some of you. To others it will appear out of step with the modern temper. But more than one research project has demonstrated its truth. Researchers from the University of Chicago have documented that there is "more emotional satisfaction and physical pleasure in a monogamous relationship" than with multiple partners. On one level, an affair may be an admission that something is wrong. You may think the new-partner sex is better, but I can almost promise you that it is not as good as sex *could* be at home if you made a go of it. The exploration between your own sheets may be more complex and emotionally demanding, but the Chicago folks offer an explanation for the more satisfying payoff: "This may be due to having learned what excites and pleases that partner."

Other research on sexually experienced women and multiple sex partners confirms these conclusions. In one study of close to a thousand nurses around the country, women with many partners reported the least amount of psychological satisfaction. If one of those partners offered something better, wouldn't the woman attempt to stick with him or her? The authors, taking one aspect of successful intimacy, said that "women with one partner indicate that their partners often delay orgasm until after their own first orgasm."

Marriage by itself is associated with more and better sex, according to Chicago's National Opinion Research Center. Their random and extremely reliable study discovered that 41 percent of married couples have sex at least twice a week, almost double the rate of non-cohabiting people, and 75 percent of married women "always or usually" achieve orgasm during sex compared with 62 percent of single women.

You may find surprising this ex-hippie's plea for monogamy in these times. But I feel that sex is one of the most important family values, not just for producing families but for keeping them together. Many divorces are triggered by a straying partner and perceived ennui in the primary sexual relationship. A sexual problem is often at the root of marital woes. One partner is having an affair, the other partner might be turned off to sex, one partner pushes the other away. On and on, in variations as complex as human emotion.

Researchers have compared monogamous relationships with those where one partner is having additional sex outside the primary relationship. More pleasure and emotional satisfaction from sex were reported by those who did not stray. Great sex helps keep couples—and therefore families—together. Simple as that. As far as I'm concerned, anything we can do to break down the barriers that keep people from enjoying this most precious of natural acts has got to be good.

Do not interpret my exhortation in favor of monogamy to mean I favor a sexually repressed culture. Repression is unhealthy at best and dangerous at worst, and there is plenty of independent research to support that view. Teens in the more sexually open countries of northern Europe and Scandinavia abstain from sex longer, are virgins at an older age, and have lower rates of unwanted pregnancy and abortion and fewer sexually transmitted diseases than American teens.

THE DEVIL DOESN'T MAKE ME DO IT

Sexuality, what should be the greatest ongoing celebration of our primary relationship, has become twisted into a sales tool and marketing device. Meanwhile open, frank discussion of sensuality is often repressed in our culture. On the air I once partly blamed our

puritan ethic for creating sexual guilt and was taken to task by a listener who felt that I was blaming fundamentalist religion for our
national sexual problems. Just look at our philandering television
evangelists and religious leaders to put that one to rest. Any religion
that formally or informally denies our sexual natures is out of step
with reality.

The reaction that intrigued me the most came from a man in
Oklahoma City, who faxed me a letter, along with a story from a conservative Protestant magazine: "I could not disagree more strongly
with [you for blaming] American hang ups with sex on the puritans
and the Mayflower. . . . You know as well as I do that true sensuality
isn't hot-and-heavy groping with a stranger. It is a celebration of two
people in a committed relationship. . . ."

This is what the religious magazine had to say:

What more divine gift of celebration do we have than lovemaking?
Even those married couples who can't afford to splurge on grand
meals and fine wine can feast on each other. . . . Yet notice how nonsexual we are in our living. We run from the cold, impersonal sex of
our surrounding culture only to act as if lovemaking were some
shameful secret. The joy of sexuality doesn't permeate our lives like
it did in earlier eras. . . . Modernity has not only turned us into
shameful animals copulating with strangers, but Christians—who
should be the best lovers, the most sexual—are quite stiff and on
feverish guard lest anyone actually commit a holy kiss. . . . This is a
sign of our spiritual immaturity. A more mature, Christian culture
could honor public etiquette knowing that lovemaking is a private,
but not a secret thing, while still leading lives blossoming with celebration of the amazing gifts of sexuality.

In case you have always wondered about sexy religions, I offer you
this from several recent surveys: The vast majority of Catholic women
approve of sex for the sake of pleasure; 68 percent of Catholics have
sex at least once a week, compared with 56 percent of non-Catholics;
three out of ten Catholics have bought erotic underwear, compared
with two out of ten non-Catholics; and 64 percent of Catholic women
scored high on a sexual playfulness scale, compared with 42 percent
of non-Catholic women. "Playfulness," by the way, included experi-

menting with sexual techniques, swimming nude, and bathing or showering with a spouse.

This is a nondiscriminatory book. Other religions have statistics that fascinate as well. According to a University of Chicago survey, the women most likely to have orgasms every time are conservative Protestants. Jews have the most sex partners of any religious group.

So it seems religion does not stop us from fully exploiting our sexual selves. I lay much of the blame on the pace and stress of modern life, which I think distorts and represses sex. A quick-fix, fast-food culture demands quick-fix sex, accompanied by the media's grotesque imagery, all designed for short-lived and shallow titillation. People are either too fatigued and stressed or lack the patience and willingness to make the effort. It takes time and attention to develop the openness and skills that lead to the higher sensual planes. An impatient lot, we want results *fast*, and we get frustrated quickly when that doesn't happen. Many couples do not consider sex a priority. They may scrupulously make their aerobics classes but turn to excuses in dealing with sex.

Interestingly, what Americans say about sex is far different from how we behave, and it is that chasm that must be bridged before we can come to terms with our sexual selves. Those researchers in Chicago compared sexual attitudes and practices in the United States and Great Britain. They interviewed many thousands of people in both countries, and the gap was both extraordinary and revealing.

The survey portrayed a shamefully intolerant America. A much larger portion of Americans than Brits have absolute and unbending opinions about extramarital sex, nonmarital sex, and homosexuality, among other areas. For instance, nearly 25 percent of Americans feel that premarital sex is "always or almost always wrong," compared with 8 percent of Britons. Yet the percentage of Americans that had five or more sex partners in the previous year was twice as high as in Britain. Twice as many Americans as Brits had more than twenty-one sexual partners over a lifetime. The authors believe that this disconnect between attitudes and practice hampers public health initiatives aimed at preventing sexually transmitted diseases, some of which America has at ten times the rate of Britain.

SPEAKING THE UNSPEAKABLE

On this side of the ocean, we glory in sex on one level and hide it on another, deeper plane, thus distorting its power. The only aspect of sex openly discussed is its dangers. We excel at warning of its supposed evils but are lousy at extolling its virtues and joys. How can children ask about sexual issues—from birth control and STDs to abstinence and orgasm—if sex is not discussed freely? When we implicitly label a subject taboo, then reticence will become the prevailing current. The blatant use of sexual imagery in our media does not indicate openness. Most sexual imagery is used to sell us products that have nothing to do with sex, and that tells you the depth of the distortion. If you doubt me, watch an hour of TV commercials, or thumb through any major magazine. Analyze the various images.

America's sexual dysfunction rates indicate that we are not a sensual culture. The official term is ISD, or inhibited sexual desire, and it comes in many forms. Some suffer from it in all sexual settings, others only in certain situations. Some people will not initiate sexual activity, others will not respond if their partner initiates it. Some people will not initiate but will respond once involved. Although we do not have clear and accurate numbers, experts generally believe that ISD has become more common over the past decade. A national survey of sex therapists reported about one in three couples complaining of discrepancies in desire.

The most common sexual complaint doctors hear from patients? Loss of interest. Depressed libido affects many people. Men tend to report more complaints about the amount of sex they experience, while women complain about the pleasure of the sex. Couples therapy by a professional familiar with the issue and its dynamics can help solve the problem. Part of the treatment includes homework, such as "pleasuring exercises." Many couples who have allowed anger to creep into their bedrooms are instructed to refrain from sex during initial phases of treatment. That in itself puts many on the path to recovery.

SORRY, GODZILLA

Most books that discuss sex feature the obligatory anatomy section. I am going to skip the plumbing and glandular and move to the part that seems increasingly to concern everyone, especially men. Penile size may well garner more ink than almost any other sexual subject, aside from breasts, of course. I assume that the explosion of explicit, X-rated media has increased the anxiety of the average American male. When I was in medical school, I was taught the reigning myth of the time, that basically all men are the same size when erect. Some men, I learned, look bigger when they are not erect. Most men are adequately endowed enough to complete the act of copulation, which in the end is all that really counts.

This does nothing to allay male fears. Most men have never seen another man's erect penis, so comparison is impossible. Anxiety is big. One day a male anchor at a television station where I worked walked into my office and noticed a teaching model on my desk, a clear plastic phallus used to train people how to put on a condom. It was larger than average. "Wow!" the anchor exclaimed. "That's pretty large, isn't it?" "No," I lied. "That's actually smaller than average." He didn't believe me, so I showed him a catalog for these models. One, which appeared to be a normal size in the photograph, was accompanied by ad copy that said "smaller than normal to not intimidate the patient." I felt only slightly guilty as I watched his larger-than-life ego visibly deflate. He quietly slumped out of my office.

Only recently has medical science established a normal, or average, penis size. The research was performed at the University of California at San Francisco. The goal was to help men evaluate penis enlargement surgeries. Imagine the problem here: Researchers would have to measure men while they were aroused. Researchers used patients who, during treatment for erectile failure, were given injections to induce arousal. The doctors used tape measures to ascertain length and width in the flaccid, stretched, and erect penis.

On the day the results were published, the university sent out a press release written by a staffer who had a little trouble converting centimeters into inches. She miscalculated the average erect length to be 6.1 inches from the pubic bone to the tip of the penis, one full inch longer than the actual finding. It doesn't sound like a lot, but it's a lot. Just in case you were wondering, 2 percent of the men measured less than 3 inches erect, which would qualify a man for penis lengthening.

So *does* phallus size matter? Fantasy and aesthetics aside, probably not much. A woman's vaginal musculature will accommodate a range of sizes and will contract to the same degree around a penis of almost any size. In addition, a woman's clitoris is the primary physio-logical stimulant for orgasm. In fact, physical contact is not even nec-essary for some women. Gynecologists have confirmed reports of women who are capable of having orgasms without being physically touched, by the stimulation of their imaginations alone.

Before leaving the male size thing behind, I must say that attempts to correlate penis size with other body parts—the nose, fingers, feet, and toes—have not impressed me yet. Scientists at the University of Geneva came close, though, with elegant genetics research in mice, which found a common gene controlling the development of the penis and the digits. Even testicle size has come under some scrutiny. An evolutionary biologist at the University of Manchester in England documented that men with larger testicles engaged in sex more often, had more sexual partners, and produced more hardy sperm. Just something else for you to worry about.

There have been studies on clitoris size as well as the size of other female appendages, although the subject has attracted very little research interest in recent decades. Perhaps the last great tome on this aspect, a book entitled *Human Sex Anatomy*, was published in 1933. It tried to correlate various dimensions of the female genitalia with sex-ual activity. Was the distance shorter between the clitoris and the vaginal orifice in prostitutes, women with strong sexual urges, and those with multiorgasmic capabilities? Were their clitorises larger or longer? In an era when doctors could not easily obtain permission to photograph patients, the text is full of drawings of female and male genitals in an attempt to launch the nascent field of sexual science. Although the text reinforced many older myths and drew no sustain-able conclusions, it did pioneer a new and invaluable—if still under-valued—interest in the study of human sexuality.

Perhaps the female shape has been of greater concern than clitoral or vaginal size. A study of the length and width of the vagina in more than one hundred pre- and postmenopausal women uncovered no relation to sexual functioning, desire, satisfaction, orgasm, or pain during intercourse.

One of my medical school professors, a gynecologist, was among the first to attempt to construct a three-dimensional image of the interior shape of the vagina. Obviously this was before the age of computer graphics. He wanted to prove that this orifice is like all sphincters in the body that guard their vulnerable openings. Such entryways are narrower at first and then larger past the sphincter, somewhat like crawling though a small cave opening into a larger cavern. The professor asked a patient if he could perform a simple experiment. He inserted a plaster-filled condom inside her vagina, planning to remove it after it hardened into a perfect cast of the interior. The anatomy lesson about the vagina's muscles should give you a clue about the outcome. I have always wondered what this hapless doctor told his patient as he raised the hammer and chisel to relieve her of the plaster cast, which obviously could not be removed in one piece.

The most misunderstood part of female sexual anatomy must be the hymen. Doctors in the Netherlands are performing hymen reconstructions for young women, often immigrants from Mediterranean and African countries where a woman must prove her virginity with blood on her wedding night. The operation is simple and the women satisfied, but there was an uproar initially over the ethics. Some people argued that the doctor was directly involved in deceiving the husband. Others saw it more from a feminist perspective. The physicians, they complained, were reinforcing an ethos that allowed men but not women to be sexually experienced.

For me, the hymen is compelling from a medical perspective. Is bleeding on first intercourse inevitable? Certainly not for Western women. Whether sporting activities or tampons are to blame, one survey of forty-one professional women found that almost two-thirds did not bleed during their first intercourse. Another report found that the virginal state could be confirmed in only 57 percent of the virgins examined.

I cannot end a discussion of size and sexual organs without a nod to breasts, that crazy obsession of men and women both. I get a lot of calls from women about breast augmentation, and for a time I used the following study to dissuade them: Male and female subjects rated photos of models, who made their breasts larger from photo to photo by stuffing their bras with cotton. Although breast size did not affect the ratings of their overall likability or personal appeal, smaller-breasted women were rated higher on competence, ambition, intelligence, morality, and modesty. Better still, the ratings by men and women were indistinguishable.

Every time I referred to this study, I inevitably got a deluge of letters from Ph.D.-waving D-cupped listeners protesting my insult to their mental abilities. In fact, I have since changed my mind about breast implants, based on floods of mail from augmented women who swear to astonishing improvements in self-esteem and erotic adventure. I have learned that it is fruitless to question people's desire for plastic surgery.

THE BIGGEST SEX ORGAN

Look not between thy legs for the primary sexual organ. Look between thine ears. It is the brain.

Whether we like it or not, our sexual urges are neurologically programmed. Parts of the brain are capable of turning us on and turning us off. By neurosurgically altering these portions of the brain, doctors have been able to create an ongoing menagerie of sexual mismatches. I saw the films in medical school, showing the normal incompatibilities between species thrown awry by tampering with the sexual centers of animals' brains. There was a mouse trying to hump an unsuspecting cat, and a cat trying to do the same to a poor mouse. Most unnerving was the sexually supercharged monkey that picked up a mouse and used it unmercifully to whack its own genitals in a pathetic attempt at a sexual relationship. What may seem like a tragicomic mismatch to us was a matter of undeniable urgency to the monkey.

The point is that sexual urges are a matter of neurophysiology. We cannot and should not blame or judge people for their sexual feelings. These urges are like eating and sleeping and lie beyond the control of any morality, religion, or cultural institution. How we *act* on them, of course, is another matter.

That said, it should come as no surprise that men and women are more alike than we once believed. After all, we share the same primary sex organ and have other similarities as well. Early in the development of the fetus, the undifferentiated sex organs of the male and female are the same. This unisex stage is actually more female-like than male. A primordial furrow with a round protrusion at the upper end develops. In the female, it becomes the clitoris, in the male, the glans. The deep furrow runs vertically. On its sides, a secondary ridge emerges, destined to become the labia minora of the adult female and the shaft of the penis of the male. The outer, secondary ridge becomes the labia majora of the female and forms the scrotal sac in the male.

As these shapes move about during embryological development, they drag the nerve and blood supplies with them. None of this is lost on surgeons when they perform transgender surgery. In a male-to-female operation, the glans is moved into the clitoral position, and the scrotal and shaft skin are moved to create the labia and the vagina. The postoperative results are astounding—done well, you have to look very closely to see the difference from nature-made. This does beg the question whether the sensations of sex really are that different between men and women.

THE NEWS YOU'VE WANTED ALL YOUR LIFE

For centuries societal dogma has carried the overt and covert message that sex is bad for your body. Throughout history sexual expression and excesses have been blamed for poor health. To the ancient Greeks, celibacy aided the pursuit of philosophy and virtue. In I Corinthians 7:1, Paul warns, "it is good for a man not to touch a woman." Early in this century, Kellogg warned of the evils of masturbation and the draining of precious body fluids and led a celibate life even in marriage. Throughout Asia, a man who can keep his semen to himself is thought to enjoy greater vigor and well-being.

Yet it appears with growing certainty that an active sex life can be a sign of overall good health or even, as two recent reports claim, a *cause* of good health. Both pieces of research were published in *the Journal of the American Medical Association*. The first studied the connection between sexual activity and certain symptoms of menopause, especially atrophic vaginitis, an annoying and painful dryness, shrinking, and inflammation of the vaginal mucosa. The fifty-two women in the project were split between two categories. "Sexually active" was defined as engaging in intercourse at least three times a month; "sexually inactive" was defined as less than ten times a year.

Researchers found a striking correlation between vaginal deterioration and sexual activity: the more active the woman, the less her deterioration. "Some support for the adage 'use it or lose it' was obtained in this research," the authors noted wryly. One could argue that women in discomfort would be less likely to have sex in the first place, but the women having less sex attributed it to circumstances beyond their control, usually lack of an available partner. They would have had sex if they could. "The results of this study suggest that regular sexual activity during and after the menopause does have a beneficial effect in terms of reducing vaginal atrophy," the researchers added.

A couple of years later, men thrilled at headlines declaring that the more orgasms they experience, the longer they live. Similar objections were raised that men who were ill might be less likely to have a great deal of sex. The scientists who conducted the research insisted that their methodology accounted for those concerns.

Scores of studies look at longevity and its association with factors ranging from diet to exercise to income, but relatively few examine longevity and sex. A major European study in 1983 found that mortality dropped for men with greater frequency of sexual intercourse. It also found that the enjoyment of intercourse reduced mortality for women. Quantity for men and quality for women? Sounds a little like reinforcing old stereotypes. A Swedish investigation found that early cessation of sexual intercourse increased mortality of men and that sexual dissatisfaction of women was a risk for heart attack. Again, though, these studies are tainted by the argument that people who are sick are less likely to have sex, let alone satisfying sex, and are more likely to die sooner anyway. The association may simply be that healthier, more vigorous people have more sex.

Perhaps the largest single known cohort of celibate adults—nuns and priests—can help. One retrospective survey of more than ten thousand priests detected increased rates of heart attack and cirrhosis of the liver, a disease related to alcoholism. Nuns had lower rates of heart attacks than the lay population. But in both populations, other lifestyle habits are so different from those of the general population that comparisons are difficult. For instance, the conclusion about nuns could be best explained by the fact that very few nuns smoke.

The best study on record was conducted by researchers at Queens University in Belfast in the Welsh town of Caerphilly and five adjacent villages. Between 1979 and 1983, nearly a thousand men aged forty-five to fifty-nine were recruited for the project. First they were medically examined, tested, and surveyed about intercourse and frequency of orgasm.

After a decade, the researchers tracked deaths and heart attacks.

Men with the lowest frequency of orgasm had twice the risk of death from all causes—most significantly from heart attack. Initial interviews on hand, the authors could take into account the subject's health as well as socioeconomic status and other factors. After weeding out other considerations, they concluded that the men with the greatest frequency of sex had a 50 percent reduction in mortality. That puts sex right up there with eating five servings of veggies a day and all the exercise you can handle. If further studies confirm this finding, the authors propose public health campaigns with the message that sex is useful beyond fun and procreation.

How sex positively influences health remains a mystery. Perhaps it lies in the energy expended during the activity. It's known that just a touch of exercise, such as brisk walking, has a profound effect on health. I am aware of only one attempt to estimate the calories burned during sex, and that effort seems to be an underestimate. Nevertheless, a major compendium of the energy costs of human physical activities equates sex with walking. Pardon me for getting personal, but the breathlessness and heart rate that can be reached during "vigorous" sex certainly rise beyond those of a stroll in the park.

Another possible mechanism could simply be the overall effect of well-being on health, or the inevitable reduction in stress that should accompany sex. One study of 2,460 Danes looked at quality-of-life issues. Sexual problems, including dissatisfaction and lack of a partner, dropped quality-of-life scores significantly below the average of the population.

I can tell you that efforts to document the benefits of sex on pain have produced extraordinary findings. Many people report that back pain and arthritis seem to improve or disappear during sex. Psychologists at the State University of New Jersey measured a woman's threshold for pain and found it more than doubled during orgasm. Further investigation may have localized the source for this to the vagina itself. A constant pressure on the anterior wall of the vagina also doubled subjects' threshold for pain. The researchers speculate that this reflex may help with the pain of childbirth.

The same researchers tried to map the nerve pathways that trigger this analgesic response. They studied women with spinal cord injuries at various levels who were given a device to stimulate themselves. Vaginal and cervical self-stimulation decreased perception of pain even in women with spinal cord injuries, suggesting that this reflex, unlike other pain reflexes, does not course only in the spinal cord. Obviously we have a lot to learn.

As for headaches, you may want to reexamine *that* excuse. Indeed, sex can cause headaches in some susceptible people, but it appears that the opposite effect may be more widespread. In several studies, a neurologist at the medical school of Southern Illinois University asked women about sex when they had a headache. Significant numbers claimed that sex cured their headache, gave them "good, long-lasting relief," or temporarily eased the pain. It sure beats popping an aspirin. If you ask me, pumping up your sex life to improve your health and lengthen your life sounds like a lot more fun than eating sprouts or trudging on your treadmill.

THE PLEASURE PRINCIPLE

One of our obsessions as a culture seems to be trying to figure out what exactly is sexually weird. Where do we draw the lines between normal, adventurous, erotic, playful, whacked-out, and insane? I once had an experience that opened my eyes to worlds out there that I had heard of but never imagined. I still don't understand much of what I saw, but it forced me to consider the variation in sexual expression among "normal" people.

A talk-show host from the Los Angeles radio station that carries my show was taking his broadcast to a sex club in San Francisco. He asked me along for "medical help and perspective." He had been tipped off ahead of time that he might encounter some dangerous practices during the broadcast that could require medical intervention. Actually I think he was just scared to go on this adventure without professional support.

This club had various rooms, each with its own theme and ambience, for patrons of various inclinations. The door on each room had a glass window. One of the many rules of the house was that a visitor could watch but never knock on the door or enter uninvited. Another stated that condoms were mandatory, even for married couples. Small paper cups filled with lubricant were everywhere. I was familiar with some of the equipment in the rooms—gynecology examining tables with stirrups, for example. Others—like slings and straps of leather and metal hanging from the ceiling, and a giant human-size roulette wheel—I had not seen.

Fortunately, there was no need that night for medical care. My role was that of straight man. There were many funny moments, despite my discomfort at some of the things I watched. The first room we peered into held a naked middle-aged man. He was chained to the walls of a simulated dungeon. "I'm a bad boy," he screamed repeatedly, delighted to be met each time with the crack of a leather whip wielded by his . . . partner.

His *partner*?

What's good for the gander. . . . In another room we watched a naked woman being flogged by her boyfriend. Red welts rose on her back with every snap. My companion and I recoiled in unison at each lash and subsequent cry. At one point the woman slipped and hit her knee accidentally against the bed frame. *That* pain induced her boyfriend to drop his whip and fondle her tenderly.

When her pain had passed, her boyfriend moved on to an electrical device. First he splattered her back with an alcohol-based liquid. As he zapped her, the spark ignited the liquid, and a blue-and-gold flame licked up her back for a couple of seconds. We were assured by the woman that "regular sex" followed the light show. We did not stay for that denouement.

Throughout the club, patrons expended great ingenuity on a quest to induce or receive pain. Does all that come under the definition of sexual health? Except for a few isolated scenes that fit my particular definition of appropriate behavior, I was really uncomfortable most of the evening. My inclination was to condemn all this, yet I did not see anybody giving or suffering pain or harm that was not of their own choosing. For them, all this was sexy. From a psychodynamic perspective, being restrained or tied up by one's partner seems reasonable. It's also rather popular, judging from many of the media images that surround us.

Maybe restraint helps to relieve some of the guilt that accompanies sex in America. After all, you can't be held responsible for what happens when you are tied up. I do not endorse any of this obviously, but I am convinced there is a danger when we harshly judge others' sexual expression. I'm willing to live and let live as long as the basic rules of sexual health are obeyed. Remember the British imperative: "the enjoyment of sexual activity of one's choice without causing or suffering physical or mental harm." In the case of a sex club, harm is rightly defined by the participants.

Although it may sound selfish, therapists advise that we do better to follow our own desires rather than worry about what we think our partners want. It makes sense—you can relax because you know each other and are playing by the same honest rules. If your enjoyment hinges solely on your partner's response to your actions, you automatically limit your pleasure.

This philosophy implies intimacy and experience. Perhaps bondage, then, serves as a shortcut by addressing some of these needs without the effort and skills necessary for true intimacy. If it sounds as if I'm struggling to understand all this, I am. I do know that outlawing or repressing sexual activity between consenting adults, like any prohibition, will get us all in trouble. Not to mention that tastes change. Much of what we once considered hippie, underground, weird, and alternative is now mainstream. Maybe in the future, brides will wear black leather. A paradox of the bondage movement is its breadth. One of the largest recent surveys of American sexual habits, conducted by the Janus Report on Sexual Behavior in 1993, found that "people who identify themselves as ultraconservatives are three times more accepting of sadomasochism in sex than either ultraliberals or independents."

WHO YOU CALLING WEIRD?

We grapple constantly with where to establish the border between pathological and nonpathological in sexual behavior. Officially it comes down to intensity of feelings and the distress caused by those feelings. Cross a certain line and mental disorder is diagnosed. But the line has shifted considerably in recent decades. Surveys have found, for example, that most people's sexual fantasies are shot through with themes of dominance and submission. Life is tough enough without adding a burden of guilt over dreams that may actually be normal and within the range of possible exploration. The vast majority of people with these feelings are not considered abnormal anymore. I offer you this to put you at ease: You do not have to feel weird because of thoughts and fantasies.

Let's take foot fetishism. You can imagine the challenge in tracing the scientific or psychoanalytic origins of this practice. One intriguing theory relates to a mother's affection. If she withdraws her love or presence from a young child, whatever occupies the child's consciousness at the time can become the fixation. At one point in development, a crawling child's world view is mostly of adults' feet. If a mother disappears emotionally or physically at that time, feet may become the child's sexual focus later in life. A male patient with a neck fetish once told me that his mother had sent him to live with his grandmother when he was a child. Bereft of his mother, he distinctly remembered his grandmother's bare neck as he was bounced on her lap. It became the only shred of physical contact left after being denied contact with his mother's skin. As an adult, he was extremely aroused by women's necks.

Humans seem capable of an incredible range of sexual expression that comes under the aforementioned definition. On my short-lived TV talk show, we took on the fetishists. (Yes, yes, partly in a vain effort to topple Oprah in the ratings. We tried to do it in a manner that could be deemed socially responsible. You see how long we lasted.) We had the following guests: a man aroused by a whipped-cream pie thrown in his face, a woman whose partner would wrap her body, mummy-style, in duct tape, and a fellow who wore his diapers to the show. Strange as it sounds, this bizarre adaptability of our sexual natures could have positive repercussions for reproduction. Being able to pass on our genes at times of adverse or unusual circumstances offers a major survival advantage for humans. That said, I hope we don't all have to wear diapers to ensure the survival of the species.

But adaptability is a marvelous trait. I once saw a teaching video for sexologists who deal with disabled patients. It featured a quadriplegic man, paralyzed and numb from the neck down, making love to his girlfriend. She first carried him with great difficulty from the wheelchair and plopped him on the bed. She then rubbed herself to orgasm on his thighs while nuzzling his neck, which was where he had learned to experience orgasm. Patients with spinal cord injuries have the ability to shift the sensory source of orgasm from the genitals to other body areas. It may not be the adaptability of species Darwin had in mind, but it's a gift nonetheless.

Throughout history, entire civilizations have been taken by strange mass sexual practices. China is perhaps the greatest example of cultural sexual programming, and for a practice we cannot call healthy because of the physical suffering involved. Most people do not realize that the abusive custom of foot binding basically began with erotic appeal.

Practiced for more than a thousand years, this mutilation was designed to make young girls marriageable and sexually appealing to men. The total length of a properly bound adult woman's foot could total less than three inches, and that was the pinnacle of female erotic appeal. Poetically called the "golden lotus," the foot became a woman's most private part, revealed only to her most intimate partner and treasured equally with her genitals, if not more. Her lover would fondle, stroke, lick, suck, and smell her feet at the peak of the lovemaking act. Foot binding destroyed a woman's ability to walk properly, yet even the resulting awkward gait was considered highly sensual. The practice only yielded to reform early in the twentieth century. Even today one occasionally sees older women with these tiny feet on the streets of Beijing. First-hand lyrical descriptions of the golden lotus in Chinese poetry and literature should remind us that people can adapt their sexuality to fit a variety of political and social situations.

MAN SMART, WOMAN SMARTER

As we all know, men are sexual Neanderthals who have neither the time nor the inclination for romance. After all, romance just gets in the way of the quick in-and-out for which all red-blooded males lust.

In case you think that way, and I am sorry if you do, fascinating and unlikely recent research has shown it to be untrue. The proof? Researchers have found that men and women are equally turned on by romance as portrayed in erotic videos.

In the mid–1980s, a new genre emerged: erotic films written, produced, and directed by women. These films are far different from the traditional fare produced and directed by men. As one of the pioneering female producers described her films, "the sexual partners have equal roles as far as sexual desire and sexual pleasure are concerned; the actors are really attracted to each other, prolonged foreplay is an important ingredient, and there is not as much emphasis on intercourse as in male-oriented erotic films."

Researchers in Amsterdam wanted to prove that women would be more turned on by the female-oriented videos. They chose excerpts from two films, one made by men, the other by women. The male-made film was set in a brothel and depicted heterosexual sex between strangers. No time was spent on foreplay or nonsexual details. The female-made film depicted an elevator in which a man and a woman met. Progressively over the next four minutes—an eternity in screen time—they glanced, stroked, kissed, and undressed each other.

Researchers hooked female subjects to devices that measured pulse and blood flow in the vagina. The viewers then watched both videos. As their physical measurements were taken, they rated themselves on their subjective erotic responses. While the women said they were more turned on by the female-made film, their genital arousal was the same for both films.

The researchers were surprised that the male-made film was genitally arousing even though the women found it to be an emotional turn-off. A complete explanation awaits further research, but it seems that men and women are more alike than we thought.

Maybe the real lesson is that we need to broaden our vision of what we find to be sexy.

THIS MAGIC MOMENT

Men and women indisputably part company in one area of sexual physiology—the orgasm. The inner landscape of the orgasmic experience is, so far, off limits to science. How do you measure a moment so varied and complex? How do you quantify an internal quest that can be manipulated and boosted with practice in a close and trusting relationship? Well, there is one glaring gender difference: Women can have multiple orgasms and men usually cannot.

Researchers in the 1950s estimated that 15 percent of women actually experienced this phenomenon but guessed that most women were capable of it. More recent investigation at the University of Wisconsin found that as many as 42.7 percent of the women it surveyed had experienced multiple orgasm. That study also distinguished certain differences between the single- and multiorgasm groups. Those reporting multiple climaxes were more likely to be stimulated by sexual fantasies and erotic literature and films. They were more likely to employ a variety of stimulation techniques with their partners. We're not talking ancient Tantric sex secrets here but fairly mundane practices such as altering the position of intercourse and having their clitorises and nipples stimulated by themselves or their partners during the sex act. "Adventurousness led to multiple orgasms," the researchers concluded. By the way, it was not determined whether these women experienced more emotional satisfaction from sex.

I get bombarded for this on the air, but another difference between male and female sexuality is ejaculation. Until proved otherwise, supposed female ejaculation is in reality a well-documented urological phenomenon known by the self-explanatory name of orgasmic incontinence. The loss of urine during sex or orgasm is fairly common. Yet the vehemence with which so many women and their partners object to this evaluation tells me the degree of embarrassment involved. There is no undiscovered gland, furtively hidden and capable of holding the volumes of fluid supposedly ejaculated. This is urine, plain and simple, and it is no big deal. That said, some women may produce considerable secretions during sex, which in turn may ooze during contractions of the musculature. Oozing is not the same as spurting.

WAKE UP AND SMELL THE SIGNALS

As technology improves, science may be better able to measure subtle forms of sexual communication. For example, olfactory researchers have been on the trail of pheromones for decades. Pheromones are crucial chemicals that send complex information from individual to individual. It is via pheromones that insects and other critters sense each other. Extraordinarily few molecules are necessary for this transmission. You cannot smell pheromones, because an insufficient number of atoms are involved to register in your nose. Yet sexual readiness is one of the prime states communicated through pheromones. Scientists have been desperately seeking evidence of pheromones in humans.

As you might expect, pheromone potential has been lost neither on researchers nor on perfume manufacturers. Some people claim that women synchronize their menstrual cycles by smelling each other's clothing, and that men attract unsuspecting females by wearing pheromone-containing aftershave, the modern answer to the medieval love potion. The evidence until now, though, has been poor and unconvincing. Nevertheless, current research efforts are intense because ultimately the payoff could be monumental.

Researchers at San Francisco State University conducted a fascinating experiment. They recruited thirty-eight heterosexual men for a study to test "whether a male pheromone added to their aftershave lotion would increase romance in their lives." Some of the subjects had their aftershave spiked with a patented synthetic pheromone; others were given a placebo. The scientists then measured six sociosexual behaviors.

An increase in two most intimate behaviors was documented among the pheromone wearers—sexual intercourse and sleeping with women. These behaviors obviously require the willingness of a female partner. Smaller increases were also measured for other partner-involved behaviors, such as petting, affection, kissing, and informal dates. Individual sexual activities—masturbation, for example—did not increase. It was not completely proved, of course, that the pheromone did indeed increase the sexual attractiveness of these men. This was one very small study. If its results are accurate, it represents one of the greatest findings in the history of psychosexual research. Obviously more investigation in larger studies is needed, and you can bet these studies are coming. Meanwhile I suspect we will see a pheromone-containing product on the market any day now.

Don't misinterpret my skepticism as doubt that our noses are involved in sexual signaling. A well-known smell-and-taste research center in Chicago claims to have shown that certain odors can increase blood flow to the penis (decreased blood flow is a primary cause of sexual dysfunction in men). Better get ready for some funky perfumes: While all the odors tested did boost blood flow, the stars were pumpkin pie and lavender. Again, these were small, unconvincing, and poorly controlled experiments, but watch for more news soon.

A more convincing investigation of humans and smell examined the qualitative aspects of our bodies' odors. People take great care to mask and perfume these natural fragrances, some of which nature undoubtedly gave us for sexual attraction. Most folks are deconditioned from responding to these natural stimulants, much to the joy of the fragrance industry. Yet the aromas of a lover's armpits or even genitals can be attractive to some individuals. German scientists decided to test it out. Their conclusion was fairly odd.

A group of men and women were rated on physical attractiveness. Each then wore a T-shirt for a week without washing it. The T-shirts were given a whiff by a panel and the resulting redolence rated with numerical scores, ranging from fragrant to fetid. The men rated the T-shirts worn by the most beautiful women as sweetest smelling. The women rated all the men's T-shirts toward the malodorous end of the scale, except the women who were ovulating. At that special time of the month, these same T-shirts moved up the attractive-scent scale.

Science has also attempted to unravel the more social aspects of sexual attraction, although, as you can imagine, research in this area is difficult at best. The most universal signaling of sexual availability by females is not a wink and a kiss blown across a crowded room. Researchers videotaped a series of interactions between men and women and concluded that the most telling behavior involved women touching their faces and tossing their hair with the hand.

Another example of nature's subtle sexual magic revolves around the display of female flesh. Women attending a lecture and a disco were rated by observers and computers on the tightness of their clothing as well as on how much bare skin they exposed. The same women were also tested to determine their exact phase in the menstrual cycle. During ovulation, the women displayed more skin and wore tighter clothes.

FLIGHTS OF FANCY

Sexual fantasizing would once have fallen into the "strange practices" category. No longer. Fantasy should be regarded as a sexual asset rather than a threat. Exploring fantasy takes a degree of security and a freedom from sexual jealousy that many couples never reach. Keeping fantasies to yourself is fine, but it is more fun if you can share them. It's all in the mind's eye, but that vision is a wondrous, and wonderfully liberating, thing.

In 1974 researchers surveyed a group of suburban housewives about their fantasies during intercourse. The most common themes were those of "submission and a fantasy lover." We can assume their eyes are closed during those fantasies. What exactly is the difference between the fantasy and the reality? If it were reality, would she be as relaxed and free of anxiety? Wouldn't the tension, anxiety, and likely guilt of such a moment diminish the experience? In other words, the fantasy is likely to be much better than the reality. Now suppose that instead of hiding the fantasy the way most people do, she were able to openly share it with her partner who, because they have a secure and intimate relationship, participates and plays the role of the strange lover. Imagine the possibilities. The ability to fantasize with your love play is the greatest protection against infidelity. Why would anyone want to stray when they can have a different lover every night and never leave home? To reach these upper echelons of sexuality one must take sex seriously and treat it as an ongoing creative adventure. The nuances and pleasures can be endless.

The first rule of any sexual relationship is to establish a baseline— that which pleases and interests you—and use it to move on. Would you really be happy if your partner was disgusted by performing oral sex yet performed it on you anyway? Isn't it more pleasing to know that your partner is doing something because he or she enjoys it? That has to be better. Get over this hurdle and you will find it easier to relax and enjoy what you are receiving. You will stop taking responsibility for and *worrying* about your partner's pleasure. Sex and worry do not make comfortable bedfellows.

My drift here should be obvious: The real barrier is communication, or rather, lack of communication. Talking about sex is the most difficult part of sex. If we could peek into America's bedrooms, we might find an occasional grunt but little talk. Most people are afraid to ask for what they want. They fear rejection, or worry that they could offend their partners by implying that they have not been satisfied. Some couples, though, would sound as if they're having a conversation rather than sex, guiding each other along undiscovered roads. Post-coitally, they talk more, dissect and discuss the experience and their reactions. Sex is a team sport. It must be learned. The next step on the ladder is knowing what your partner wants, so you can mix experimentation with the well and happily proved.

There is no one way for all. My sense is that for sexually successful couples, sex is never the same. It is always changing and is never, never predictable. Growth is a worthy sexual goal, in my view.

By now you must be getting the message that nothing is as sexy as talk. I firmly believe that the fundamental skills to send your sex life rocketing are verbal intimacy and sexual communication. Researchers have affirmed the critical role played by this elusive talent. "Communication can enhance sexual arousal, is necessary for the initiation and refusal of sex, and is related to sexual satisfaction," say researchers at the University of Helsinki. "Couples that maintain a high quality of communication about sex are more likely to have a satisfying sexual relationship. . . . Sexually assertive women reported higher frequencies of sexual activity and orgasm, rated themselves as having greater subjective desire, and reported greater marital and sexual satisfaction."

Yet most people never even get to the "faster . . . slower . . . harder . . . softer" phase. If you care about your sexual health, face your fears and talk about sex. Start slow and easy: "Hey, honey, what did you like when we just made love? Should I do that again?" It will pay off later when you're ready to tantalize each other with scary questions like "What do you fantasize about when we make love?"

Ask for what you want, and ask your partner to do the same. If all that is too direct, make it a game. Experiment. Be creative. Instead of arguing about whether it's a left-hand turn off the highway to Aunt Trudy's house, make a sexual bet with your spouse. The loser gives the winner what she or he wants. Give sexual IOUs for presents.

If you need some help, every city now has retail establishments that cater to sexual creativity. No longer "porn stores," most are owned and run by women and offer an astonishing array of accessories and ideas. If that's too intimidating, check out a local lingerie store together, or just take a cruise through the Internet. Reading books that catalog other people's fantasies should tell you how normal, or maybe even boring, your fantasies are. You would be amazed at the changes over recent years. Video stores report more women renting erotic films than men. There's something for every taste.

Keep in mind, please, that we are all individuals and will find our own solutions as long as we rank sex as important to our mental, spiritual, and physical existence. We must make the commitment to grow and to explore our sexuality. It must become as important as anything else in our lives.

Use sex well. Program it into your hectic life. Schedule it, if necessary. Make it a measure of the priority you place on your primary relationship. It can be a delightful antidote to the stress you endure in the rest of your day. Can you honestly think of any other antidote that could come close to being as much fun?

8

SOME GERMS ARE YOUR FRIENDS

You Shouldn't Always Avoid Them

———

You've got potatoes in your ears."

How could that be? Yet my mother insisted. She would stretch my ears between her fingers and in her best professional voice declare the presence of spuds where they couldn't be. It is one of my earliest memories, the warning that maternal torment was imminent. A washcloth, sandpaper equivalent #200, would descend on my tender young ears. "You've got a ring around your neck" was another warning that the Cloth of Torture would soon follow. I wasn't trusted to do a thorough job myself, so Mom did the scrubbing. I tried to talk her out of it. Oh, how I tried.

I whined. I pleaded. I begged. "It's dead skin, Ma," I whimpered as her hand worked at my neck like a fresh piece of pine being smoothed into a staircase rail for the Rockefeller mansion. Some friends and I figured that if you wet your fingers and rubbed hard enough, the darkened dead skin would melt away, leaving renewed pink fresh flesh to frustrate Mom. Before heading home, I would scrape my neck raw, hoping to remove enough outer flesh to pass inspection. It never worked.

When finally I was old enough to assume the duties myself, I tried the standard shortcuts—no soap, for one—but never slipped past Mom's keen nose. I was always being sniffed—I felt like a puppy. If my hair didn't "smell dirty," then I simply "smelled like a little boy," guaranteeing a round-trip ticket to the tub. All those hours in the porcelain gave me time to develop a valuable gift for holding my breath underwater. I can still go two to three pool lengths on one breath.

I decided to use my skill for the greater good of children everywhere. Once, when Mom came to check on the progress of my second mandatory bath of the day, I was in the midst of setting the world's "tub breath-holding record." There I floated, facedown and unmoving. I heard my mother shriek. Seizing the moment, I stiffened, thinking I could turn her horror to my permanent advantage. Alas, an unsuccessful jail break. I lost my bathtub privileges and suffered years more before I was trusted again to harvest potatoes and obliterate neck rings myself.

Thus I learned that the world was awash in germs. Certain items were not to be touched because of—horrors!—germs; certain foods were not to be eaten because of germs; certain parts of the body . . . well, let's not go there. There were important exceptions and inconsistencies that, of course, made no sense, even to my young, unformed mind. Kisses were OK, and I got plenty of those, smothering wet ones, from every relative between here and the Old World. Yuck.

Now I'm an old doctor, and I know that what *really* matters is not the dirt but keeping track of the unseen critters that can harm you and knowing what you can do about them. I'm the first to admit that it's hard to know about those countless germs and not react at all. How could I—potato farmer that I was raised to be—not be "germ conscious"?

I don't blame anyone for getting a little paranoid about germs. No argument from me that they are there and they can harm you. All told, fifty thousand people each day die awful deaths from germ-related diseases. Germs cannot be avoided, and that means you have to be conscious of them. I use my foot both to flush in public restrooms and to pick up the seat and was gladdened by a recent survey that found most of you do, too. One entrepreneur who could feel our pain recently introduced a device called Sani-Grip, a 4-inch aluminum handle that attaches to the side of the seat for nontactile lifting.

Do I go too far? I use the paper towel to dry my hands and to turn off the faucet. I learned that in medical school. After all, what's the sense of washing your hands if the next thing you do is grab the bathroom faucet to turn it off? In the operating room of older hospitals, the faucet is activated by a handle you move with your knee, and the soap dispenser is a foot pedal, so you don't have to touch either with your hands.

You'll never catch me using someone else's toothbrush, no matter how romantic the moment.

A GERM-WARY MEDICINE MAN TELLS ALL

Medical school didn't make my germ-consciousness easier. You may find it strange to hear a doctor voice this, but I never liked the grungy stuff. It must have something to do with my childhood training. In one of my first classes as a new medical student, we were commanded to save a day's worth of our urine for an upcoming class on urinalysis. With newspaper and shopping bags hiding our specimens, we converged on the class. Beforehand I had overheard a conversation in the cafeteria that launched me into a panic: The professor was going to order us to taste our urine. I knew that this was a basic and simple old-time test for diabetes, sugar in the urine. But this was the twentieth century, I protested to myself.

As it turned out, I had overreacted. It never happened. What I had misheard was an apocryphal story of the same professor dipping a finger in the urine and licking. He then asked the class to repeat his action. The students dutifully complied. "The most important skill of the physician is careful observation," the sage teacher then told them. "Had you had been paying attention, you would have noticed that I dipped my index finger in the urine but licked my ring finger."

I was spared that time, but I had to work to stay clean. I always divided the medical specialties into "wet" (urology, gynecology, obstetrics, gastroenterolgy, and pediatrics) and "dry" (psychiatry, ophthalmology, and radiology). Being bled, peed, pooped, and salivated on in the middle of the night just never caught my fancy. Bodily fluids don't attract me. During my stint at Bellevue Hospital in New York City, where the clientele was notorious for diseases run amok, I routinely confronted incisions and drainage of appalling surgical abscesses and infections. Excuse me, but we're talking cupfuls of foul pus from these infections, which smelled as you would expect and made me wish I'd gone to law school.

Yet you have to touch even the most filthy and smelly of patients. I handed patients specimen jars and had cups handed back to me that were overflowing with urine. I remember one mentally challenged patient whom I asked for a urine specimen. As usual at supply-starved Bellevue, we had run out of cups, so I gave him a test tube. He returned a few minutes later after complying. Before I could protest, he was shoving the foul tube into my hand. He thought I had requested a stool sample. You can understand why I am still proud of being probably the only doctor in history to finish training without performing a proctoscopy.

There was a bright side to this aspect of medical school training. I learned about "sterile technique." I liked that, all the different ways to put a barrier between yourself and the patient's germs. I was a quick learner in putting on rubber gloves. It's actually not that easy. You've got to keep the sterile outside, outside and the inside, inside, and ne'er the twain shall meet. Masks and gowns were OK with me, too. You never know what these people are carrying.

THE UNSEEN WORLD WITHIN

Maybe people were better off, psychologically, before we learned that we share this planet with countless trillions of earthlings we cannot see. Imagine the surprise when in the mid-1600s, a humble cloth merchant in Delft named Antonie van Leeuwenhoek peered through his incredible homemade lenses and saw what no human being had seen before—a whole new world. Van Leeuwenhoek was a talented, unschooled lens grinder. He scraped his teeth, put the results under his primitive microscope, and became the first person to describe the bacteria he saw. It took two centuries before these tiny creatures were proved to cause disease.

It is reasonable to fear infectious diseases. They can harm us, as I will discuss shortly. But we are more freaked out than we need be.

Germs have a wholesale bad reputation that is undeserved. Germs are everywhere, from hot volcanic vents under the sea, to the pillow you sleep on, to—maybe—Mars. We are peacefully infested with micro-organisms. A microbiology professor horrified me with the notion that if every bit of our flesh, every atom and molecule, were suddenly to disappear, a perfect image of our bodies would remain, comprised of all the microorganisms that live in and on us. Immediately upon birth, a baby's body is colonized by a vast jungle of tiny critters: bacteria, parasites, fungi, yeast, and viruses. The first invaders come from Mom and the rest from others who touch and breath on the baby. After a few weeks of life, a pattern of microorganisms is established that remains with us all our lives. Their names would fill pages and pages of this book.

This is a fundamental part of the human condition. Although the role played by many of these creatures is not known, it seems in many cases that they are necessary for life, not merely contributing to it. Some germs perform critical functions. Germs make vitamin K, which is a vitamin essential for blood clotting. Germs in the intestines help produce vitamins B-12, B-6, and B-2, folic acid, biotin, and pantothenate. Other germs produce ammonia that may be available for our bodies to produce amino acids.

In fact, people raised in too germ-free an environment are left with a weak immune system and higher rates of certain diseases such as diabetes and asthma. English and Scottish researchers found that subjects with more siblings and older siblings all living in crowded conditions had *lower* rates of various allergic diseases, including eczema, asthma, hay fever, food allergies, and runny noses.

Researchers found a clever demonstration of this phenomenon among young people who tested positive for hepatitis A, a reliable marker for overcrowded residence and unhygienic practices including poor food-handling and hand-washing. The presence of antibodies to hepatitis A in the bloodstream is considered a sign that an individual was raised in a relatively unsanitary environment. Italian researchers checked military recruits for hepatitis, then tested them for all allergic sensitivities and diseases. Those who had had hepatitis at some point in their lives had far lower rates of allergic diseases.

How else are your resident germs your friends? They fight off bad disease-causing counterparts that attempt to invade their space. Think of it as a tight housing market. When pathogenic microorganisms—bad germs—want to move into the neighborhood, the long-term residents battle to beat them off so they cannot hurt the town.

An example familiar to every woman occurs when she treats an illness with antibiotics, which suppress bacteria. An undesired result may be a vaginal yeast infection. That happens because the antibiotic also kills the usual harmless bacteria in her vagina. The yeast, which resides there anyway but in lower numbers, senses a population vacuum and moves in strong. Reestablishment of normal bacteria like lactobacillus beats back the yeast. Now you understand the yogurt cure. The germ in yogurt is the lactobacillus bacterium.

Your body is a true freestanding ecosystem. Germs have certain niches based on their particular habits. If they like oxygen, they hang out where oxygen is plentiful—on your teeth, for example. If they do not like oxygen, they nestle in the space between your teeth. Most germs hang out around openings and in those parts of your body accessible to openings. The inner organs and bloodstream are relatively sterile. Everywhere else? Look out. The skin is covered with germs, especially the warm moist places. The eyes, ears, and respiratory tract are loaded. The vagina and digestive tract—population explosion. The contents of the colon carry up to a hundred billion germs per gram.

I know that you may not find this a pretty picture. For instance, there are more bacteria in your mouth right now than there are people on the earth. That makes it the most bacteria-ridden region of your body. If you are a brusher and a flosser and have a relatively aseptic mouth, each of your teeth has between a thousand and a hundred thousand bacteria on it. If you rarely pick up your toothbrush, or wouldn't recognize floss if it wound itself around your nose, then I'm talking between a hundred million and a billion bacteria on each tooth. As many as five hundred separate species are hanging out in your mouth, each with its favorite piece of real estate. Some love the crevices and furrows of your tongue, where they are capable of manufacturing some funky odors. (The origin of much bad breath is the tongue.) Others love the pockets between the gums and the tooth, or cheeks and tonsils. When you kiss, you give free transportation to these little friends back and forth, a sort of oral student exchange program. You carry microbiological remnants of every person you've ever kissed. In case this isn't enough for you, I'll come back to your lovely mouth a little later.

THE GERMS ARE COMING! THE GERMS ARE COMING!

Fear of infection leads folks to do some strange things. For a while, a number of women inexplicably and accidentally kept torching their kitchens. When firefighters arrived at one home in Salt Lake County, Utah, they were amazed that the lady of the house had started the fire by microwaving her undies. She had heard it was an effective way to prevent vaginal yeast infection.

True, this is an extreme example, yet many of our everyday responses to germs are irrational, ineffective, and anxiety-provoking. Ever patiently position those paper toilet liners in a public restroom? Ever hover over the seat instead of sitting down on it? Disease is not spread by toilet seats. New mothers scrupulously sterilize baby bottles, but breast-feeding moms do not sterilize their breasts. People worry about doorknobs, pay phones, taxicabs, and dirt, yet kiss each other with aplomb, exposing their mouths to an invasion of foreign armies.

Americans spend eleven minutes in the shower or twenty minutes in the tub every day, more than anybody in the world, yet those activities do not decrease the spread of disease. Civil engineering and the benefits of modern plumbing, sewers, and sanitation have probably played a greater role in beating back these plagues than medicine's enormous strides—but because of toilets, not showers. Until the late nineteenth century, when plumbing and hot water became available, infectious disease from bodily fluids and excrescences was the leading cause of death.

Most of our illogical reaction to this parallel universe is purely emotional, a response to something we cannot see, which goes a long way toward explaining our fear. Because we can't see them, we imagine germs as the larger-than-life creatures in those electron microscope snapshots, where they are uglier than anything Hollywood can scare up. It's not unlike early in the Cold War, when those invisible Communist hordes were plotting to invade and seize our country from us. Remember our reaction?

We have become a nation of germaphobics and understandably so. Not only are they an invisible menace, but the talk shows, TV reporters, and media health mavens tell us that we're losing the war. Every week, it seems, there is a new offensive. This is another of my fat file folders. Here's the prepackaged salad story, first circulated at a convention of investigative, consumer, and beat television reporters. These folks gather at regular intervals, where they are fed prepared stories to take back to their local markets. There the story runs as if the reporter generated it. Is it a scam, you ask? I think you could make that case. At the very least, it's a deceptive practice by the reporter.

In any event, the salad story went like this. The television station bought some prepackaged salad fixings from the local grocery store and carted them over to a lab for tests. You got it, the lettuce had germs. Voilà, instant scare story, just like we like 'em in TV. But there was some context missing here. As you now know, our world is covered by a sea of squirming germs, most of which are not only benign, but a necessary part of life. No food—natural, fresh, or raw—can be sterile unless cooked, so it's normal for germs to show up. There has never been an outbreak of disease from prepackaged salads, yet those local TV types had their viewers convinced that an epidemic lurked around the corner. Prepackaged salads, by the way, are washed with antiseptic chlorine solutions. That should make them even safer than regular water-washed produce. The package can legitimately claim that the contents don't have to be washed before serving.

Then there was ebola, the viral disease of the week. I got more calls on my radio show than I could handle. People worried that this African illness would invade by airplane. Public health officials tried to inject reason but were helpless, their voices drowned out by the media din. Diseases like ebola that quickly make their victims deathly ill do not allow time for those victims to get on airplanes.

Flesh-devouring strep bacteria have floated around the world since the eighteenth century. They are no more common today, yet you might think they are standing poised to strike you and your loved ones. Each case in the United States warrants headlines. Actually, I never heard the term *flesh-eating* associated with these germs until the media made it up. On June 10, 1994, *USA Today* warned FLESH-EATING BUG SWIFT, DEADLY; HORROR STORIES SEND CHILLS ACROSS NATION. This necrotizing fasciitis can be horrible, no doubt, but it is not likely to happen to you. A little later, stories correcting these misimpressions got lost on the back pages. They noted that one in four Americans carries the germ, usually with no harm.

THE GERMS *Are* COMING, SO CHILL OUT

Without doubt, germs can and do cause diseases. But please keep that truth in perspective. In 1920 the eight most serious disease groups were influenza, pneumonia, kidney disease, stomach disease, syphilis, diphtheria, whooping cough, and measles. Most are infectious diseases, and thanks to the era of miracle drugs and vaccines, these are not our biggest problems today. Antibiotics and vaccines heralded an era of better health and a new sense of security.

We have been spoiled by our triumph. Now the media, among others, announce every little outbreak of any new bug, no matter what its significance or insignificance. They tend to make everything sound scary.

Yes, an airplane has spread tuberculosis, in one very unusual circumstance, with a sick patient on an extremely long flight who transmitted the disease only to those sitting nearby. Yes, the wife of a pizza maker contracted yeast vaginitis from baker's yeast. Yes, a shower transmitted Legionnaires' disease at a hospital in South Dakota. Yes, an infant contracted meningitis from the family dog after the pooch licked his face. Yes, 11 percent of the soil in the backyards of private homes in Baltimore tested positive for live eggs of a dog worm that can infect children. Yes, public parks and sandboxes were worse. Yes, cats can pass toxoplasmosis to pregnant woman, possibly affecting the fetus.

All true. But if all those germs are out there just waiting to get you, why aren't you and everybody you know sick all the time? All these odd infections are rare, and there's nothing you can do about most of them. They are random, and you stumble on them randomly. Your body adjusts to the presence of many other germs it encounters. For instance, half of you have already had toxoplasmosis, a parasite you probably caught from undercooked meat but that can also be passed to pregnant women by cats. You never knew you got it, and you probably never will. Meanwhile, are you going to stop breathing on an airplane? Quit eating pizza? Run away from household pets?

Doctors and health care workers, with their host of meaningless rituals, do not help to calm the germaphobic waters. They wipe your arm before drawing blood or administering an injection, but that does nothing to prevent infection. Surgeons don't just *wash* their hands before an operation; they do a *surgical scrub*. Why the word *scrub*? Because it is done with brushes, which it turns out are no more effective than soap alone. Someone may shave your abdomen before surgery, yet that may actually increase infection. A regular razor may stir up germs deep in the skin, which are then carried into the wound during surgery. The surgical face mask does not prevent infection during an operation. Swedish doctors performed 1,500 operations without them. There was no greater rate of infection.

Manufacturers, ever sensitive to new markets and potentially profitable paranoia, constantly answer the call of our nonneeds. Who can blame them? One recent poll found that 96 percent of adults worry about bacteria and germs, up from 77 percent in 1995. And 87 percent have used an antibacterial product. The find-a-need-and-fill-it geniuses have responded with new inventions on which these germ phobics can waste their money. Hasbro, encouraged by sales of an antibacterial 1-2-3 High Chair, introduced a line of fifteen antibacterial toys for tots. These products are made from plastic bonded with antiseptic pellets. This material is antimold, antimildew, antifungus, and antibacteria and has been used in some surgical equipment. Now it is headed for use in athletic shoes, cutting boards, and carpeting.

Antiseptic sheets, pillow cases, sprays, soaps, and lotions of all sorts jam supermarket and drugstore shelves. Half of all consumers will buy the antibacterial version of cleanser, detergent, and soap when they make their selection. Antibacterial hand gels, most containing ethyl alcohol, are best-sellers, racking up as much as fifty million dollars in sales a year. "A consumer that used to think, 'My hands are dirty,' now thinks, 'My hands are dirty because they came in contact with something,'" said an executive with Dial Corporation.

One doctor, Stuart Levy, a researcher at Tufts University, has warned that these manufacturers are marketing based on parents' fears. He worries about the harm down the road caused by introducing bacterial resistance to these substances. It's the same mistake made by overprescribing antibiotics. "Products, including cutting boards and other kitchenware impregnated with antibacterial chemicals, could be killing off weaker germs, [thus] helping to breed bacteria that cannot be eradicated by standard antibiotics," he cautions.

Other researchers at Tufts found bacteria resistant to pine oil disin-
fectants and household cleaners. These germs also turned out to be
resistant to tetracycline, ampicillin, and chloramphenicol—all common antibiotics.

Of course, you *can* wash anything. Germs adhere to fabrics by forming a gluelike encrustation. High temperatures in a washing machine
and an effective detergent will give them the heave-ho. New fabrics
that get "clean" with low-temperature washing, the disappearance of
efficient phosphate detergents, and washing machines with energy-
saving low-temperature options complicate the battle. Researchers
have found that bacterial contamination of fabrics actually *increased*
with newer detergents and lowered temperatures. Terry cloth had the
most germs.

UNCOVERING THE ENEMY

One of the collective feats of modern medicine has been proving that
diseases could be caused by organisms we could not see. At first it was
thought to be the notion of crackpots. The great cholera epidemics of
London in the mid-nineteenth century offered the first opportunity to
demonstrate the path of disease.

Cholera is a diarrheal disease that dehydrates and usually kills
between half and three-quarters of its victims. When it hit England,
no one knew that germs spread disease or that they could be spread
by water or anything else. A simple investigation by Dr. John Snow, a
nineteenth-century British physician, uncovered this fundamental
knowledge of infectious medicine. Snow unfurled a map of London
and placed a dot on the location of every death during one of the outbreaks. Within days, five hundred dots were clustered around the
Broad Street water pump in one neighborhood. But strangely, one dot
was isolated in another area. Snow tracked down that case: a woman
who had moved to another neighborhood but had a taste for water
from the Broad Street pump, so that water had been delivered to her
new home.

Snow went the next step, convincing the local authorities to shut
down the pump. Immediately the disease subsided in that neighborhood. Further investigation uncovered a ruptured sewer pipe that had
contaminated the Broad Street water supply. Thus the discovery that
water could transmit this killer of millions of people around the

world. Yet despite this elegant and unassailable scientific truth, the public balked at Snow's breakthrough. Then as now, old ideas were hard to change. Think of that when you hear people complaining about chlorination, which has effectively put an end to this scourge in the developed world.

Still more radical a notion lay ahead: people could transmit diseases to each other. In the 1840s, as Snow in London struggled to understand cholera, an obstetrics assistant at the Allgemeines Krankenhaus (General Hospital) in Vienna noted a strange situation. The death rate from postpartum fever among new mothers was more than five times greater on wards staffed with medical students than on those staffed with midwives. The assistant, Ignaz Semmelweiss, speculated that the medical students were carrying this disease into the ward. The source, he reasoned, was the morgue, where the students often performed dissections before going on duty. The midwives did not do dissections.

Semmelweiss detected a pattern: A row of patients would be examined by the medical students. Within a day or two, a new cluster of fever would occur. His suspicions deepened with the death of a friend and colleague who cut himself during an autopsy on a woman with postpartum fever. Semmelweiss attended the autopsy of his friend and noticed that his organs looked like those of the women who died of the fever.

Semelweiss insisted that the medical students start washing their hands (an action that, remarkably, medical personnel still balk at today) using chlorinated lime before touching any pregnant women. The death rate quickly dropped below that on the midwives' ward. Despite these results, he was violently opposed by orthodox obstetricians. He was demoted and hounded, forced by the opposition to flee Vienna. His story had a tragic end. The rejection and controversy, too much for this sensitive and intense visionary, drove him to a mental asylum, where he died at age forty-seven, only two weeks after his admission. I keep a photo of his washbasin and use it in television pieces to remind viewers of this hard-fought battle over infection.

Semelweiss had no idea that bacterial infection was the actual cause of postpartum uterine infections. That came a little later, with Joseph Lister. Lister was a prestigious physician in Glasgow. Obviously doctors were accustomed to seeing pus in a wound, but no one had demonstrated that pus could transmit disease. Lister noticed that patients' broken bones healed well if the skin was not broken as well. If it was broken, pus—or as we now know, infection—developed. Lister also saw pus result after operations. He thought it was, literally, in the air. He sprayed carbolic acid on wounds during surgery and it worked. He got lucky—he didn't know it would kill germs, but it did. In 1867 he described eleven cases in *The Lancet*, the British medical journal. As with Semelweiss, indifference and hostility followed from his colleagues.

But it was Louis Pasteur who took medicine to a new plane, with his germ theory of disease. While helping a local alcohol manufacturer solve some problems, he proved that bacteria—tiny microscopic creatures—were responsible for fermentation and that some of them liked oxygen and others did not. He also discovered that heating wine for a few moments at a temperature of 108 degrees Fahrenheit destroyed the fermenting germs. The process became known as *pasteurization*. He later went on to save the silk industry by figuring out that a devastating silkworm disease was infectious and could be prevented by removing the contaminated food source.

Pasteur also made a critical leap for disease control of anthrax in sheep and cholera in chickens. Earlier in the century, Edward Jenner had played with a technique from China and the Middle East called *variolation*. He tried pricking the lesion of smallpox in one patient, then lightly pricking the skin of another person with the same needle to immunize the second person by inducing a mild case of the illness. It did not work all the time—sometimes transmitting a severe case—so the technique was not generally accepted.

But he kept at it. Milkmaids, it seemed, were resistant to smallpox. Jenner thought that perhaps they had unwittingly caught cowpox, a close relative of smallpox. In 1796 he extracted some matter from a cowpox lesion on the hand of Sarah Nelmes and inoculated the hand of eight-year-old James Phipps. He then inoculated young James with a virulent smallpox virus. Phipps did not develop the disease. Jenner had discovered that one disease actually can prevent another.

Pasteur built on Jenner's discovery. He found that he could produce harmless weakened cultures of anthrax and cholera that, when injected into animals, conferred immunity against the virulent powerful forms of the same germs. In 1881 in front of an audience of skeptics, he injected live anthrax into sheep that had weeks before been injected with the weakened form of the same disease. The sheep lived. He called his technique *vaccination.*

The lives and works of these and other giants of science should never be forgotten. I hope you can understand why I get so outraged with the glib actress on the talk show who wants us to dump centuries of struggle, fought for at the cost of many lives, because she doesn't "believe" in vaccination.

WHEN FEAR MAKES SENSE

We have beaten smallpox and polio, but bubonic plague and cholera are still out there. Worldwide each year, 17 million people die from infectious disease. The breakdown is staggering in its breadth: 4.4 million succumb to pneumonia and other respiratory diseases; 3.1 million to diarrheal illnesses such as cholera, typhoid, and dysentery; 3.1 million to tuberculosis; 2.1 million to malaria; 1.1 million to hepatitis B; 1 million to AIDS; and 135,000 to intestinal worms. While wealthy, spoiled naysayers warn mothers not to vaccinate their children, more than 1 million children annually lose their lives to measles. Another 46,000 die from neonatal tetanus (the *T* in the DPT shot); whooping cough kills 350,000 children (the *P* in the DPT shot).

Even when they do not kill, infections wreak wholesale havoc. Tropical diseases—from malaria to river blindness to leprosy to elephantiasis—currently infect 500 *million* of the earth's inhabitants. The Western world doesn't worry much about these diseases. It will beat them the same way it beat the others—by applying logic and science and rejecting hysteria and ignorance. All our impressive advances aside, though, it is no time to let down our guard. Look at how science continues to struggle with AIDS.

Where are the germs most likely to nail us? They can be anywhere. Researchers at Georgetown found between 1 and 4 germs per page on books, although these germs were not particularly virulent. Airplane headsets carry 60 germs per unit before you put them on. After an hour of wear, there are about 650. Best not to talk about pay phones. Testing done in one parish uncovered a variety of pathogenic bacteria on half the communion cups shared during mass. Federal inspectors looked at 2,461 shared cosmetics (lipsticks, blushers, and eye shadow) in department stores and found that 5 percent had high amounts—

10,000 germs per gram—of bacteria. One mascara sample contained a nasty bug called *Pseudomonas*, capable of causing a blinding corneal disease. Studies of germs on paper money consistently find bacteria. Among medical personnel, stethoscopes, pens, bow ties and regular neckties, tongue depressors, lab coats, and otoscopes are loaded with germs of various ilk, and hospital carpeting is another source.

Not enough? Scientists have found 14 million germs on the body of a single cockroach. One of its turds carries 7 million germs. An Israeli study of flies and diarrhea found that just controlling the number of flies in hospitals led to far fewer cases of gastrointestinal illness.

I must be blunt—the source for many diseases, including cholera, hepatitis, and *E. coli* infection, is someone's large bowel. These diseases are spread by linking up our digestive systems and our mouths or, to be accurate, another person's digestive system and our mouth. Breaking that connection has driven much of public health for more than a century. It is an ongoing battle.

One intrepid researcher at the University of Arizona, Charles Gerba, has made a name for himself by going where others dare not tread: the bathroom. He claims that, aside from coughing and sneezing, germs are most commonly spread in the mist of the toilet flush. His studies find that with each flush of the toilet an invisible mist belches from the commode and covers the bathroom, including your toothbrush.

Isn't there a low-tech solution here? Can't you just shut the lid? Dr. Gerba says no. Closed, the inside of the lid gets covered, and when you then open it, you create a slight vacuum that creates a minicloud. Gerba has found that the cleanest toilets are in your home, libraries, and hospitals. I'll bet you can guess the worst: gas stations. By the way, the middle stalls are the most contaminated, while the stall closest to the door is used the least (and, not incidentally, likely to have more toilet paper). Also, when picking your next hotel, note that bathrooms in cheap hotels had more germs than in pricier locales.

Funny thing, toilets. We need them; we dread them. The vast majority of women in one survey admitted that they hover like helicopters over public restroom seats and never sit down. Ironically, this is bad for your health, ladies. The bladder cannot empty completely when you squat rather than sit, increasing the risk of bladder infections. You're better off having a seat.

Don't forget that people are covered with germs. To do us any damage, these germs must be in high enough numbers and able to enter our bodies at the right place and time. People, surrounded by disease-causing armies, are constantly invaded and constantly fighting off infections. A healthy immune system does its job to keep you from getting sick. If not, you would be ill most of the time.

YOUR AMAZING IMMUNE SYSTEM

It's your primary defense against germs.

It's an extraordinarily complex armada of cells, some of which produce antibodies, while others engulf and kill microorganisms. The antibodies are molecular assassins that disable and kill germs. But it is naive to assume that it is healthy simply to turn on or boost the entire immune system, as so many new supplements and herbal concoctions claim to do.

Many parts of the immune system function by suppressing other components of the same system in a complex network of checks and balances. If you could actually supercharge the immune system, you would wind up with autoimmune diseases such as arthritis and lupus—conditions where an overly aggressive immune system attacks the body itself. You don't want an across-the-board acceleration of immune function.

Another way the immune system can overreact is when antibodies, designed to attack germs, mistakenly take on healthy tissue as well. A child with strep throat can develop rheumatic heart disease and arthritis because the antibodies specifically designed to kill the streptococcus germ also attack tissues of the heart and joints. Autoimmune diseases may be rooted in this type of antibody misfire.

A healthy immune system usually accompanies a healthy person, but some of the relationships are paradoxical. For instance, stress can cause an increase in germ-fighting antibodies, at least in the short term.

Then there are unique situations where germs do not turn on the immune system at all but rather suppress its actions, as in HIV. Allergic diseases are also manifestations of an overactive immune system. The point is that it's not as simple as the marketers would have you think to boost your immune system as a route to good health.

KNOW YOUR ENEMY

Before you can know which germs really pose a threat and how best to fight them, you need to know the differences among them. For all germs are not alike.

The little beasties appear in three guises. First, the bacteria. These are simple single-cell creatures. Their shapes vary—round, spiral, or rodlike. They divide and divide and divide, and stick to surfaces in a variety of ways. These traits enable them to infect many parts of our bodies, from lungs (where they can cause pneumonia) to bladders (where they can cause urinary tract infections) to cuts and wounds.

Second is the basic fungus, a complex of cells either strung together in a chain or gathered in a group. Unable to move easily, they need to hitch a ride to travel around your body. A yeast, for example, is a single fungus cell.

Finally, the virus. This germ has no sex life and cannot live without us. It is not a real cell and is infinitesimally smaller than a single bacterium. A virus has the remarkable ability to invade one of your cells and rewire the cell's genetic blueprint, or DNA, into a virus factory. That infected cell is converted into a viral assembly line, stamping out identical copies of the virus. Neat trick. In a lab, you can grow bacteria in a petri dish by sticking a few of them on food or other nourishment. No can do with a virus. It takes living matter, such as cells in culture, eggs, protozoa, or parasites.

How do these little guys get you? They come from many directions.

The infections most likely to hit you *and* make you miserable are colds, flu, and food-borne illness (and the latter's cousins, various diseases spread via that unsavory fecal-oral route). Learning to do what you can to prevent their onset will give you more time to be merry and less time to waste on germ anxiety.

COLD COMFORT

Best to start with the common cold, precisely because it so common. Colds are relatively easy to diagnose, although allergies can mimic their symptoms (hint: allergies may make eyes itchy and red; colds do not). Although colds are viral in nature, I know of one nonviral organism whose symptoms masquerade as a cold. *Mycoplasma pneumoniae* is a bacterialike organism that, according to the Centers for Disease

Control, breaks out every four to seven years. It triggers a coldlike syndrome, with hacking cough and sore throat but an uncoldlike headache. The bad news is that it can cause pneumonia. The good news is that, unlike the cold, it can be treated with antibiotics.

Really the most confusing thing about colds is the name. My mom still warns me to bundle up or "you'll get a cold." My dozen years of medical training will not dissuade her. "Don't tell me," she snaps. "I'm old and know more than you do. Virus schmirus, button your coat." I gave up arguing years ago. I can still feel that washcloth. . . .

Fortunately, she didn't write this book. Most Americans, 62 percent to be exact, still buy this weather thing, and with good reason because you *do* get more colds in the winter. But that does not mean they—or my mom—are right. Scientists think colds actually are more frequent in winter because people spend more time indoors. When researchers discovered that the cold virus could live on your hands for four hours, they figured that was the primary way colds spread. This is what most people tell you today. Read on.

In experiments on weather and colds after World War II, subjects stood naked or fully clothed outdoors in brisk weather for two to four hours and were then exposed to a cold virus. The results were the same in both groups: one-third got colds. Adios, Mom, so much for your insistence that that the cold weather "lowered my resistance."

The history of cold research has been long, fascinating, and full of scientific mystery. Before World War II, science thought it understood the common cold, although the virus had not yet been isolated. "Coughs and sneezes spread diseases," warned British wartime public-health posters. "Stop the germs by using your handkerchief." Medical textbooks taught that colds are spread by talking, coughing, and sneezing.

That airborne thinking started to erode with more study. The greatest cold research institute at the time was the Common Cold Unit at Salisbury, England. Thinking colds were spread by touch, scientists there inserted fluorescent fluid in the noses of volunteers and watched it spread quickly, first to the hands and then to everything these people touched. Children with fresh and juicy colds were invited into the lab to play card games with volunteers, who quickly got colds. However, after the kids left the lab, a new set of volunteers used the same cards and did not contract colds. Did hands transmit the cold or not? Apparently not.

Another experiment positioned children with colds at one end of a hut separated from volunteers by a blanket as a fan circulated air throughout the building. The volunteers got colds. Spraying a mist of virus in the faces of volunteers transmitted the colds. The touch-transmission theory was now on the ropes. But it had not gone down for the count.

New studies showed the virus on the hands of cold sufferers and everything they touched. It had been assumed that the virus died quickly once it got as far as the hands, but in fact it survived well. The touch theory then got a bigger boost when researchers placed hidden cameras to observe respectable churchgoers in a Sunday school class and supposedly hygienic medical students during a class lecture. The subjects were seen frequently picking their noses and rubbing their eyes. From their hands, went the theory, to others. Still, nobody was seen picking their neighbor's nose, so touching others as the cause and colds as the effect had still not been proved absolutely.

It took a poker game to nail this one.

In 1987 scientists at the University of Wisconsin gathered thirty male student volunteers susceptible to a particular cold virus. Some were given colds in the lab, then put around the card table in a small room with uninfected subjects. First, though, the uninfected players were divided into two groups. One group was fitted with either a three-foot-wide, flat, plastic neck collar or an arm splint to prevent them from touching their faces. The second group were free to touch their faces. Everyone played cards through the night.

The cards got sticky and gooey with mucus. If hands are the primary transmitter of colds, then this would be a slam dunk: The poker players unable to touch their faces would get no colds and the unrestrained players would fall like flies. Yet the same percentage—roughly two-thirds—of *both* groups got colds. And back we went to the future.

It seemed again that airborne transmission was the real culprit—coughs and sneezes, not touch. The same mucus-tainted cards and chips were then passed to another group of totally unrestrained players, who played the night away. None of them caught cold. Transmission by hand is just not that efficient. Please don't quit washing your hands (more on that shortly). But short of wearing masks in cold season, as people do in some countries, your only recourse is to avoid breathing. I don't recommend that either.

There was a final blow still to come for the touch-transmission theory. Volunteers infected with colds were put at one end of a hut, healthy subjects at the other. They were prevented from physical contact by a wire mesh barrier. Fans kept the air moving. That's right, the colds easily spread from one group to the other. Sneezing or blowing the nose produces droplets of just the right size to imbed in the nose. So the final word, it seems, is that although touch is capable of transmitting the cold virus in certain circumstances, air droplets may be the most efficient way to spread this most common of our infectious diseases.

It *is* true that we have more colds in winter, but not because we don't bundle up outdoors. More time spent inside means more contact with other people's sneezes and cold-carrying hands. Also, going in and out-of-doors in the winter creates condensation in our noses. This wetter environment makes a more hospitable place for survival for the virus that lands there.

One additional item: There are five hundred or so cold viruses that we know of. When you catch one, you become immune to it forever. Each new cold you get is from a different virus. This may be one reason that older people get fewer colds. They've become immune to larger number of viruses over the course of a lifetime. Parents of small children will get more colds as their children bring home more viruses.

THE ITALIANS CAN KEEP THE WORD *AND* THE VIRUS

Funny word, *influenza*. We stole it from the Italians—it means "influence"—because early observers thought this ubiquitous disease was somehow influenced by the stars. The flu is so confusing that three times the number of people who actually have the flu think that they do. Its symptoms are fever, chills, cough, headache, and muscle ache. Yet one survey found that nearly half of those questioned thought the list included nausea, vomiting, and diarrhea. Flu causes none of those three. There is no such thing as the stomach flu. If your stomach is upset, you do not have the flu.

Mild cases of food-borne illnesses are often mistaken for the flu. That's not to imply that flu should be dismissed. In an average year, the flu kills between ten thousand and thirty thousand Americans. Those in contact with many people are more likely to catch the flu. Among employed individuals, 36 percent reported the flu in 1997, compared with 23 percent of the unemployed. The story is similar in households of five or more individuals. Residents of metropolitan areas run a greater risk than those living in rural environments, as do those living in homes with children under age twelve. Curiously, only 17 percent of seniors reported the flu the season of the survey, the lowest rate of all surveyed. As with colds, seniors have greater immunity to more viral strains because they have been around more flu over the years. But it is also the age group most vulnerable to death by flu.

Many of us dismiss the flu as little more than a few days of inconvenience, a reason—albeit a miserable one—to stay at home and watch *I Love Lucy* reruns. For a little perspective, you might ask elderly relatives if they remember the Spanish flu of 1918.

It began as a minor outbreak in Fort Funston, Kansas. Within a month it had spread to Europe, carried by American soldiers off to the final battles of World War I. Along the way, the virus mutated. By the time the scourge had passed, it had taken 675,000 American lives, more than the combined total lost in both world wars and the wars in Korea and Vietnam. Around the world, twenty million people succumbed. It was truly horrifying.

Eight decades later, researchers still struggle to understand the genetics of this virus. The name, Spanish flu, is a misnomer. Like most flu, it most likely originated in Asia. The flu virus begins with birds, especially ducks. The ducks hang around pigs, which are even more prone to the illness. In China the proximity of ducks and pigs allows various viruses to infect cells in both species. Human flu virus and duck flu virus live in the throats of pigs. They pass their genes back and forth, constantly reshuffling DNA, until new strains emerge, which then infect nearby human populations. An epidemic is born. New and unique strains are bred every generation or so.

Flu virus is extraordinarily tenacious. One study found that a virus survived between twenty-four and forty-eight hours on hard, nonporous surfaces, including stainless steel and plastic. Cloth, paper, and tissues were less hospitable, although the bug still lasted eight to twelve hours. The little menace could jump from steel to human hands for twenty-four hours but only for fifteen minutes from tissues. The virus survived on hands up to five minutes after being transferred from some of these surfaces.

How can you prevent flu infection? The best methods are to avoid touching your face and to wash your hands frequently. There are no guarantees, obviously, particularly because you can't know when the virus is lurking about. But you will be surprised at how effective that two-pronged strategy can be.

WHAT'S MY SNIFFLE?

When is a cold not the flu? When is the flu not a cold?

Colds cause sneezing. Flu does not. Flu causes fever, malaise, and headaches. Colds do not. There are no definitive diagnostic differences other than fever and sometimes sneezing. The aches and pains, the feverish chill, and plain old feeling worse should make the diagnosis. But beware, many other infectious diseases begin with identical symptoms. Just one example—the initial infection of HIV (human immunodeficiency virus) often produces flulike symptoms. Still, when you do get these symptoms, it's more likely to be a flu than anything else.

But just so you won't say I didn't try to help you figure it out, here is a handy reference chart.

SYMPTOMS	COLD	FLU
Fever	No	Yes
Sore Throat	Yes	Yes
Muscle Ache	Yes	Yes (especially legs and back)
Headache	Mild or no	Yes
Malaise	Mild or no	Yes
Cough	Yes, hacking	Yes, with sputum
Runny Nose	Yes	Yes
Sneezing	Yes	No

FOOD DOESN'T ALWAYS NOURISH

Sooner or later, diseases from food will strike most people. Most of the time doctors do not routinely react to your diarrheal illness by ordering cultures and looking for specific germs. It's expensive and time-consuming. Besides, most gastrointestinal illnesses go away by themselves. These illnesses are often food-borne but get written off as "stomach flu." Studies between 1948 and 1971 showed roughly one food-borne stomach illness per person each year. Since then, that rate has risen to 1.4 illnesses per person per year and still higher in some parts of the country. The real rate is certainly higher because the vast majority of food-borne illness goes unreported.

One reason you are getting these stomach bugs is that increasing quantities of our food come from foreign countries, where agriculture and food-handling standards are different. Call it the revenge of the global economy. As we ask people to eat more fruit and vegetables, we must expand our imports from abroad. More than one-third of all cantaloupes, three-quarters of green onions, and nearly all cucumbers grown in Mexico are sold in the United States. During some seasons, 70 percent of the produce in your local grocery store came from south of the border. You no longer have to travel to get traveler's diarrhea; It's traveling to you. Our growing affection for gourmet undercooked delicacies only makes us more vulnerable.

To what degree are chicken, eggs, and other foods contaminated? In a word: very. The most serious and persistent food-borne illness is salmonellosis, which sickens between two and four million Americans every year and kills two thousand of us. The bacteria come from chickens' intestines and are difficult to control. More than half the raw chickens in the United States become contaminated during slaughter. Cooking kills it easily, but that's not enough to stop you from getting it.

Another salmonellalike germ that may be new to you is *Campylobacter,* which infects two million people each year and kills a thousand of its victims. Half of these cases are due to chicken. Consumers Union found this germ in 63 percent of the chickens it tested. In addition, nearly 2.5 million eggs sold each year are contaminated with salmonella. That may sound like a lot, but given that Americans consume 47 billion eggs a year, it actually works out to 1 contaminated egg in every 20,000. That's not as worrisome as the rate of infection among their clucking mothers. You will not eat twenty thousand eggs in your lifetime.

As always, some germs are worse than others. *Escherichia coli,* a bacterium, lives happily in everyone's intestines and causes no trouble.

Your healthy colon is inhabited normally by trillions of them, and they account for one-third of stool weight. Their presence just means fecal contamination. Traveler's diarrhea is the result of exposure to a strain of E. coli that your body is not accustomed to—it doesn't bother residents of the host area. There are, however, many subtypes that aren't so benign. The worst is E. coli 0157:H7, which can be fatal in a high percentage of cases. Closely associated with cattle intestines, the germ spreads fecally to beef during processing and to other foods, such as raw milk, apple cider, salami, lettuce, and all produce fertilized with manure, including potatoes, radishes, and alfalfa sprouts. It even shows up in yogurt, sandwiches, and water. In many cases we are not exactly sure how it gets there. It can survive acid conditions and, worst of all, can infect you with a dose of less than ten organisms. By comparison, it takes hundreds of other food-borne germs to do their nasty work. As with salmonella, thorough cooking kills these germs.

Indigenous cultures have long had their own ways of dealing with these germs. Conventional thinking held that the use of spices was developed to mask the flavor of spoiled food. Paul Sherman, a behavioral ecologist at Cornell University, believes that spices were adopted, in fact, not for flavor but to suppress and kill germs. Germs grow better in hot climates, precisely where people tend to eat spicier food. Sherman and a student developed their theory after reviewing ninety-three cookbooks of traditional recipes from around the world.

Really want to help prevent disease in your life? Try shutting your mouth. After all, it *is* the dirtiest place on your body. The most common chronic infection among our species is gum disease. Far be it from me to threaten the bond between mother and child, but the germs that cause periodontal disease may at first come from your mother. There seems to be a critical period when Mom, while cooing and kissing her baby, transfers these critters. Fortunately, with proper oral hygiene they can be kept at bay.

As you know, our oropharynx—or mouth and nose—is capable of spreading the most common and stubborn of human infections, the common cold and the flu. Now perhaps you can understand why the human bite may be the worst animal bite of all. Any human bite that breaks the skin should be respected, cleaned scrupulously and ideally seen by a physician. A common infection method is the "clenched fist injury"—either on purpose or by accident, your fist slams into someone's tooth. Doctors studied forty-two such hand wounds. Among the patients, thirteen waited at least two days to see a doctor. Of those, ten experienced either lengthy hospitalization or permanently disabled hands. Only three recovered to the point of full range of motion or at least painless motion. The rest sought treatment within twenty-four hours—usually including heavy antibiotics—and all recovered the full range of pain-free motion.

There are other kinds of bites. One medical review of five cases of human bites to the penis uncovered the possibility of major abscess and gangrenous progressive infections. "Victims of human bites to the penis often do not seek timely medical attention, and dangerous progression of infection may ensue," warned urologists at the University of California at San Francisco.

You may take a break and go brush now.

PROTECT THAT SEX

I find it strange that in an era of germaphobia, we tend to ignore an entire class of bug that can easily strike us: sexually transmitted diseases. Possibly one-half of the American adult population has been infected with one of these many illnesses, yet many don't know it. The irony is that almost nothing is easier to prevent. Right now, there is only one reliable device: the condom.

The condom is weighted with so much baggage that it almost breaks under the pressure. It's not considered sexy. Its users don't really want to talk about it (if people have trouble talking about sex, they don't exactly jump at the chance to discuss the little rubber thing). Men will hurriedly turn their backs and fumble with these less-than-user-friendly packages. If you use your imagination, you can make them sexy and part of the fun for both of you (sorry, we're mainly talking the guy here; female condoms are not widely available yet).

A quick primer:

While latex is the standard material, polyurethane condoms are now on the market and promise more sensitivity. Most condoms don't come with instructions, and surveys find that most men use them inappropriately and make common errors, like not using them soon enough, unrolling them backward, or unrolling them before putting them on. When you finally get it right, make sure to squeeze out the air bubble at the tip. Also, consider a small amount of lubricant on the inside at the end to increase sensation. And make sure to hang on with your hands when withdrawing to prevent the condom from slipping off.

Oral sex is one sexual act in which people may inadvertently spread STDs because condoms are not commonly used. The most common STD, chlamydia, has been found in the mouths of one in thirty hetero-sexual men and women. Oral sex has also been implicated in the transmission of gonorrhea and syphilis, among others. Yeast infec-tions in women have been linked to oral sex with men who have the yeast organism in their mouths. The National Cancer Institute recently published the finding that while oral cancer is mostly linked to cigarette smoking, the more sex partners smokers have, the more likely they are to develop such malignancies. The offending organism here is the human papilloma virus (HPV), an STD that infects more than one in ten Americans. Sexual health professionals are still unsure how to treat and deal with this growing new problem.

In the end, the best advice is to know your sexual partner. Also, take latex out of the closet, and you'll both have more fun keeping those germs out of your bed.

LIGHTEN UP ALREADY

I'm trying to guide you through the germs and diseases of which you should be most aware. There are loads of others—they fill libraries— many of which show up in our world but are unlikely to show up in your life. They are scary sounding, new and exotic and when they appear, and the media runs wild. Legionnaire's disease, Hantavirus, Lyme disease, flesh-eating strep, toxoplasmosis, Giardia. It's not impossible to arm yourself against these diseases and others, but in most cases they are outside your control. Once you start trying to pre-pare for all eventualities, you can drive yourself nuts. And we don't want that, do we? But I will throw out a couple of items for those of you who prefer paranoia to common sense.

Being careful and wearing appropriate clothes and footwear may protect you from the tick that could give you Lyme disease. One expert suggests a better way—if you are willing. Henry Feder, a physician from the University of Connecticut Health Center, accepted an offer from a nudist colony to conduct a summer seminar on Lyme disease. He found three hundred nudists and, remarkably, not one with a single tick bite or Lyme disease. His conclusion: The best protection is no protection. You're better off walking around nude. Ticks like to sneak under your clothes. They don't like the exposure on a nude body.

If you prefer to be in the buff in the privacy of your own Jacuzzi-outfitted hotel room, think about this before dipping in a toe. Lurking in the pipes of the whirlpool jets are remnants of intestinal contents of the couple who rented the room yesterday. These tubs are constructed so that the residual water in the pipes cannot be flushed or cleaned by anyone but a professional who specializes in whirlpool tubs. It is unlikely that the hotel or resort takes that kind of step between guests.

Remember when ulcers came from stress? From sources like your fire-breathing boss, or your fire-breathing mother-in-law, or your fire-breathing kids? Well, it was none of the above. Ulcers are triggered by *Helicobacter pylori*, a bacterium that many people carry and never know about it. Unfortunately, we don't know how it spreads. It might be through kissing. The bacteria has been found on chopsticks and houseflies and in the mouth. It is common in families and can spread by hand to mouth. It may also cause allergies, halitosis, and who knows what else. Ulcer surgery is much less common these days because it makes no real sense for treating an infection. Heavy antibiotics and acid-suppressing drugs do the trick.

THE SOURCE OF MOST EVIL

What is the dirtiest place in your house? (Hint: Don't bother looking under the kids' beds.)

It's your kitchen, by far. The drain of the sink, believe it or not, is worse than the rim of the toilet—even for fecal coliforms like *E. coli*, which by definition come from the colon. The ultimate source is raw meat, poultry, and other foodstuffs that are contaminated before they make their way to your kitchen. In fact, *E. coli* is rarely found around the toilet but is plentiful in the kitchen, scattered on sponges, dishtowels, counters, and ground zero, the drain. Remember Charles Gerba from the University of Arizona? Evidently he lost his interest in toilets—after all, how much of *that* research could anyone stomach?—and turned to sinks and sponges. He studied one hundred homes in each of five cities: New York, Los Angeles, Boston, Miami, and

Chicago. He found pathogenic germs in 70 percent of them, and salmonella and staphylococcus in 20 percent.

It gets worse. One drop of water from a dishcloth carries a million times more germs than surfaces in a bathroom. If the kitchen sponge stays moist, as they usually do, the number of living germs will not decrease for two weeks. Even while the sponge is drying out, germs can survive for two days until it does. How many are we talking? A milliliter of liquid squeezed from chef's little helper can harbor a million germs.

Don't walk out of that kitchen yet. Ever thought about your cutting board? Is it plastic or wood, and why? Most people who think about it assume plastic is cleaner, figuring that germs can't cling as easily to plastic as they can to wood. Wrong, I'm afraid. They may not have brains, but germs adapt by forming biofilms that help them stick to all the nooks and crannies on the plastic. Put that board under a microscope and you'll find invisible cities nestled in what look like thousands of Grand Canyons. Wood is more porous and may absorb germs deeper into the surface and somehow kill them. Researchers at the University of Wisconsin watched germs on both types of boards. After three minutes, the germs on wood had died. The germs on the plastic were alive and thriving—they actually grew overnight. Microwaves will further sterilize a wooden board, especially when it is wet. It doesn't work on plastic because microwaves don't raise the temperature of plastic. For that, you need a hot dishwasher.

DR. DEAN'S OLD-FASHIONED, SCIENTIFICALLY SOUND GUIDE TO NONPARANOID SENSIBLE RESPONSES, TREATMENTS, AND CURES

We know those germs are always out there, waiting in the wings to infect you with the flu or a cold or strike at your tummy. There *are* some sensible responses when the germs get you down, or even before they strike. There are things you should not do, too, so let's consider them.

You have a cold? Poor baby. Do us both a favor and don't go to the doctor. You may not want to hear that, but I must say what should be obvious. (Have you figured out that much of the time, that's what I do for a living?) Despite the presence of almost a thousand over-the-counter remedies for the symptoms that accompany a common cold, we still do not have a cure. I don't care how much you trust your doctor, even if he looks and sounds just like Dr. Welby. He, or she, can't do anything for you that you can't do for yourself, which is basically to bundle up and wait it out.

This leads us to one of the more embarrassing examples of the overzealous application of modern medical technology. Researchers at the University of Kentucky found that 60 percent of patients with a condition diagnosed as a cold by their physician filled a prescription for antibiotics. While the prescriptions were mostly for amoxicillin, eighteen other antibiotics were used. Adults were more likely to get a prescription than kids; urban physicians were more likely than rural doctors to prescribe them. Americans spend nearly thirty-eight million dollars a year treating their colds with antibiotics.

This is preposterous and so contrary to rational medicine that it requires more careful examination. Colds are caused by viruses. Antibiotics are effective only against bacteria. They do nothing—*nothing*—against viruses. That doesn't mean doctors are giving out a harmless placebo. There is a real danger in using antibiotics where not indicated. They only kill the germs susceptible to that particular antibiotic. The rest survive and take over. They learn to eat that antibiotic for dinner. In other words, they become antibiotic-resistant. In the end you lose, because the next infection you get may no longer respond to the antibiotic. So you may stay sick or get sicker, when you otherwise could have been cured. Your antibiotic-swilling neighbor also contributes to the growing population of antibiotic-resistant germs around us.

There is no controversy or doubt about this. Why, then, do doctors whip out those pads and send you scurrying to the drugstore? Occasionally, from misinformation. Some doctors genuinely believe that antibiotics will reduce the chance of a bacterial infection moving in secondarily. There actually is some evidence that one out of five cold patients also has bacteria in his or her nasal secretions. If treated with antibiotics, the patient might improve more rapidly. The problem, though, is that it takes days to get a culture back from the lab, and by then you are better anyway. Ultimately it is inappropriate to prescribe antibiotics to all comers on the chance that this scenario fits some of them.

Other doctors may misinterpret symptoms, such as colored mucus, and diagnose an already incipient bacterial problem. One study found that doctors assigned great importance to the color of mucus, even though there is no real association between the type or severity of infection and the color of the mucus.

The main reason your doctor gives you antibiotics is that you expect them. The public still sees them as miracle drugs. Doctors figure that if they don't fulfill that expectation, you will feel ripped off. They interpret certain of your signals as a desire for antibiotics. For example, asking for "something to help" will lead to a prescription. A physician's assistant, in a piece for the *Journal of the American Medical Association*, put it nicely:

The problem is quite simple. Patients expect to receive antibiotics for colds, upper respiratory-tract infections, and bronchitis. Health care professionals give the patients what they want because of their increased clinical workload, rather than take the time to explain why antibiotics are not needed. Managed care organizations contribute to the abuse by competing for business and by encouraging practitioners to make patients happy so they will not switch insurance companies. Fear of complaints also influences this practice. Patients are happier when they are given the antibiotic prescription that they expect—telling some patients they have a viral infection and antibiotic treatment is not indicated makes them angry.

So applaud rather than knock your physician when he or she does not prescribe antibiotics for your cold. And for goodness sake, don't beg for them.

Antibiotics are coming under scrutiny even as a routine treatment of sore throats, a condition for which they are no longer automatically recommended. That makes sense to me, because sore throats are mostly viral. Some researchers are even considering that antibiotics may not always be the best treatment for strep throat. Treating every strep throat with antibiotics decreases the body's ability to develop resistance and makes people more vulnerable to reoccurrences. Bronchitis, sinusitis, and infections of the bladder and ear do not automatically warrant antibiotics anymore either.

Is there anything else to be done? Interferon excited us for a while because it seemed to end colds more quickly, but it irritates nasal membranes. Inhaled steam was thought to work but eventually failed the test too. Remember Linus Pauling and the vitamin C craze? After twenty-one placebo-controlled studies at dosages of 1,000 milligrams or more, the evidence still is not consistent. It does seem reasonable to believe that vitamin C may reduce the severity and duration of cold symptoms by 20 percent, although it does not prevent the cold itself. At the very least, it will not hurt you, and a lot of people still believe in it. A little placebo is not a bad thing.

Could the cure reside in zinc? It came on like gangbusters, but questions remain. For instance, how does sucking on a lozenge affect a virus in your nose? Snorting zinc would make more sense. It's tough to conduct controlled tests for a simple reason. Zinc has a distinctive, often terrible, taste, so subjects can distinguish between the placebo and the real thing. In addition, a recent study, conducted on children and paid for by a zinc-remedy manufacturer, found no benefit for kids.

Echinacea is popular among the alternative medicine set. Sorry, but again the results are incomplete, inconsistent, and unimpressive. As I told you in Chapter 5, the most recent controlled experiment found it ineffective in preventing colds. Hot echinacea tea may feel good because of the tea's heat. The herb is being peddled as a cold preventive, and there is some suggestion that it can boost the immune system. But as you now know, boosting the immune system is the last thing you want if you have arthritis or other autoimmune diseases, because these diseases stem from an immune system on overdrive.

Basically, you are left with over-the-counter medications. Experiment until you find the kind that seem to work best for you. But be aware that decongestants and antihistamines that dry secretions can do their job too well, leading to thicker mucus, dry, irritated membranes, and cough. Personally I prefer an assault on the stuffy nose, which I find to be the worst aspect of a cold. I use judicious amounts of nasal spray, two or three times a day tops, for only a couple of days. Otherwise you wind up with a stuffier nose than you had at the start. Spray tackles the problem directly, where pills affect your whole body and can cause unwanted changes in throat and pharyngeal tissues.

If you follow me into spray country, though, I have two warnings: First, follow directions and do not use more than the recommended usage. Second, spray and withdraw the nozzle, then release the pressure. Otherwise the bottle will suction cold virus from your nose right back into the bottle, where it can survive up to fifty days. You can also look for a metered pump-delivery system.

Other cold-fighting tips: Don't get dehydrated (that thickens the mucus); to avoid it, drink fluids, then drink more fluids, and follow that by drinking more fluids. Hot, dry, indoor heated air makes your cold worse by thickening mucus and irritating your nasal membranes. Humidity is better. And lastly, chicken soup is good for you. There really was a study that found mucus clearance rates were improved by this magical elixir. "It vouldn't hoit," and if you're Jewish, it might guarantee you a spot in heaven. Or at least eternity next to my grandmother. You could do worse. She was a nice lady.

It would be lovely to find a way to avoid the whole damned mess. But lest you think that hiding in your bedroom all winter is the way to go, consider this: Researchers found that the more diverse social contact you have, the fewer the colds. Susceptibility increased, by the way, among those who smoked, slept poorly, did not drink alcohol, had low vitamin C levels in their diet, and were introverted. All this may seem to fly in the face of the more-contacts, more-colds theory. Actually, it raises the important issue of resistance and stress.

Previous research found that psychological stress can increase your risk of a cold. A large family or many friends can help with stress, but this research found that a diverse network was better. If your only defense against stress at work is to be trapped by a large family, you may not do as well as someone who has a diverse social support network that includes not only relatives but also friends, neighbors, co-workers, and folks from religious and recreational organizations. Sometimes a large family can make life more stressful. It's also possible that more exposure to different people and their germs eventually toughens up your immune system.

Other than hibernating, the most effective actions you can take to avoid colds are to wash your hands frequently, avoid touching your face, and steer clear—politely, of course—of sneezers and coughers.

SHOO FLU, DON'T BOTHER ME

Many of you take vitamins and eat organic food to prevent illnesses like the flu. But you do not take advantage of the most effective preventive out there—the flu shot, which can reduce your chances of catching that bug by 70 percent. Of course, if everyone did avail themselves of the opportunity, there wouldn't be enough to go around. It's supposed to be reserved for the elderly and those with preexisting conditions, including heart and lung disease and immune dysfunctions, that leave their victims at higher risk of being killed by the flu.

Producing the vaccine is a bit of a trick. Long before the winter flu season, experts must juggle predictions and guesses as to which particular strains of flu are going to be next year's monsters. It's a crucial art because they take those strains and put them into the vaccine. Sometimes they hit it on the head and sometimes they miss. But it's still your best opportunity to minimize the effect of this disease.

Some strains of this virus are particularly nasty. While the media gets us stirred up about wild, exotic, and especially rare infectious diseases, you should always keep track of the prevailing flu. Actually, flu can finally be treated by a doctor with a new generation of drugs that must be taken at the first sign of symptoms. But for some reason, this very safe class of drugs has not caught on in the United States. Most Americans don't even know that we now have antiviral compounds for flu virus just as we have antibiotics for bacteria. You should talk your doctor into a prescription before you need it so that it will be handy in your medicine cabinet when you first detect symptoms. These drugs—amantadine or flumadine—must be taken at first sign of flu, so you need to know those symptoms. There is a potential downside here. While drugs such as rimantadine can prevent the flu or shorten its symptoms, the person you pass the virus to will most likely receive a virus that is resistant to this drug. First one to the medicine cabinet wins.

As for herbs, there really may be some help on the way. Elderberry extract, to be specific. In a double-blind, placebo-controlled study in Israel, a proprietary extract of elderberry (*Sambucus nigra*) improved flu symptoms and speeded time to cure faster than placebo. I have not seen other studies on this, but it would be a positive development if future research did confirm the Israeli finding.

You want an effective treatment for food-borne illness? Don't get it. Gerba, the Arizona kitchen-and-toilet king, believes that 90 percent of food-borne illnesses from your home could be prevented just by incorporating two key functions into your work: Wash your hands after handling meat, and use paper towels to clean up, throwing them out immediately after you are done. I always yelled at my kids for using half a roll to clean up a spilled drop of milk. I've since shut up. As for those germ-ridden sponges, you can sterilize them by popping a dry cellulose sponge in the microwave for thirty seconds, or sixty seconds when wet. Take that cotton dishrag and nuke it for thirty seconds if dry and three minutes if wet. Better still, buy a bag of new ones and launder them often.

I've reviewed, oh, some four trillion lists of safe food-handling tips. I think this one, ten simple food preparation rules from the World Health Organization, is among the best and most reliable.

1. Choose foods that are processed for safety. While some foods, like fruits and veggies, are fine raw, others are not. As we learned a century ago, you should not drink raw, unpasteurized milk (leave it for the health nuts). Poultry treated with ionizing radiation is best, though we seem illogically to worry more about the radiation than we worry about the salmonella. Consider yourself warned.

2. Cook poultry, meat, and fish thoroughly. Learn what thoroughly cooked looks like, and when in doubt, put it back in the oven. Overcooked is better than undercooked. I know raw foods are in at the moment, but gastrointestinal diseases are *always* in.

3. Eat food immediately. As soon as food cools, the germs grow.

4. Store cooked foods properly in a refrigerator that's chilled to at least to 40 degrees Fahrenheit.

5. Reheat cooked foods thoroughly. Germs form during storage, so heat those babies to 158 degrees Fahrenheit.

6. Avoid contact between raw and cooked food, a common error. Do not use the knife you just used to cut raw chicken for other food. Especially do not use the same cutting board without cleaning it first.

7. Wash hands repeatedly. Then wash them again.

8. Keep kitchen surfaces clean, and I do mean clean.

9. Protect foods from insects, rodents, and pets. Need I tell you why?

10. Use bottled water if you have reason to doubt the purity of what comes out of your tap.

Take another look at point 7. It has come up frequently in this chapter, no? There is a reason for that, and it's not just that I don't know how to edit myself. The one universal and most important preventive in the spread of infectious disease is . . . washing your hands. That makes it worthy of some extra attention.

Any parent knows how hard it is to get kids to keep those paws clean. Researchers divided 305 school-age kids into groups. Some of them washed their hands four times a day, the rest did their usual thing. The hand-washing group missed 23 percent fewer days due to infectious diseases. That broke down to 24 percent fewer missed days from respiratory illnesses and 51 percent fewer days from gastro-intestinal problems. Very impressive, just from hand-washing.

How about you? Do you wash? Of course you do—if somebody else is watching. So say studies done in public restrooms. In a recent report, 95 percent of those surveyed said they always wash their hands in the bathroom. In fact, 68 percent *really* did. Women, at 74 percent, were much better than men, at 61 percent. My problem with this study is that in most situations, the people knew there were other folks in the restroom. Sometimes the researchers sat in stalls, but just as often they stood at the mirror and pretended to comb their hair.

In another report, researchers tried it both ways, making their presence known in some cases and disappearing in others (they hid in the stalls, lifting their feet so the subject thought she was really alone in the bathroom). Thus busts the myth of Ms. Clean. When they knew they had company, 90 percent of the women washed their hands. But when they thought they were alone, only *15 percent* washed hands.

Doctors know better . . . not. Did you hear the one about health workers who don't wash their hands? In fact, researchers replicated these conditions at a medical conference of—are you ready?—infectious-disease experts. These doctors were just as bad. In fact, most of them did not wash.

It is a widespread problem. Hand-washing studies in hospitals are downright shocking. Health workers washed their hands 27 percent of the time before they put on the gloves to poke you. Oh, what difference does it make as long as they wear gloves? Oops, turns out they changed gloves only 16 percent of the time between patients! Uh, excuse me, but what is the point of wearing them if you don't change them? Who are they trying to protect from germy patients—themselves or you? Hospital-borne infections can be nasty, and it's no surprise that we have such a problem with patients catching infections in hospitals.

Next time, before you worry about your doctor's medical education or patient survival record, you might just want to ask: "Hey, Doc, did ya wash those mitts before laying 'em on me?"

The art of hand-washing is in the technique and timing. You should wash before and after you prepare food (especially raw meat, chicken, and fish), eat, go to the bathroom, have sex, wipe your nose, cough, or sneeze. That should remove 95 percent of the germs. Now the technique. A hurried dab of soap is no good. Lather up with warm water; cold is better than none at all if you have no choice. Make sure you rub those hands together. Paper towels are best for drying, but just make sure you do dry. Wet hands hang onto germs. Regular soap is dandy; it cuts oils and prevents germs from sticking. You don't need expensive antibacterial fancy-pants soap. Make hand-washing a routine, like seatbelts.

I know this book is about eating, drinking, and being merry, but if you're stuck in bed for ten days with the flu, miserable with a cold, or trapped on the commode with a stomach bug, you can't be relaxing and enjoying life. Sorry, some things you just have to pay for.

9

HANDLING THE MECHANICS
WHO KEEP YOUR ENGINE
PURRING SMOOTHLY

T he point is to live a healthy life, have fun, and spend as little
time as possible in your doctor's office. Obviously that doesn't
always happen.

Much of the game, as I've been telling you, is out of your control.
Blame your genes, the chemicals in your food, the misalignment of the
moon and the stars, your lousy childhood, or an imbalance in your
bioenergy frequency. At some time or times, your body will let you
down. It will have minor quirks. It will have major breakdowns. It
may rebel and make you downright miserable. It may cure itself, or it
may not be cured despite all the tricks medical science has its disposal.

When problems arise, or to offset their arrival, you are going to be
hopping down for a visit to a doctor of one kind or another. That

means a relationship with folks who will help you do what you must to try to keep your health on track. The alliance you forge with them works very much in both directions. You have undeniable responsibilities in the relationship, and you have legitimate expectations of fair, honest, and competent treatment.

I know that many patients, especially older folks without much social support, consider a visit to their doctor as they would a visit to a friend or neighbor. They want hand-holding and personal contact with another human being. But for many of us, a visit to the doctor is at best inconvenient and anxiety-provoking and at worst potentially devastating. Personally I avoid doctors like the plague. I've been lucky so far, knock wood, and have not needed them for anything other than the occasional minor disturbance. I know that it won't always be that way.

I'll deal a bit in this chapter with preventive maintenance, but much more will involve doctors because they are the mechanics who tinker with your body and, when things go right, keep it on course. Judging by the continued popularity of television medical dramas, the public seems forever to be fascinated with doctors. A recent Harris poll awarded us the most prestige of any profession in the United States. Almost 90 percent of those surveyed ranked doctors as having either "considerable" or "very great" prestige. Nobody else came close. This is about more than prestige, though. You should be comfortable with them, understand what to ask them, and know how to ask them for what you want. To do that effectively, you must understand a bit about the world that makes them.

WHO *ARE* THESE PEOPLE?

Some of the most creative and brightest folks I have met have been doctors. But those are the rarer birds in the flock. Stereotypically, medical students are seen as the science-nerd types, devoid of outside interests. It's an apt description of many, considering the emphasis on grades and academic performance for those heading to medical school. Medical training is intense, and quickly draws the aspiring doctor's focus from the outside world. For a time in the 1960s, medical schools bought into the fad of looking beyond the typical science major and admitted literature and art graduates as well. Medicine needed "well-rounded" doctors, the argument went. Schools soon learned the true value of that fad. Roundedness just did not substitute for a good basic science background.

Peer with me through the windows of Cornell University School of Medicine, circa 1963, when I set off with some other twenty-one-year-old kids—that's all we were—on our education. My class was a mixed bag. We had brilliant, outgoing winners, success stamped all over their faces; we had withdrawn, quiet gnomes with all the personality and charm of clams. At the time I wondered how the clams could ever relate to patients, at least while the patients were still breathing.

The bag was just as diverse intellectually, which probably reflects our ongoing difficulty with figuring out who makes a good doctor. I remember many who really struggled with their studies. Some worked very hard and diligently for average grades. Some seemed to get decent grades with hardly any effort. The great equalizer was the staggering mass of information everyone had to learn.

No matter how hard you tried, there was no way around learning the nerves and arteries, the metabolic fates of the amino acids, and all the rest. All the rest. You cannot imagine, unless you have been through it, what that implies; the sleepless years of—yes—blood, sweat, and tears. What was not obvious to me at the start was the need for so many different skills beyond a memory to help in learning lists of things. How do you judge the skills necessary to look at swirls of tissues under a microscope and make a diagnosis? What to make of the klutz who could not tie a surgical knot fast enough? Or the hapless student who fainted the day we learned to draw blood, using each other as guinea pigs? Or the fresh-scrubbed student who masterfully kept a family calm during emergency surgery on their newborn?

Grades aren't everything. Some of my intellectually average classmates have become brilliant internists and distinguished surgeons. Some of the geniuses turned into confused losers. Recent studies of affirmative action students who got into medical school with lower grade point averages confirm that they go on in their careers as smoothly as others. We have no measure. Sheer brilliance, no doubt, helps in making diagnoses and in research. But it is not the whole picture.

I must admit that I suffered through the process, almost ten years of backbreaking work. I had an attitude problem that affects my feeling about doctors to this day. I don't do well with authority, and much of my antipathy to the process came from my disdain for the absolute power wielded by those above you in the medical hierarchy. A resident doctor, one year ahead, has absolute authority. Then there are the professors and real doctors. With notable and welcome exceptions here and there, the arrogant and the pompous rule. It's boot camp, not medicine.

Personally I found the experience horribly dehumanizing. It changed me. It has to change anyone. Different as my classmates may have been, we all got to the freshman class of an Ivy League medical school in the same way: competitive and, in some cases, avaricious instincts. We needed those skills to survive. Some medical schools begin with freshman classes that are two and three times larger than the class that will graduate. Medical residencies begin with worse odds. The dictum is as basic as it gets: Kill or be killed.

I remember one of my classmates ratting on several of us for not dissecting a cadaver to the exact specifications of the teacher. I confronted him outside the lab, but his story melted my anger, even as it disgusted me. He came from a small town in Pennsylvania, had worked like a dog to get to that lab, and had been looking over his shoulder all his life. "Do you realize how people just below me on the ladder would love to have my spot in this class?" he pleaded. Add to this boiling pot the intellectual pressures of absorbing immeasurable tons of information, and the fact that patients—actual human beings—depend on your knowledge and abilities.

One story in a medical magazine says it nicely, just in the headline: CAN A NICE PERSON MAKE IT THROUGH MEDICAL SCHOOL? That should tell you a lot.

THE DOCTOR FACTORY

I entered medicine for naive reasons: I enjoyed people and loved the information. Little by little, though, the system made the patient the source of all our problems and stresses. When I finally emerged, the patient had become my enemy.

Young doctors in training brag to one another about their "great cases." These are patients with exciting, unusual, and dramatic diseases. Whether a patient gets better or not, or even survives, becomes secondary. As we move down the assembly line, we begin to resent and become uninterested in folks with routine problems. The patients now are projects to complete, continually cycling through stainless-steel hospital beds. One hour empty, the next occupied. You don't have the time to care or involve yourself with whoever is lying there. Get the tests ordered, the paperwork done, and move on to the next one before rounds because you're going to be grilled over how much you know about a long list of the patient's possible diseases. The idea of the doctor leading rounds is to pick, pick, pick until this presiding genius finds something you didn't know and then exposes you as a fraud before your peers. Not a very constructive process.

The race to keep up with the onslaught of new knowledge thrown at you, as the hours and the responsibilities grow, ultimately factors the patients out of the equation. They are cells and organs and diseases, not people. We refer to them as "I got a hot appendix on 3B and a bleeding ulcer downstairs." Medical school is a time of great insecurity in the face of illness and death, as well as our ignorance. Meanwhile the expectation of the patients is that we know everything. It's almost instinctual to react as if you do know everything. Doctors must appear to know it all to instill confidence in their patients.

This came up with my very first living patient. After two years of medical school, it was time to move beyond cadavers and on to the real thing. We paired off and went to see our first real sick people. In a teaching institution, the patients experience endless physical exams, from students, interns, residents, and even some real doctors. While it might seem abusive, in my experience most patients love the attention. More important, this is where the finest medicine is practiced. Here many minds focus on the problem. The patient's every move is scrutinized and considered. That does not happen routinely in the real world. I saw insightful diagnoses made because we all pitched in and contributed.

My partner and I nervously walked down the corridor and found our patient's room. He was an older gentleman suffering from lung cancer. We entered and introduced ourselves as "doctors." I felt like Dr. Kildare. We were going to examine him. He asked if we could first raise the back of his bed. Absolutely, we answered. Tens of thousands of dollars on a medical education so far and neither of us knew how. We fumbled like Keystone Kops, pretending we knew what we were doing. "It's down there," our patient finally said, pointing weakly to the folded handle tucked under the bed.

We took his history, a critical stepping-stone in the process. When did his illness begin and how? What did it feel like and where? Were his bowels moving? His eyes seeing? His lungs breathing? For an experienced physician, this step would take several minutes. It took us an hour. Time for the exam. When we got to his throat and mouth, we did as we had been taught, removing his dental plate to examine his palate. My partner politely placed the plate in the wax-paper denture cup on the bedside table.

Hospital etiquette dictates that you pour a little water over the plate to keep it from drying out. The water carafe and the urinal were both stainless steel, side by side on the table. My partner deftly clasped the wrong carafe and poured urine over the patient's dentures. I choked back my horror. The patient figured we must know what we were doing. We were *doctors*, after all. My partner immediately launched into a wholly convincing scientific explanation of new research that confirmed the sterilizing qualities of human piddle. The dentures would be germ-free after a little urine soak. Even I almost believed him. We proceeded with our physical and left our patient suitably impressed with modern, up-to-date hospital care. We did switch his dentures to water before we left.

Amid the cutthroat competition, we would try to help each other when we could. Once, a fellow intern suffered a bedside interrogation about foods that can distort the results of a blood test he had ordered on his patient. "What else could the patient have eaten that could give you a false positive on this test, Doctor?" the chief resident demanded of the poor intern, who was literally sweating to avoid the three words every one of us dreaded ("I . . . don't . . . know"). I knew the answer—bananas. Hidden behind his inquisitor, I imitated a primate eating a banana, scratching my armpit. The intern's eyes lit up with the answer.

"Monkeys," he sputtered. Kill or be killed, yes, but we all died inside for him.

A year later I finished that phase of training. The biggest event in our lives during this most impressionable of times was the free black bag (with logo) a drug company gave to each of us. Of course, we already had our white lab coats, which we all donned with great pride. If we were lucky, it would confuse a myopic nurse or new orderly into saying "Hello, Doctor" and thus make our day. There were also moments of deflation. Shortly after I started to wear my coat, I strode proudly to a nearby deli for lunch. A patron approached and asked me if our corned beef was rare today.

LEARNING IN A WAR ZONE

The first major guerrilla attack I saw on medical education was not even written by a doctor. As part of his campaign to humanize medicine, Norman Cousins, the late editor of *The Saturday Review*, figured out that it all begins with the training. In 1981 he wrote a groundbreaking piece in the *Journal of the American Medical Association* entitled "Internship: Preparation or Hazing." Calling the process "a human meat grinder," he asks if the way we train doctors "has the effect of dulling the sensitivities of the physician or fostering feelings of resentment by an intern toward a patient who has a propensity for feeling his sharpest pains at 3 A.M.? What kind of judgment or scientific competence is it reasonable to expect of a physician who hasn't had any sleep for 32 hours. Is the workload at times not so much a sampling of later challenges as it is an exercise in what I can describe only as disguised hazing at best and systematic desensitization at worst."

Nearly two decades later, we continue to struggle with the answers. Some states have passed laws to limit the work hours of doctors in training. For the most part, they are ignored. But various studies have shown the toll that this system takes on its victims. In one survey among resident physicians, most indicated that their "attitude toward patients had changed while in training." Nor was it a change for the better. Many wished to spend less time answering patients' questions and dealing with direct patient care. Other studies have found significant rates of serious depression among medical students, considerably higher than among the general population. Complaints are frequent of exposure to repeated verbal and physical abuse from superiors and sexual harassment. These findings have been constant and consistent.

From this training, we expect caring, compassionate caregivers?

It should come as no surprise that many physicians are unhappy with their chosen lot in life. And the numbers have gotten worse with the years. Recent surveys are fairly consistent in finding that one-third of physicians would choose another profession if they could;

more than half would not recommend that their children go into medicine. After all, this is not an altogether pleasant environment in which to work. It's no surprise we wind up all over the emotional map. You have to develop some coping mechanisms. For many, that means an aloof stance, a distance from the daily realities of the profession. Disease is not a happy thing. The more serious side is when a doctor's dissatisfaction leads to drug and alcohol abuse. The vast majority of doctors complain of too much paperwork, the interference of third parties, and not enough time for their patients or their own families. That said, most physicians still seem relatively satisfied with medicine, but there are too many who are not happy.

Be on the lookout for this syndrome. Unhappy professionals do not give the best care. Would you rather have a surgeon sloshing around your chest cavity who feels depressed and downtrodden, wishing he'd gotten an MBA instead of a medical degree, or one who whistles while he works and is glad for the privilege of practicing medicine? There are no hard-and-fast rules here, but trust your instincts as best as you can. You know when people seem happy or depressed. Don't be intimidated by the supposed power and prestige of doctors. Look at them as critically as they are supposed to be looking at you. As a patient, I fear the power the doctor has over me. As a physician, perhaps I fear it more because I know how deep and at the same time how precarious it is.

WHO WAS THAT MASKED MAN?

Everybody wants Dr. Welby as a primary care physician. Or at least Dr. Kildare.

I can tell you already get my message. Of course, as human beings doctors can be arrogant and aloof as well as caring and warm. You, as the patient, must accept this range, know what it means, and learn how to play it to your advantage. I have seen arrogant types, capable of infuriating patients with their lack of charm, who also happen to be brilliant surgeons; I have seen back-slapping, happy-go-lucky types who are complete quacks but adored by their patients. The best neurosurgeon I know has the reputation of a drill sergeant among his patients but is held in sterling regard by other doctors. If I needed brain surgery, he'd be the man. God forbid your child needs brain surgery, but who do you want here?

Most of the time, though, people deal with doctors over minor maladies and really need the sense that they are cared for. Frankly, many doctors never had that ability before they entered medical school and were worse when they got out. Do not automatically assume that doctors lacking warm personalities are bad doctors.

One could argue that the healing environment needs human caring and warmth. One could also argue that we aren't there to hold your hand but to try to repair your health. Doctors are human beings, not gods. They can only get off the pedestal when patients get off their knees. If your expectations are way too high, you are disappointed and angered easily when doctors don't deliver what you think they should. A good physician wants you as a partner. The doctor did not make you sick. *You* must take responsibility for your illness and your health.

Doctors are highly trained specialists who can *maybe* fix you when you break down and help keep you from further breakdowns. They are not your mommy. They should treat you with the respect you deserve, and vice versa. It's tough-love time because the financial squeeze is on. For many people, health care has now gone out to the lowest bidder, and your doctor is stuck in the middle. You need to know who your doctor is in order to get the most out of your encounter, to expect what is reasonable.

The truth of the matter is that the routine practice of clinical medicine is not that difficult for those of moderately vigorous intellect. Many doctors I know complain that they are bored. Much of medicine is fairly cookbook stuff, especially in these days of managed care. If patient A has symptom B, we perform test C, which, if positive, merits treatment D. Unless grossly and obviously different, aches of the head, stomach, and back all fall into the wait-and-see bin. If they get worse, we order a routine test, often performed and interpreted by others. If the test is positive, the problem will be treated in standard fashion or treated by specialists. Superior intellect is called in when other doctors are stumped by a diagnostic conundrum. Great research breakthroughs are usually made by better minds.

If there is any single shortcoming within the profession, it is a fault that's easy to remedy: failing to stay current with developments in the field. These days I occupy a privileged position. I have no practice to chew up my time. Essentially my current job comes down to reading medical articles and I am completely obsessed by it. Ditto for my assistant and radio and television producers. Between us we review hundreds each week, thousands each month.

I admit I never did that in practice. I was too busy and frankly not interested. Medical journals went from the desk to the wastebasket, with no reading in between. Now I have the privilege to study journals in all the specialties. Nothing amazes me more than to discuss a new research report on the air that could really change the treatment of a particular disease, see the finding show up on the cover of *Time* magazine, and still, months later, get calls on my show from listeners saying that their specialists never heard of this "new" treatment. Not only is that dangerous, it is unethical. Most states have justifiable requirements for the continuing education of doctors, who must report the number of conferences they attend. The universe of knowledge out there is far beyond the scope of a single practitioner, or all practitioners, for that matter. I spent years and years of my life learning a smattering of what there is to know about my ultimate specialty, which concerned a round 1-inch ball in the head, the eyeball. Whole libraries are filled with what is known just about this little globe.

I am heartened by a doctor's desk piled high with journals that have been read, underlined, even torn apart. It serves as one vital measure of a doctor not bored with the field. Be encouraged by your doctor's messy desk.

Then there are those three critical words you want your doctor to be able to say: "I don't know." Yes, but . . . Doctors do have such a hard time admitting their mistakes. We may not deserve or welcome the pedestal, but often we secretly relish the height. You usually defer to us. We also know we deal with the most precious of commodities, life itself. We do noble battle against death and pain. We come to believe in society's deification, when it is not vilifying us. Gods never admit when they're in the dark. You expect us to know, and we learn that it's relatively easy to fool most of the people most of the time (lest you forget, the denture soak?). We delude ourselves into believing that if we do not know something—and there is much that we do not know—then you will not trust us.

Doctors must know when they are in over their heads. Being stubborn or too pigheaded to get help is just plain bad medicine.

SHOW THE NICE DOCTOR THE MONEY, DEAR

Everyone knows that all doctors care about is money. They make too much of it anyway.

Sorry, but grab the dynamite. That is one myth I have to blow up. I'll risk accusations that I'm a shill for my profession. There is no amount of money that would get me to return to practice, and my refusal would have nothing to do with my current income. The *average* doctor makes around $100,000 a year. (I'll spare you the calculator—for every doctor at $150,000, there is another at $50,000). Certain specialties pull in more dough than others; certain specialties make their practitioners work harder for less money. A doctor earns a lot more money by doing an hour-long procedure or operation than by spending an hour with a patient and making a brilliant, life-saving diagnosis.

Generally, though, I have a hard time understanding how to judge such things in a capitalist society. A tall guy makes millions of dollars to stuff a ball in a hoop, yet we begrudge an equally talented surgeon his lucrative fees. Stars who play doctors on prime time make scads of dough. Money is an important part of the incentive for prospective doctors. Who would go through the years of extraordinarily costly, rigorous, and exhausting training if surgery paid $25,000 a year? Whether you like it or not, in America financial incentives motivate the best and brightest to compete for the slots.

Decades ago, I looked across the on-call room at a friend of mine, his eyes underlined with the same black bags as mine. We were about to grab an hour's sleep while pulling an all-night rotation at our hospital. We were thirty-one years old, married with children, deeply in debt, and sleeping on uncomfortable bunk beds. We were in the thirteenth year of intense post–high school education. People driven enough and smart enough to go through all that could make more money in a variety of fields.

You may be sensing an attitude here. Consider the reflections of Dr. Christopher Sanford, a second-year resident who wrote a sympathetic piece for a medical journal about his efforts to "attempt to make sense of the toll" of his career choice:

During medical school, medical students work ridiculously long hours as their relationships deteriorate, social skills erode, and debts mount. After graduation the stress and hours increase. The average intern, if honest, will tell you that he hates his life. A common way to be compensated for their toils is obvious ... cash money, preferably in large amounts. Most applicants probably really mean what they say at medical school interviews about wanting to be doctors to help people, but after witnessing how little can be done for many patients, how many people don't want to be helped, and the obscene toll taken from their own lives, another reason must be found for going through the many years of hardship, and for many, money is the answer.

THE PRICE OF BEING WRONG

Doctors are human. Humans make mistakes. Therefore ...

Doctors may be glorified mechanics, but the price of their mistakes can be far higher than an oil leak. As the mother of a friend of mine, who worked all her life in hospitals, liked to say: "Doctors bury their mistakes." There is truth to that, although it is not quite that simple. When you look at intimate surveys of doctors spilling their guts about their errors, you can spot some situations that you may be able to avoid.

In one rare portrait of the field, fifty-three family doctors allowed themselves to be taped describing their most memorable error. The mistakes included delayed or missed diagnoses, surgical mishaps, and chaos in medical treatment. The causes of their errors fit into four major categories. I have listed them below, each with a quote from a doctor in the survey.

- Physician stress: being pressed for time, distracted or fatigued, or being angry at the patient or the family. Some errors occurred when the physician avoided an intervention because of cost. "I just didn't stop to think about all the possibilities. I mean I knew about [the disease]. They teach that in medical school. I was just in a hurry . . . to get to the next patient."
- Process-of-care factors: pursuing a particular diagnosis too aggressively and not considering other diagnostic categories;

not being aggressive enough in pursuing a particular diagnosis; the doctor didn't take the patient seriously enough; insufficient or incorrect information from the patient's history, physical, or lab work. "I guess because of his relatively young age, the thought of cancer didn't even come up. . . . I flat-out didn't think of the connection of bone pain, secondary to cancer."

- Patient-related factors: patients minimizing their symptoms; doctors trying to minimize their patients' discomfort; doctors fooled by hypochondria; errors related to doctors' dislike of the patient or friendship with the patient. "She was very obnoxious to my nurse, who said: 'This is not a very nice lady.' . . . She got up off the examining table and she had a hundred questions. She stood there and they were more bizarre questions, and with each question I got more and more irritated."

- Physician ability: doctors lacking relevant knowledge or reaching beyond their capability; pride in their own abilities got some in trouble. "I wasn't completely competent (yet) when it came to technical things. . . . I was fearful of looking as incompetent as I was, so that I didn't feel that I could call on the people that I really needed to help me."

The doctors were asked how many mistakes they could recall making and how many resulted in death. The mean number of mistakes per doctor was 10.7; the mean number of death-inducing mistakes was 1.2.

I offer these trade secrets not to frighten you but to increase your understanding of that person you call "Doctor." My hope is that you will see how human they are. Think about your line of work and mistakes you have made. Substitute the specifics of your job, and in one way or another, your mistakes were probably for the same reasons. It will be helpful for you to remember that your doctor's best judgment can be thrown off by stress and confusion and other normal irritants of life.

SQUEEZE THE MELON FIRST

What is a good doctor? I don't know, and neither does anyone else.

In a recent survey, patients said that what they value most in a doctor is willingness to spend time talking about nonmedical subjects. True, it may please you when they discuss your roses, but does that make them good doctors?

In the profession, we struggle with this all the time. I wish there were a Doctor Olympics, where mystery patients would be presented to a panel of doctors competing against one another for the correct diagnosis. How about surgery competitions, where judges give scores for performance, style, and technical difficulty? I have seen surgeons whose hands truly danced across open chest cavities, deftly twirling instruments and sutures, hitting their mark like champion figure skaters. But does that automatically mean they are performing better surgery for their patients? More important, do they know when it's appropriate to perform surgery? In the past, we believed that "faster is better" because patients remained under anesthesia for less time. Once my surgical partner and I proudly timed ourselves on a certain eye operation. We clocked in at fourteen minutes, while other surgeons labored long and hard, almost clumsily, over the same operation. But decades later, I cannot say for sure that our outcome was necessarily better.

In routine day-to-day practice, it is virtually impossible to measure outcomes objectively to determine the characteristics of a good physician. It all really comes down to the particular service you want. The colonoscopist snaking a tube through the twists and turns of a colon needs a sharp eye, ever on the watch for the slightest irregularity. A hyperactive personality would be good at that, a person with good hand-eye coordination—maybe a lot of practice with video games as a kid would help. The pediatrician who can calm a child in order to get a clear look down her throat or in her ear may do better for the patient than the valedictorian in the same doctor's specialty, better suited to make great discoveries in the lab.

One measurement is death rates in critical surgery, but that is full of problems. Years ago, the state of New York ranked eighty-seven cardiac surgeons by the death rate of their patients undergoing heart surgery. Of course, the doctor at the bottom of the list panicked when the state said his death rate was too high. At his low point, he had 13 deaths in 265 operations. But that was early in his career, when many young surgeons routinely accept the tough cases. "You earn your stripes by taking anything that comes," he told the New York Times. Some of his low-rated colleagues left the state.

High-risk patients suffer higher death rates, as you would logically expect. The state tried to factor this in by adjusting for risk factors such as previous heart attacks. Heart surgeons responded by over-reporting risk factors, making the patients out to be worse than they really were to protect themselves from poor scores. But the worst aspect of all this was that sicker patients were turned away and sent out of state so that they would not show up on the annual tally. It's just a fact of medical life: You can do a perfect surgical operation and the patient dies. Doctors need tremendous professional security and self-esteem to keep going. That young doctor with the highest death rate zoomed to a perfect, no-death record for the next two years.

It seems logical that malpractice claims would be a good way to weed out the good from the bad. Researchers compared urologists listed in the 1994 edition of *The Best Doctors in America* with plain old neighborhood urologists. What do you think they found? Well, 77 percent of the "best" urologists had been sued, compared with 49 percent of the undistinguished types. Still more revealing, 44 percent of the claims against the superstars finished in payments to the complaining patients, compared with only 29 percent of the claims against the regular doctors. Further proof, as far as I'm concerned, that such lists are a laugh.

About the best you can do in selecting your doctor is to make sure that anyone who advertises as a specialist is board certified in that specialty. This is your most reliable assurance of quality. After internship, doctors can obtain a license from the state where they want to practice medicine. Technically, that license enables a physician to work in any specialty. Preposterous as it sounds, performing plastic surgery, for example, fresh out of internship is not illegal and does happen. To gain national board certification in a specialty, doctors go back into residency training for an additional three to seven years. At the end of all this, they sit for a rigorous set of examinations, often both written and oral. At least then you can trust their credentials.

It's also fair to ask them how many times they have performed the particular operation you need. Beyond that, go with your best judgment and that of the physician you trust, who referred you in the first place.

EVERY DOCTOR'S NIGHTMARE

You cannot imagine how much doctors fear and loathe malpractice complaints. These complaints sink physicians in an emotional swamp of failure and shame and sap their self-confidence. As every doctor is taught, malpractice cases almost always begin with poor relations between the doctor and the patient. Physicians never know which patient will be the one to turn on them; which smiling, friendly, sad, or angry face will become the litigant.

In most malpractice cases, no malpractice was committed. When indeed there *is* malpractice, there often is no lawsuit. Unfortunately, every drug and every treatment—surgical or otherwise—has an expected rate of side effects. When a side effect appears, the perception is that the doctor screwed up. If this leads to a malpractice suit, the process of defense is horribly degrading for the doctor. It's bad enough when they *did* screw up. It's far worse when they know they are innocent, because they also know how easily a jury might side with the sympathetic victim.

Studies have documented the degree to which patients judge their care based on the physician's attitude rather than on objective measures of competence. Less communicative doctors are more likely to be deemed at fault for what goes wrong with their patients. This is kind of scary because not all of you need as much TLC and not all people who choose the medical profession are equipped with the same ability to communicate. How do you objectively evaluate the effectiveness of communication between a doctor and a patient? You cannot.

The vast majority—80 percent—of physicians who have been sued for malpractice report that before the lawsuit they believed their relationship with the patient was open and honest. Only 40 percent of the patients doing the suing gave the same answer. At least one reading of this situation finds that medical training emphasizes skills of reading, writing, and speaking. The fine art of listening, which requires interpretation and evaluation, generally gets ignored. Yet a doctor spends more time listening than doing anything else.

I have learned this lesson over and over on the radio because all I can do is listen. I am still amazed by the number of correct diagnoses I have made over the years. I assume the callers' doctors missed them because they were distracted by the physical presence of the patient and the option to do tests.

The first time this happened to me was with a young caller under treatment for allergies. Her face was swollen like "the moon," she said. She tried to explain it the same way to her doctor, but he ignored her. I was struck by her use of the word. We use the term *moon facies* to describe a particular disease. Had she noticed any other changes, like facial hair, stretch marks, menstrual abnormalities, or a fatty hump on the back of her neck? Yes to all. Bingo. I told her I thought she had a disease called Cushing's syndrome, caused by a tumor of the pituitary gland, at the base of the brain. Months after neurosurgery, she sent me photos of her wedding, her swollen, distorted body returned to normal. I had an advantage over her doctor: All I could do was listen. While I believe that a lot of this has to do with a doctor's personality, there is still a lot that can be changed through training.

KEEPING YOUR DISTANCE

I love to argue, so why not with myself? Are we emphasizing bedside manner too much? A few years ago, I wrote an article for the *Journal of the American Medical Association* asking whether physicians shouldn't learn acting skills so they could at least look as if they care. It only *sounds* cynical. In many specialties, if the practitioners truly did care, they would be depressed all day as one battle after another is lost against particularly deadly and virulent diseases. You learn that the first time you lose a patient for whom you have let yourself feel more than professional interest. Years after my piece appeared, the prestigious British medical journal *Lancet* advocated that acting classes be taught in medical school so that doctors learn "just when to provide a perfectly timed, compassionate look." Let's face it—some doctors have this ability, some do not. Can you really teach this?

I stopped practicing medicine because I never learned how to substitute emotional distance for actual feeling. After some training in general surgery, I decided to specialize in the eye. I loved using my hands for delicate work, and this was far from the mainstream of medicine. I liked that most physicians look at eye surgeons as a breed apart. So three years more of residency, and I hung out my shingle as an eye surgeon.

I had a patient on whom I performed a cataract operation. A cataract is any cloudiness in the lens of the eye. In those days, you opened up the cornea, flapped it back, and with a tiny forceps grabbed the lens—nothing more than a sac of gel with a very thin skin—and carefully pulled it out. The lens is attached to the eye behind the iris by thousands of radial-like fine fibers called zonules, which must be broken to get the lens out. You can't just yank all at once. Instead, you pull on one side of the lens to break them in one quadrant and, with a complex motion of the hand, rotate and pull the lens at the same time to sequentially tear the zonules, loosening them all the way around (it's like the old trick of tearing a phone book apart). If your flimsy grip is still good enough, you then gently pull out the lens.

This is delicate work, and you always exhale in relief when you see the lens perched at the edge of your incision. I was proud of myself that day. It went without a hitch. I was confident of my "good hands" and felt a talent for this kind of thing. But in the subsequent weeks I stood by helplessly as this patient's sight slowly deteriorated. She suffered a rare but not unknown surgical side effect, which happens to some patients sooner or later despite our best efforts. It had nothing to do with my technique. But I was devastated, never regained my surgical confidence, and quit the practice of medicine forever. Looking back, I realize how overly sensitive I was. You see how scorecards don't always tell the whole tale.

Yet skills aside, the way doctors communicate with you is critical to what you think of them. Surveys show that most people think doctors could do better at explaining the treatment options and the reasons they recommend a particular therapy. People do not care so much about the length of the visit—short and sweet works for many—but feeling cared for is their first concern. Half of those surveyed simply wanted the doctor to ask if they had more questions. Unfortunately, many doctors fear that too many questions will make it harder to finish with you in the allotted time. They are right to worry. Remember the survey that found many patients most satisfied when their visit was spent chatting with the doctor about nonmedical subjects?

One of the most positive aspects of our medical traditions is the commitment to tell the patient the whole truth and nothing but the truth. The average American patient demands no less. If you deplore the current doctor-patient relationship, consider the Japanese. Four out of five patients who die of cancer there are not told what they have before they die. Fewer than one in five are consulted about terminal therapy. Commonly, two consent forms are prepared before cancer treatment or surgery. One, signed by the family, has the real diagnosis. The other has a less serious diagnosis and is designed to mislead the patient, who doctors hope will thus have a more positive outlook. In 1995 the Japanese Supreme Court supported a doctor's right not to inform patients of their cancer.

SMILE, AND YOUR DOCTOR SMILES WITH YOU

You benefit in unseen ways when you're satisfied with your physician. Obviously there is a lot to be said for a positive healing environment, although give me the drill-sergeant personality with great hands any day. But when it comes to taking doctor's orders, the issues are different. Studies have found that medical advice is followed much more by people who are happy with their doctors. We're not just talking taking two aspirin. One group of four hundred hypertensives and two hundred diabetics were asked to assess their doctors for interpersonal skills, technical expertise, and accessibility. The hypertensive patients who rated their doctors as excellent were more likely to stick to low-salt dietary regimens and take their medications. Diabetics satisfied with the amount of time the doctor spent with them adhered more to proper diets. The availability of the doctor by phone also increased compliance.

History between doctor and patient also plays a part in the relationship. The longer the ties between doctor and patient, the lower the rate of hospitalization and the shorter the hospital stay. A doctor who knows the patient well will know better whether the patient can be managed at home. The patient should need fewer office visits, and many problems can be managed over the phone. It is also easier for the doctor to motivate patients to change bad habits. Prior research has found that longer relationships increase patient satisfaction and all of its benefits, which leads to fewer broken appointments, fewer lab tests, and a decrease in emergency room visits.

Yet that critical long-term relationship is increasingly destabilized in these days of managed care. From the beginning of health care in America, the ability to choose your doctor was a feature of the fee-for-service system. Today, some health plans assign a primary care physician to you or limit the list of whom you can choose. This practice could be penny-wise and pound-foolish. Researchers compared patients who chose their primary care provider to patients who were assigned a doctor. Who do you think wound up happier? Those who picked their own were up to 20 percentage points more likely to be extremely satisfied with their care, and the freedom to choose was central to that satisfaction.

GENDER CHOICE

With more female doctors finally in the marketplace, it is not sexist to ask whether gender should figure into your selection of a physician. But is it sexist to ask if gender makes a difference in certain specialties? In this, as in all of life, generalizations can be true for large groups, but they never reliably describe an individual.

Surveys show that most men prefer male physicians and most women prefer female doctors. Women believe that female doctors are more humane; men believe that male doctors are more technically competent. By the way, patients with no preference quickly came up with one when their problem was anal or genital.

Surveys also show that female pediatricians spend 29 percent more time with patients, compared with their male counterparts, engage in more social interaction, encouragement, and reassurance during the physical exam, and collect more information from children. Parents were more satisfied with female doctors, but the kids liked doctors of their own sex.

In general, female doctors spend more time learning about a patient's family and social milieu. One study from the University of California at Davis found that "women physicians not only spend significantly more time focusing on such preventive care as Pap smears, testicular exams and scoliosis screening, but also communicate with their patients in a way that leads to more patient satisfaction." Not unexpectedly, male doctors communicate more easily with male patients. Yet male doctors are also more likely to misperceive the motivation for a patient's visit when the patient is female—especially when she comes with an endless catalog of complaints.

Neither patient nor doctor is excused from sexist attitudes regarding the more intimate aspects of both our lives and our anatomy. The gender of your doctor may determine the competence with which you receive certain screening tests. For instance, according to surveys, female doctors are more likely than males to be "very comfortable" performing breast exams and Pap smears on a woman and taking her sexual history. They report less comfort taking a sexual history from a male patient. Here is the worst of all: Only 6 percent of female family physicians and 13 percent of female internists felt that their skill was excellent in performing a prostate exam. That compared to 49 percent and 37 percent respectively for their male colleagues (still shockingly low figures). Clearly they all could use some sensitivity training in their sex-related professional skills.

By the way, if you have a choice in another medical area—picking a hospital—those with more specialists and higher volumes of procedures have higher success rates, lower death rates, and shorter patient stays. Generally, for complex cases, teaching hospitals are your best choice. These are hospitals associated with universities and medical schools where the intellectual rigor is of the highest order. These institutions, though, struggle with conflicting missions in the managed care environment. They are expected to deliver first-rate care cheaply, train young doctors, sponsor research, and offer broad services to indigent populations. They are an important resource that needs to survive through the current upheavals in health care.

WHEN TO BUG YOUR DOCTOR

I am a terrible medical consumer. Then again, maybe I'm a good medical consumer. The point is, I have been to the doctor twice in the past decade. I hate the idea that my life could end up in the hands of someone with whom I am hardly close, yet who may have the power to save my life. I think that idea partly explains why doctors make such bad patients. As a doctor I know things that can go wrong that you've never thought of and don't want to. When doctors become patients, they must confront the loss of power that they normally wield when they are on the listening side of the stethoscope.

Be aware, though, that most visits to doctors are unnecessary. Most of the time, the problem is not physical illness, or it is something that will go away by itself. Fatigue, headaches, indigestion, colds, and backache are for the most part routine complaints that usually do not require medical care. Of course, the lines get blurry here. What have you got to lose by trotting down to the clinic for every symptom? So you get a little neurotic and distraught over every little symptom and find yourself camping out in the HMO lobby. After all, you might have something serious. Isn't the loss merely time and money?

Doctors, when pushed by your frustration with minor symptoms, will start to order more tests, and that can backfire on you. Angiography to pursue what the doctor is pretty sure is heartburn can be dangerous. Laparoscopies—to peer inside your abdominal cavity—as part of a search for the causes of minor symptoms carry a real risk as well.

Avoiding doctors altogether is not in your best interest. Conversely, running to the clinic for minor symptoms wastes resources. Finding the balance would offer contemporary medicine's biggest savings. There are simply too many colds and flus clogging the system and too few blood-pressure checks and mammograms being performed.

The question, then, is when should you go to the doctor? In general, if you have a symptom that you have had many times before and that did not lead to trouble, you can rest assured that it is not cancer, or another dire warning. On the other hand—oops, *this* is a new pain—that would warrant a visit. You know how your back aches at the end of a long day. Trust me, the pain in your back from kidney stones is far different. If it is a symptom you have experienced for a long time, but it has gotten more severe or changed qualitatively, come on down to the doctor store.

OK, you've got this pain, or new symptom. Test time, courtesy of Mayo Clinic. For the following symptoms, what do you do: Head to the emergency room, call your doctor for advice, or just wait and see?

- Chest pain or upper abdominal pain or pressure?
- Sudden, severe headache with no prior history?
- Unexplained weight loss?
- Dizziness, sudden weakness, or sudden change in vision?
- Vomited once in six hours, no fever, pain, or other symptom?
- Lump in breast?
- Suicidal or homicidal feelings?
- Blood in urine?
- Abdominal cramps, lasting two weeks?
- Difficulty breathing or shortness of breath?

All set?

For chest or abdominal pain, straight to the ER. Thousands die every year because they get fooled. The signs of a heart attack can be subtle or overt. Nausea, sweating, faintness, and pain in your jaw can all indicate a heart attack. Listeners have often heard me recount the case of the man who suffered pain in his tongue during sex, told his doctor, yet both missed this symptom of heart attack. Be aware that with any of these symptoms, it is unlikely to be a heart attack. If it's not, it is probably esophageal problems like heartburn, or an arthritis-like inflammation where the ribs attach to the breastbone, or sprains of the chest wall. Heart pain is usually, but not always, a feeling of pressure or heaviness, not sharp and stabbing. Pushing on the chest wall does not make it worse. This is one symptom, though, where it is better to overreact than not to react at all.

Headaches are very common and emergency rooms are jammed with them. But the key with this is its suddenness and uniqueness, especially if any other symptoms accompany the headache, like difficulty staying awake, talking, or concentrating, or weakness or numbness anywhere in your body. Hop down to the ER.

Weight loss? Make an appointment. Unplanned weight loss is a serious symptom, but there is nothing we can do about it in the middle of the night.

Feeling dizzy or weak or suffering a change in vision without a headache and we still want to see you right away. These are common early signals of a stroke and tragic if ignored because we can help if we catch them early. Afterward is often too late.

Repeated vomiting? You should immediately come for a visit. A single episode is likely to stay that way. So in that case, hang on.

A breast lump means you should call for advice. While you are dialing, remember that at least 80 percent of lumps are *not* cancer.

Suicidal thoughts are often a missed opportunity for medical intervention. Head to the ER.

Blood in your urine is definitely worth a call. In the toilet bowl, it looks like a lot more blood than it actually is and freaks out a lot of folks. It could be serious but is not an emergency.

Two weeks of cramps is too long for routine problems. Get on the horn and ask for help. If the cramps suddenly become worse, go to the ER.

Shortness of breath is a serious symptom, and you should pay a visit.

One of the hardest decisions for parents is when to take a feverish child to the pediatrician. There are guidelines that describe how high a fever should be and for how long before making that appointment. The higher the fever, the less time it should be tolerated; lower fevers can be tolerated longer. It is rare for a fever to mean something ominous.

There is even a school of thought that says we are too quick to treat a fever. After all, this is nature's way of fighting infection, and if we automatically try to lower body temperature, we may be prolonging illness. You should follow two important strategies with fever, though: Administer liquids to replace the increased loss of natural fluids from sweat-inducing higher temperatures, and call the doctor before making a trip to the waiting room. He or she will know whether you need to schlep over for a visit.

WHAT, YOU'RE *STILL* GOING TO GO?

If I haven't scared you off, you should think a little about the coming encounter with your doctor. You should know exactly why you are going for the visit and write down the three most important questions you need answered. Studies have found that such readiness actually lessens patient anxiety. I promise that well-thought-out questions will help your doctor to help you. Doctors say they are more likely to be in the dark over why you are there when you have multiple concerns, like a skin rash, weight management, and high blood pressure. Make it clear to your doctor why you *are* there.

That said, you do not want to show up with three legal-pad sheets of questions, both irritating and distracting the doctor from what is really important. It is the quality, not the quantity, of your questions that counts. Never be too embarrassed to ask about medical problem. One in four patients admits that they have been too ashamed at times to discuss health problems or symptoms with their doctor. Sexual dysfunction, sexually transmitted diseases, incontinence, prostate problems, menopause, depression, and birth control are all on the top-ten list of questions patients say are too embarrassing to ask. Not surprisingly, then, many of these are among the most undertreated conditions, despite all the ways medicine can help.

But shame is just one reason for reluctance, according to surveys. People also fear bad news, possible treatments, and wasting their doctor's time. Many people worry that their symptoms are unimportant. Yet even when the visit apparently goes well, all is not as it seems. A

Mayo Clinic report found that 68 percent of the patients surveyed could not recount the doctor's diagnoses after returning home. The problems frequently diagnosed yet forgotten or ignored included hypothyroid, colorectal polyps, obesity, osteoarthritis, and tobacco abuse.

It seems a strange notion, but patients and physicians might be talking past each other. I know you are accustomed to complaining about doctors, but you might not be aware of the other side. Patients can be a real pain. The polite term in the trade is *difficult.* You should care about this. If you don't, you may find your care compromised. Frustrating your doctor puts you at risk.

Difficult patients, according to a review by the University of California at San Francisco, account for up to nearly one-third of the patients at primary care practices. This study uncovered that seven of twenty-one difficult patients had at least one diagnosable personality disorder, primarily dependent-personality disorder. More technical terminology refers to these folks as dependent clingers, entitled demanders, manipulative help-rejecters, and self-destructive deniers. Our less technical expressions for these patients include crocks, turkeys, GOMERs (get out of my emergency room), and heartsink patients (your heart sinks when you see them come in the door).

I know that "we are not supposed to dislike people," as one internist in an Australian study put it. The relationship between negative attitudes and substandard care is not clear, but common sense tells you that you cannot possibly get the same care from two doctors if one does not like you. Human nature does not change with a medical degree.

Most doctors hate certain medical conditions: mental illness, alcohol and drug abuse, obesity, back pain, sexual behavior—related conditions, headaches, and hypochondriacs. Doctors' frustration levels rise with conditions for which there is no cure, that are difficult to cure, or that can be blamed on the patient. These include accidents, suicides, and sexual child abuse. There are some social characteristics of patients that doctors said in a survey do not make their hit parade: dirty, smelly, aggressive and hostile, noncompliant, demanding, lying, and sneaky. Oh, what the hell, take the whole list and see if you fit: self-destructive, self-pitying, suspicious, doubting, overdependent, overbearing, arrogant, complaining, manipulative, snobbish, VIP, wealth-flaunting, self-diagnosing, overly familiar, gushing, litigation-prone, health nuts, medical faddists, selfish, egocentric, garrulous, boring, know-it-all, stupid, ignorant, and immature. We're not done yet. Deadbeats, habitually late, lazy, loud, rude, poor morals, promiscuous, religious bigots, and fanatics all made the list.

If you see yourself here, clean up your act. You're a mess. Your good health may depend on it.

TOO MANY TESTS, TOO MANY MISTAKES

Most patients still expect long laundry lists of routine tests on a regular basis. In recent years, though, that list has been steadily whittled away. Those routine cardiograms and chest X rays that your parents got every year just don't happen anymore. Many tests have been deemed too expensive for the number of cases they detect. Others falsely alarmed so many people that they caused more dismay than they were worth. Consequently, the recommendations for routine screening procedures change frequently as each medical group draws its own conclusions.

Searching for diseases in patients with no symptoms yields little information, so many doctors now believe that your time with a physician is better spent talking about how to prevent disease. The HMOs have not made it simpler. Although it sounds brutal, doctors must ask which tests will pay for themselves in the long run. That means weighing the cost of the test against the cost of treating the illness when it arises. A review by the congressional Office of Technology Assessment revealed that only three procedures pay for themselves: prenatal care for poor women, testing for some congenital disorders of newborns (hypothyroid, phenylketonuria), and childhood immunization.

To be fair, money is just part of the formula. For example, there are terrible problems with certain tests, which make retesting necessary. When a test comes back positive for a disease, and further testing reveals that in fact you do not have that disease, the original finding is called a false positive. When the test comes back negative—indicating that you do not have the disease—but further or repeat testing determines that you indeed do have the disease, the original finding is called a false negative. The better the test, the fewer false positives and false negatives. The greater the number of unnecessary tests, the more likely it is that we come up with false-positive findings, which lead to more testing. You can end up with side effects from the testing itself.

Some tests are used as a screening device to see who would benefit from more expensive and accurate tests. We expect a high false-positive rate with these tests. The unnecessary anxiety they cause comes with the territory, yet we have a hard time dealing objectively with this in medicine. A twenty-four-year-old woman feels a lump in her breast; her doctor thinks it is benign but orders a mammogram anyway to reassure her. The mammogram shows the lump, and the radiologist reads it as benign. But the patient knows these tests cannot be 100 percent sure and easily talks the doctor into a biopsy.

Most breast biopsies are not cancer and are in a sense unnecessary but performed to offer a worried patient some reassurance. Doctors are quick to do them because ultimately it is in their best interest and often yours. Throughout years of practice, physicians will perform hundreds of biopsies in cases where they feel relatively sure there is no cancer. Sooner or later, one of those biopsies will turn up positive for cancer. Had the doctor not done the biopsy in that case, he or she might well have been sued for missing the diagnosis of cancer. No doctor gets sued for ordering a biopsy, only for not doing one. So these days, find a lump and you're likely to get a biopsy. If your doctor, after a careful examination and a mammogram, insists a biopsy isn't necessary, you can probably believe it.

WHAT *IS* ROUTINE ANYMORE?

No subject in annual medical care is more confusing these days than the checkup. But most physicians would agree with me on these basics: Adults should have their blood pressure and cholesterol levels checked every year. Women should have regular mammograms beginning in their forties, recognizing that because their breasts are more dense, cancer is harder to detect but fortunately less common. Women should have Pap smears initially every year. If it's normal for a few years, and you have a single sexual partner, skip it every other year.

All middle-aged patients should have a simple test for stool blood, which can pick up colon cancer. Many doctors recommend a colonoscopy every few years, especially if there is a family history of colon polyps or cancer. I believe all middle-aged men should have a digital rectal exam and the PSA test for prostate cancer. This definitely can pick up prostate cancer, but because many doctors aren't sure of the best treatment, they may not recommend the tests.

All this assumes you have no symptoms. If you do, obviously you should have the appropriate follow-up care with your doctor. Use these professionals wisely and as necessary. Just don't overuse them.

10

BE HAPPY

Your Body Will Thank You for It

Answer this question: How much time do you spend in any given week searching for and eating the right foods, popping the right pills, pumping the right exercise gadgets, reading the right health books and magazines?

I'll bet you can come up with a reasonable estimate. Now answer this: Do you spend as much time and effort on improving your mental health, shaping your moods and relationships, adjusting your general state of mind and attitude toward yourself? How much do you really *think* about your life?

Living a long time because you had the right genes and followed all Dr. Dean's advice is one thing; being as content as possible and enjoying your life is something else. If you are not lucky enough to live a long life—and I'm sorry, but many of you will not—you may as well have a relatively happy experience for as long as it lasts. Research is emerging to indicate that obsessions like cholesterol levels and body mass index may not be as important to health and longevity, not to mention simple enjoyment, as is our mental state. A less stressed, depression-free, happier life, the research says, will increase your chances for living longer. Better moods and more positive feelings appear to pay more direct rewards than shedding a few pounds or dropping cholesterol points.

Taking the claims of the mind-body gurus at face value tells me that this pleasure thing sounds like a lot more fun than an exercycle. So it seems that of all the advice you get from the health nags, enjoying your life looms as the most bang for the buck. Being merry, it seems, can add years to your life.

The exhausting pace of modern life leaves us little time for each other, our kids, or ourselves. We need money to buy the things that we think will make us happy. We need to work a lot to earn all that money. Do you see a cycle here? We all know people who've succumbed to the process. Sudden death from heart disease can be more common in those with certain personalities and stress reactions than in some folks who have high cholesterol.

Why is it so hard to face these realities, and even harder to do something about it? Consider the fantasy question my friends and I love to bat around: What would you do if you knew you had a terminal illness and were going to die in six months? Why do some folks say they would just continue on with life as it is, while others would drop out and head for the beach? What does *your* answer say about you?

For some people, getting happy may be as much work as a treadmill. For others, and I hope you are among them, it may be easier than it seems. I am not suggesting that you dodge your responsibilities and avoid the unpleasant but necessary tasks of your life. I *am* suggesting that you make room for some of life's pleasures. It's a twofer: Enjoy the time you have on this earth, and help your health along.

I have a friend who always greets me with the same question: "Are you happy?" Not even a "Hihowyadoin." Am I happy? It's a particularly annoying question because I never know how to answer it. Happy at that moment, with him in my face? Happy yesterday? Or a running average over my whole life? Or just for the past month? Is happiness lack of depression or optimism? Is it lots of yucks, or is it just being mellow? Psychology and psychiatry struggle constantly with this. As you will see in this chapter, happiness cannot be defined by the scientific method.

THINK LIFE

The mind is powerful enough to control the timing of its death. In case you need me to tell you, this is a rather extraordinary fact that astounded the medical community when it was initially proved. The first critical study was conducted in 1988 by researchers looking for a meaningful event that met two important criteria: (1) that it be of great interest to one group in a population and of little interest to another, thus allowing for an easy comparison, and (2) that it move around the calendar and not be linked to fixed monthly mortality patterns. They decided to study Jews and Passover. They found that the mortality of Jews in Israel fell just before Passover and rose after the holiday. Non-Jewish control groups showed no such changes. The conclusion: Some Jews were able to prolong life until after the holiday.

Obviously this is a radical concept. So in 1990 scientists at the University of California at San Diego decided to duplicate the study using Chinese-Americans and the Harvest Moon Festival, a holiday of special significance to older Chinese women. It turned out that mortality among Chinese-Americans dropped by a huge 35 percent in the week before the festival and rose by the same number during the week after the holiday. Strokes displayed the largest change, followed by heart disease and then cancer. The dip and rise did not occur in non-Chinese control groups. The rise might be the result of all the stress and overeating during the holiday, which caused an increase in death afterward. But that does not explain the dip before the holiday. The authors attributed the pattern to a short, but willful, postponement of death.

Another study of Chinese-Americans found that they die earlier than normal if they have a disease linked to Chinese astrology, a complicated system that connects the year of birth to a specific illness. For instance, according to the system, a person born in 1907 would be susceptible to heart disease; one born in 1908 to tumors. In comparing records of 28,169 Chinese-Americans with those of matched controls, a pattern developed: The more strongly the individuals were attached to Chinese tradition, the more the phenomenon appeared. Those people who believed in astrological fate and had a disease matching that of their birth year died between 1.3 and 4.9 years earlier than others who did not share that faith.

This remarkable human ability to influence the Grim Reaper's timetable seems to relate to our optimism about the immediate future. It has been suggested that this optimism is the most fundamental way to measure the quality of our life. That rings true to me, yet I find myself intimidated by both its simplicity and its wisdom. How many times have I vowed to better my own thinking about the immediate future? Modern cognitive therapists confirm that much of the time, feelings are beyond our control. However, the decisions made in response to these feelings can be controlled.

Learning how to respond to feelings in ways that are in your own best interest is the crucial skill in navigating your mental health. I'm not sure life is much more complicated than that. I just want as many of those joyous moments as I can rack up, and as few of the other kind, which seem capable of finding us no matter how we try to avoid them.

And what of pessimism, optimism's evil twin? They are not opposites. At least one study has linked pessimistic attitudes to higher blood pressure. Overall it appears to be more beneficial to avoid pessimism than to try to be more optimistic. Researchers at Ohio State University followed two groups they defined as optimists and pessimists for a year. Those who scored high in pessimism had more stress, anxiety, and poorer health. Elderly optimists had the highest level of symptoms of depression after a negative experience.

Then there's that thing about death again. Pessimism can increase the risk of early death. A seventy-year-long study by the University of Michigan began with a group of schoolchildren in 1921, following them into their eighties. Pessimists were defined as fatalistic folks who tended to blame themselves when things went wrong and who believed that one bad event could ruin the rest of their life. They expected bad things to happen and felt powerless to change them. Statistics again: They ran a higher risk of untimely death. That could be because they were less likely to avoid or escape potentially hazardous situations. No one knows for sure, but attitude does seem to matter.

WHAT'S DRIVING YOU, AND WHO IS THE NAVIGATOR?

Need advice? Turn on your radio. The airwaves are streaming with experts.

I know some of these people personally, so trust me that much of what you hear does not reflect the person behind the microphone. And yes, of course, you should challenge *my* take on the world as well. Always question authority. You hear talk-show hosts setting standards of behavior for us that they never meet themselves. You get family advice from people who can't get along with their own families. You are instructed on child-rearing by people who wouldn't know how to unfold a diaper. You are clubbed with commandments on love from cognoscenti who have never enjoyed a healthy relationship, and sex counsel from counselors who have never *really* made love.

Here we go again. The danger on these critical but often murky issues is that the formula for a happy life is different for each person. Your genetic heritage and your life experiences are uniquely you. Your happiness may not fit into a file folder that a radio hack labels "happiness" for someone else.

Some experts are aware of this confusion of expertise. Two psychologists at Cornell University, Wendy Williams and Stephen Ceci, even researched the subject after a mutual friend approached each of them for advice—and got contradictory recommendations. That experience stimulated the professors to investigate. They gathered fifty-nine true-life relationship problems from family and friends. Then they solicited solutions from more than a hundred psychologists and psychiatrists. You can imagine. Between two and five expert answers for each of the fifty-nine problems. Different experts, same problem, different advice. Their book, *Escaping the Advice Trap*, offered sage advice:

> We think lots of people take the glib advice of relationship gurus, self-help books and columnists way too seriously. They think if a so-called expert says it, it must be so. Some media shrinks bark out orders as though they're God. We want people to realize they need other opinions . . . if not therapists, at least relatives and friends who care about them.

Actually, Ohio State University psychologists seem to have figured out what makes us tick. They claim that they are the first researchers to conduct a scientifically valid survey of intrinsic human desires. In the past, psychologists tried to come up with single major, fundamental desires for us all. Freud, for example, famously figured it was sex. Not so, say the folks at Ohio State. "One size does not fit all," they wrote of their findings, a declaration that you know by now I love to hear. "There is not a fixed hierarchy of values true for all people."

To reach their conclusions, they quizzed 2,500 people and grouped their answers into fifteen categories of fundamental desires and values. The range of responses was wide, and that in itself tells you why you must avoid falling for radio shrinks and self-help books offering the same formulas for everyone. "Most of these desires are similar to those seen in animals and seem to have some survival value," they wrote. "This indicates they are genetic in origin." In other words, even as we are all human, we are different for a reason, and the reason is survival. "These desires," writes coauthor Steven Reiss, "are what guide our actions. In a sense we are studying the meaning of life."

And that meaning is . . . well, it's far more genetic than the psychobabble media gurus would have us believe. In fact, only three out of fifteen basic, fundamental desires do not spring from our genes—the urges for citizenship and independence and fear of rejection. Oh, you are insatiable, aren't you? Here's the entire list:

> Curiosity, the desire to learn
> Food, the desire to eat
> Honor/morality, the desire to behave in accordance with a code of conduct
> Rejection, the fear of social rejection
> Sex, the desire for sexual behavior and fantasies
> Physical exercise, the desire for activity
> Order, the desire for organization in daily life
> Independence, the desire to make our own decisions
> Vengeance, the desire to retaliate when offended
> Social contact, the desire to be in the company of others
> Family, the desire to spend time with loved ones
> Social prestige, the desire for positive attention and prestige
> Aversive sensations, the desire to avoid pain and anxiety

> Citizenship, the desire for public service and social justice
> Power, the desire to influence people

So if that's what we want, does any of it make us happy? Let's talk a little about that very elusive commodity, happiness.

The *British Journal of Psychiatry* proposes to classify happiness as a psychiatric disorder because it is either uncommon or "statistically abnormal, consists of a discrete cluster of symptoms; there is at least some evidence that it reflects abnormal functioning of the central nervous system, and is associated with a range of cognitive abnormalities." Typically British, it is not clear whether the authors are being tongue-in-cheek or slyly serious.

The authors claim that "happy people are often irrationally biased in favor of themselves and have an unrealistic view of their own abilities, achievements, etc. Happy people overestimate their control over environmental events ... give unrealistically positive evaluations of their own achievements, believe that others share their unrealistic opinions about themselves and show a general lack of evenhandedness when comparing themselves to others."

WHAT IS THIS THING CALLED HAPPINESS?

Fine, but what does science *really* know about happiness and joy? In short, not a whole lot. Surveying the last thirty years of psychology journals, one reporter found forty-five thousand articles on depression and only four hundred on joy. Scientists of the mind focus on pathology—disease—so nobody will study happiness unless it *is* classified as a disease (maybe the British journal was really on a hunt for research funding). Thankfully, that could change. Recent leadership at the American Psychological Association wants to refocus psychological research on the study of normal people, not just those who are abnormal.

The *New York Times* set out to chase that elusive blue bird. It's not where you would think it nests—money, education, a good marriage, family. Not even lottery winners were any happier a year after their windfall. In fact, all those factors were relatively minor sources. A great deal of happiness, readers will be pleased to learn, resides in your genes. Yes, those inescapable, immutable bundles of DNA that complicate or simplify your life, depending on your initial combination.

Remember the set-point theory from Chapter 3 on dieting, that your body has its own thermostat to keep your weight steady? Some researchers now believe that a similar mechanism works for setting happiness. Dr. David Lykken, a behavioral geneticist at the University of Minnesota, studied identical twins and found that their well-being matched up. "Half of your sense of well-being is determined by your set-point, which is from the genetic lottery," he says of his findings. "And the other half from the sorrows and pleasure of the last hours, days or weeks."

Are you catching the drift? Genes work ultimately through chemical messengers. The implication, then, is that our personalities and thus our capacity for happiness are also chemical. The field of neuropharmacology sends the same message. Pardon me for being simplistic, but why do people take drugs again? It makes them happy. Drugs from the amphetamine and cocaine class mimic happiness in the chemical way they stimulate the brain. The seduction is not the drug but the happiness it induces. Perhaps people less prone to happiness within their own neuropharmacology are more susceptible to seduction by these drugs. Freud was so excited by the magnitude of cocaine's antidepressant action that he became its addict.

For centuries, such discussions have engendered vitriolic attack from those who resent and fear the reduction of human mentality to physical causes. Heed the strange and remarkable case of Phineas Gage for further proof that our personalities—even down to the details of our dispositions and moral outlooks—have a considerable physical component.

In 1848 Gage was a twenty-five-year-old railroad foreman. His employers said he was the most capable employee on their payroll, describing him as "temperate of habit, [with] considerable energy of character, a well-balanced mind, [and] a shrewd, smart businessman, energetic and persistent in executing all his plans of action." Unfortunately, an accidental explosion propelled a 4-foot long, 13-pound steel rod through his left cheek and up through his brain. Miraculously, he survived.

But he was a different Gage. The earlier description was replaced. Now he was "fitful, irreverent, indulging at times in the grossest profanity which was not previously his custom, manifesting but little deference for his fellows, impatient of restraint or advice when it conflicts with his desires, at times pertinaciously obstinate, yet capricious and vacillating." In sum, he was not the same guy. He wound up joining the circus as a freak, then working as an itinerant farmhand. He died destitute at age thirty-eight in San Francisco. His skull still resides at the Harvard Medical School, and the lesson of his life still fuels arguments that we may not have as much control over who we are as we would like to think.

GETTING STEAM FROM SELF-ESTEEM

What the heck *is* self-esteem anyway? The concept itself was invented in the late nineteenth century by philosopher William James, who defined it as the difference between your aspirations and your performance. The idea seems simple enough. Consciously and unconsciously, we constantly evaluate ourselves, automatically forming a summary overall opinion, regardless of specific skills. You may be a great golfer or a superb bridge player, but that may bear little relation to the general judgment you make of yourself. Some people feel the world is truly their oyster; others question their very right to exist.

Experience matters. There are those who attribute success to their own efforts and those who are quick to blame failure on circumstance. Can others confer self-esteem on us? Does the respect, praise, and affection of others change this inner self-rating? Is it Mother's fault? Freud claimed that "a man who has been the indisputable favorite of his mother keeps for life the feeling of a conqueror." And if Mom rejects you?

The stakes here may be higher than feeling better about the world. Some researchers chart direct links between self-esteem and health. Low self-esteem has been related to depression, anxiety, psychosomatic illnesses, child abuse, and delinquency. Yet research on the subject lately has suffered from low self-esteem. The purity and primacy of the concept started to unravel when it was found that self-esteem did not correlate with the standard definitions of success in the world. This was so upsetting that the *New York Times* reported with shock that "studies of gang members and criminals found their self-esteem reinforced by peers and lawlessness to be as high as that of any over-achiever. . . . Some people achieve great things in life while gripped by feelings of worthlessness. Others set low standards and feel great." Oops. Perhaps low self-esteem spurs people onward. If

Napoleon were tall, maybe he would have been chopping meat in a butcher shop instead of conquering half the world.

Some people choose to avoid the whole mess by giving up and blending their self-esteem with that of other individuals or with leaders via cults or groups. Others are simply more self-critical than necessary. Such an attitude can get you into serious trouble: it can damage your capacity for happiness as well as your physical and mental health. Some psychologists say that low self-esteem is the final common pathway that determines your susceptibility to depression and can take you all the way there.

There is a standard method for measuring self-esteem, the simple ten-question Rosenberg Self-Esteem Scale. Subjects are asked to agree or disagree with the following statements, aimed at uncovering their opinion of themselves. Since we are here, you may as well take the test. Do you strongly agree, agree, disagree, or strongly disagree with these statements?

1. On the whole, I am satisfied with myself.
2. At times, I think I am no good at all.
3. I feel that I have a number of good qualities.
4. I am able to do things as well as most other people.
5. I feel I do not have much to be proud of.
6. I certainly feel useless at times.
7. I feel that I'm a person of worth, at least the equal of others.
8. I wish I could have more respect for myself.
9. All in all, I am inclined to feel that I am a failure.
10. I take a positive attitude toward myself.

Hang on for the ride. Here's how you figure it out: For questions 1, 3, 4, 7, and 10, "strongly agree" gets you 4 points; "agree," 3 points; "disagree" 2 points; "strongly disagree", 1 point. For questions 2, 5, 6, 8, and 9, "strongly agree" is worth 1 point; "agree," 2 points; "disagree," 3 points; and "strongly disagree," 4 points.

How did you do? Dr. Timothy Owens, of Indiana University, says most people score between 30 and 40. That is considered normal. A much smaller number will land in the 20s. Below 20 and you're drifting toward high rates of depression.

These currents start early and run deep. The best research I have seen to explain all these paradoxical reactions to self-esteem documented just how profound it all is for children. Psychologists at Columbia University demonstrated that by praising a child's intelligence and aptitude after they do well, to boost their self-esteem, you actually might be producing the opposite effect.

The researchers gave sets of problems to fifth graders. All the students were told they did very well, regardless of their actual performance. Some additionally were told that "you must be smart at these problems." Others additionally were told that "you must have worked hard at these problems." Then they were all given more problems. This time they were all told they did not do as well as before.

Their reactions were amazing. Those previously commended for effort attributed their poorer performance to lack of effort. But the kids praised for intelligence attributed their perceived lowered achievement to lack of ability. Nor did they enjoy taking the test. Next, both groups were allowed to choose tasks. The intelligence-praised kids picked easier ones because they knew they could do well on them. The effort-praised group, however, picked tasks from which they thought they would learn something. "Praising children's intelligence, far from boosting their self-esteem, encourages them to embrace self-defeating behaviors, such as worrying about failure and avoiding risks," wrote the authors.

The insidious effects of all this could explain the backfire a few years ago when grammar schools sought to boost girls' self-esteem and instead led them to lowered motivation and worse performance in later years. The Columbia University authors also warned that labeling kids as gifted or talented can hurt them as they try too hard to justify the label. When they experience a setback, these kids assume they don't deserve the gifted label. Rather, praise the student's efforts and hard work, not the results.

So once again, maybe we can blame it all on Mom. Throw Dad in, too, for good measure.

THE BEAST EMERGES FROM THE CLOSET

Happiness seems to be eluding us, but it's worse than that. Once again, time for some numbers, and these are doozies. Each year, seventeen million Americans suffer from depression. One in every four women, one in every ten men, and one in every fifty children will struggle with this monster at one time or another. Visits to doctors for depression rocketed from eleven million in 1988 to twenty-one million in 1993. Doctor visits for depression doubled for both primary care doctors and psychiatrists. Psychotropics, to help ease depression's symptoms, are now the most widely prescribed medications in the United States.

Sadly, depression rates have been climbing steadily around the world. Since 1915, in fact, depression in every country has risen with each new generation, according to Columbia University research. In America the risk of depression almost doubles every generation. In all countries, women reported twice the rates as men. Marital separation and divorce were the factors most consistently associated with depression. Divorced men have higher rates than married men, although rates for divorced women are no higher than for married women. Jewish men have higher rates, about the same as Jewish and non-Jewish women.

The most common mental disorders are anxiety and depression, and they are not as simple as might seem. We will deal with these throughout this chapter, but they have been consistently linked to unemployment and poverty, independent of occupational social class, according to a study at the University of Wales. Financial strain was the most powerful predictor of both the onset and maintenance of mental disorder, independent of different standards of living.

These are the five most frequent symptoms: difficulty in doing the things you have done in the past; feeling hopeless about the future; difficulty in making decisions; feeling worthless and not needed; no longer enjoying the things you used to do. Other common symptoms are sleeping troubles and insomnia, changes in appetite, restlessness, and trouble concentrating. There can be a decrease in immune function. Depressed teens are at greater risk for drugs, smoking, and alcohol.

It is critical to recognize that there is a spectrum of severity with depression, as with all medical disorders. Depression can be a fatal disease. Self-diagnosis is as inappropriate with this illness as it would be with cancer. Deep, dark depression requires expert medical care, while you may be able to tackle the milder forms yourself.

To find out your risk for depression, answer yes or no to the following statements:

- I find it easy to do the things I used to do.
- I feel hopeful about the future.
- I still enjoy the things I used to do.
- I find it easy to make decisions.
- I feel that I am useful and needed.

Any negative responses? If so, you are at risk of depression.

Being tough on yourself is another potential interstate to Depression-ville, courtesy of that self-esteem problem. How else do you explain depression and suicide in those who impress us with their power, prestige, money, and loving families? Self-imposed unrealistic standards and intense self-observation may well lie underneath the asphalt. Tragic irony that the very quality driving such individuals to high achievement—perfectionism—can also carry them to self-destruction.

I was taught in medical school that depression is a mood disorder, which seemed abstract and unapproachable to me. What is a mood? Where does it come from? How do you treat it? The new thinking about depression suggests that actually it has a lot to do with altered thinking patterns. Now *that* I can deal with. Everybody has a normal number of depressing thoughts. How could anyone live life on this planet and not have depressing thoughts every so often? A psychologist at the University of Texas at San Antonio did some clever research to demonstrate what depressed people *really* do. "The problem," Richard Wenzlaff discovered, "is that they ruminate on their negative thoughts, which evokes worse mood and which, in turn, primes more negative thoughts."

One of those vicious circle deals. The trick, apparently, is to distract yourself. In one experiment, volunteers imagined an upsetting scene. They were then instructed to spend some time writing down their thoughts but to keep that upsetting scene out of their minds. If it pushed its way into their thoughts, they were instructed to make a mark on the page. With time, most people thought of the nasty scene less and less. But the depressed subjects found the thought intruding with greater frequency. What do you think they used to distract themselves? "Ironically, depressed people seem to use one depressing topic to get their minds off another," wrote Wenzlaff. They create a chain of increasingly depressing thoughts. Here's an example: "My checkbook is overdrawn, therefore I can't pay the rent. I'll be thrown out on the street and lose my job. My spouse will leave me." That is one devastating drift of thought.

TAKE A LITTLE DEPRESSION AND DON'T CALL ME IN THE MORNING

Maybe this will make you feel better: Sometimes mild depression, which is even more common than major depression, may offer a distinct advantage. Just as people suffering from major depression have an unrealistically negative view of their world, mildly depressed folks may see the world more clearly than most. Students at Niagara University were first assessed for mild depression, then asked to predict the most probable personal events over the next two months. They could pick from seventy-five events, including the likelihood of getting a new job, falling in love, needing money, and getting sick. Two months later, the mildly depressed turned out to be more accurate in their predictions than those with no signs of depression.

The researcher who conducted this study calls these people "sadder but wiser." His conclusions followed earlier work from the University of Pennsylvania that found that nondepressed individuals overestimate their ability to control events in their lives and suffer illusions of control—unlike mildly depressed people. Another study found that depressed people are more accurate in assessing their own personal appeal. Nondepressed subjects tended to hold a better image of themselves than others held of them.

Feeling a little worse now? Good. But just a little, please.

There is a tendency today to attribute all depression to nasty chemicals. "I have chemical depression," callers tell me. I don't know exactly what they mean. Ultimately, all mood and brain functions are chemical. This notion medicalizes all depression, and it may make the drug companies happy, but it just is not true most of the time. Life experiences account for a lot of depression. There is no other explanation for rising rates. There simply is no proof that chemistry is behind it. For instance, women can get depressed after giving birth. Many have theorized that this is due solely to chemicals or hormones. If so, the rate of postpartum depression should be the same whether women have one baby or twins. Researchers compared women who had twins with women who gave birth to one baby. Sure enough, moms of twins had more depression, signaling that that life events, not only brain chemistry, can contribute to depression.

The problem is that many people don't know they are depressed. There is no blinking neon light announcing that all those symptoms add up to the great black cloud. Many who do recognize it hesitate to seek help. Unfortunately, you can't count on your doctor to detect this illness for you. Experts in Arkansas diagnosed major depression in a group of adults, then found that physicians had missed the illness in one-third of the cases—even after a year of multiple visits by the patients. To be fair, it is a difficult diagnosis to make because the symptoms are so easy to hide. But it's a tragedy when it goes undetected. There is so much we can do these days that is effective for treating depression.

Yet there remains a stigma to depression—and any mental illness, for that matter. Many people are ashamed to acknowledge it. A recent poll for the National Mental Health Association was revealing. Half of those surveyed said they or a family member had suffered from depression. An astounding 43 percent viewed the illness as a personal weakness. In other words, you blame yourself when depression hits, thus worsening the initial depression. One out of three people polled said they would not want their friends to know if someone else in their family was depressed.

Please listen to me on this: Do not keep it a secret. The single true, courageous, and positive response to depression is to get help. This means more than going to your general practitioner for a prescription. Treatment of serious depression is best left to specialists. You choose— psychiatrists or clinical psychologists—but know the difference. Psychologists, for the most part, are barred from prescribing medication and should be willing to refer you to a psychiatrist if you need pharmaceutical help. By the same token, psychiatrists are often criticized for overemphasizing psychotherapeutic drugs.

You don't necessarily need to take Prozac. The public has registered all the hoopla and mostly believes that all depression is treated with pills. Some people therefore avoid professional intervention because they don't want to be "drugged." This is not about happy pills or magic bullets. The new generation of antidepressants is extraordinarily sophisticated and really can be helpful when necessary.

But the latest research finds that talk therapy is as effective and more lasting in its effects than medication. Therapists now tend toward cognitive behavioral therapy, which tries quickly to identify strategies to change the way patients think and thus help them feel better. How Mom and Dad potty-trained you is not considered important. The goal is to teach patients skills for thinking positively and making decisions. This type of therapy can be very effective in a relatively short time for most simple and moderate cases. Unfortunately, many HMOs want the quick fix, which they perceive as drugs. Talk therapy may be hard to get in a managed-care environment.

Just in case you need another reason to confront your depression, here it is: It's bad for your health. Do something about it. It's not as intractable as you may think. With treatment, as many as 90 percent of depression sufferers can be helped to feel better within weeks.

LOVE LONG, LIVE LONGER

To quote Jane Austen, it is a truth universally acknowledged that almost nothing can make you happier or more miserable than your primary relationship. (That's not exactly what she wrote, but it certainly was one point of *Pride and Prejudice*.) Obviously the capacity to maintain those relationships evades a lot of us (including yours truly). America's high divorce rate speaks of an insidious unhappiness out there.

Although the association between divorce and ill health is well established, we really do not know how one causes the other. Remember, two events that happen at the same time do not automatically add up to cause and effect. The increases in illness, smoking, and drinking that accompany divorce could be attributed to depression and neuroses, which also destroy relationships. Even just being sick in the first place can contribute to a divorce, thus altering the statistics in such a way as to make divorce appear as the cause. Perhaps much of the ill health springs from the drop in financial resources that often accompanies divorce. It has been proved that health deteriorates right along with personal finances, and certainly we know that the stress and anxiety of divorce trigger a lot of health mayhem.

Science actually tells us quite a lot about relationships, even more than the chat-show queens. Here is the basic, most elemental truth: Being married confers many health benefits, including living longer. A review of health and marriage in the *British Medical Journal* paints a bleak picture for the health of divorced people. Divorced people of all ages and sexes have higher rates of premature death and psychiatric morbidity in all countries that keep accurate statistics. For men between the ages thirty-five and forty-five, the risk of premature death is doubled. The morbidity that follows divorce may be due to stress and loss, increased susceptibility (again) to disease, smoking, and drinking, and psychological symptoms. Divorced men have higher rates of death from heart disease, cancer, stroke, suicide, and accidents. The children of divorce also show higher rates of disease.

Even everyday arguing is not healthy. A study from Ohio State University found that marital arguments, even among older, long-term, successful, and happy couples—married for forty years—had a negative impact on their immune systems. The degree of impact was linked to the levels of hostility in the argument.

What causes so much marital discord? One-third of divorces can be blamed on high levels of conflict. Research at the University of Nebraska challenged the absolutism that pervades talk shows. Divorce is not always a bad thing. In marriages with a lot of arguing and quarreling, the children—as well as the spouses—were better off with divorce. But in the majority of divorces, the couple were actually getting along quite well before they split. The low-conflict marriages wreaked the most havoc on kids and grown-ups alike. Constance Ahrons, a sociologist at the University of Southern California, claims that kids are not damaged in half of divorces.

I'm not encouraging it, but don't think that you have to stick with a bad decision for the rest of your life. It would be nicer to know how to make the right decision. Because of our devastating divorce rates, there is growing interest in marital preparation courses, which have been shown to help lower the risk for divorce. Getting to couples in the beginning, when they are still happy, is the best time. A study of one marital distress prevention program shows that couples who took the course were still getting along better five years later.

One relationship scoring system was extraordinarily accurate in predicting which couples would remain satisfied with their relationship. Successful couples had higher scores on realistic expectations, among other factors. Satisfied couples knew each other longer before marriage and had parents and friends who approved of their union.

After taking the test, some couples decided not to get married. They did the right thing because their scores were very similar to those of couples that eventually divorced or separated.

Obviously this is not an exact science. Although these tests can predict marital success with considerable reliability, no one could ethically use them for that purpose. There are still too many false positives and negatives: they predicted failure for some couples that survived and success for some couples that failed. What emerges from them all are some generalities, but as with other aspects of health, there is no one solution for all. Just to tease you, though, one telltale sign of trouble was a husband's lack of independence from his parents. Couples did better when hubby had less anxiety, guilt, mistrust, and anger about Mom and Dad. Other signals of potential divorce are criticism, defensiveness, contempt, and stonewalling. Some signs of happiness ahead: good quality sex, good communication skills, ability to solve conflicts constructively, compatible personalities, and broad agreement on religious values.

NOT JUST TALK, TALK, TALK

Everyone's heard the conventional wisdom that better communication—in itself—leads to a happy relationship. I hate to rain on that parade, but get out your umbrella—new studies challenge that whole notion. Researchers at the University of Florida warn that communication can be transformed into pressure and blame. Some people are born worse communicators than others. That does not automatically mean they will have poor relationships. In fact, the real key was selective memory, or perceptions about the past. Successful and divorced couples alike shared happiness at the outset of their marriages. That makes sense. Why would you get married if you were not happy at the moment? But the happy couples used their memories selectively to feel good, jointly, about their early time together. It's much like the yearning many people feel for what they consider the good old days. The key was telling themselves stories they would like to believe, true or not. "It's OK not to be accurate about the past," says Benjamin Karney, a psychologist at the University of Florida, "if it makes you feel better about the present."

"Many relationship gurus insist that you focus on personal communication in your relationship," adds Karney. "Yet, that fails to consider your individual personality, family background or the kinds of challenges you face in daily life."

While we are on the subject of communication, active listening—another lauded predictor of relationship heaven—did not predict success. You know active listening: You each take turns listening and rephrasing the, other's complaints, carefully commenting, "I hear what you are saying. . . ." Studies at the University of Washington determined that successful couples almost never use this. Couples who tried to follow such advice did not have fewer divorces. "Our analysis suggested that active listening occurred very infrequently in marital conflict resolution," they found, "and its use didn't predict marital success."

You'll love this. The Washington team followed 130 newlyweds for six years and found that marital success was based on the husband's willingness to be influenced by his wife. "Getting husbands to share power with their wives by accepting some of the demands she makes is critical to helping to resolve conflict," the researchers wrote.

Wives complain more about their marriages, not because they are more emotional or focused on the relationship but because they have more to gain by speaking out and looking for more equity. Husbands benefit most from keeping things just as they are—they usually hold more power in the relationship—and they achieve this state of affairs by doing what they do best, withdrawing from such discussions.

You want my bottom line on all this? It's like depression. You should get help when you clearly need it. You run to the doctor for every ache but are reluctant to seek aid for this most important aspect of your health. By the time most couples have made an appointment with a therapist, marriage counselor, or clergyman, it's already too late.

STRESSING OUT

Life is more hectic by the hour. But why?

This is the age of technology, with electronic and mechanical wonders at our disposal that allow us to do tasks in seconds that took our ancestors hours, weeks, and years to accomplish. Yet rather than enjoy more leisure time, we are required to do more in response to the more we can do. I know it may be hard to believe, but I resisted having a computer at work or at home until recently. I figured that between voice mail, regular mail, interoffice mail, faxes, yellow sticky notes from coworkers, a cell phone in my car or in my pocket, telephones to the left and right, I was reaching out and touching enough already. Finally forced into the computer age, now my day begins with endless lists of e-mail. Now I get voice mail messages asking "Did you check your e-mail? It's important."

I'm not exactly unique in facing this onslaught from the outside. A survey by Pitney Bowes, the office-product company, compiled the following list of communications in the daily life of the average office worker: thirty e-mails, eighteen interoffice mail items, eighteen U.S. Postal Service mail items, eleven Post-it notes, four overnight letters and packages, three U.S. Postal Service express mail items, fifty-two phone calls, twenty-two voice mails, ten telephone message slips, fifteen faxes, and three cell phone calls. Nearly half the workers get interrupted six or more times an hour by messages.

You're stressed? What a surprise.

But let's look at other sources of stress. They will not be where you expect them. Three decades ago, two psychologists developed a now-famous stress scale, known universally after the inventors as Holmes and Rahe. In fact, their system changed the field, rating stress and giving different stressors a numerical score in order to predict illness. They found that patients ill with stress-related disease were more likely to have experienced specific events in the year before their illness developed. Not all the events were what anyone anticipated. While deaths in the family, divorce, injury, and losing employment top the list, other surprising events contribute to your stress quotient and thus your chance of illness: marriage, retirement, pregnancy, son or daughter leaving home, outstanding personal achievement, change in church activities, vacation, and Christmas.

Vacation and Christmas? Aren't they fun? Think about it. That's the contribution of Holmes and Rahe. Stress is not always obvious nor is it always provoked by a negative event. This list may seem a touch simplistic today. Nowadays, anger and hostility are emphasized as sources of stress. One project rated hostility among female subjects. Women defined as hostile were asked to describe a life event that made them angry. Just talking about it raised their blood pressure and heart rate higher, compared with nonhostile women describing an event that made *them* angry.

While not yet deemed as important a factor in heart attacks as smoking, hostile and angry reactions to stress are linked to cardiac disease. Here is an overview of a second stress questionnaire that weaves in hostility and anger. The questionnaire scores your responses to situations we all encounter:

- How do you react to loud stereos in teens' cars?
- How do you react to the guy with thirteen items in the ten-item express line at the supermarket?
- How do you react to the elevator that just won't come? (Me? I push the button fifty times. *That* makes it move faster.)
- How do you react to traffic?

If you're upset just reading the list, you're putting an unhealthy strain on your system.

IMMUNE TO STRESS

Finally something that's easy to measure. Immune-system response is a piece of cake and can be measured in the laboratory. There are many mechanisms to explain how and why stress affects the immune system. Nerves go to immune tissues, as do hormones secreted during stress. Behavior also changes with stress: increased drinking and smoking, lack of sleep, less exercise, poor diet, and poor adherence to doctors' orders. Exposing subjects to just a few minutes of a stressful task triggers a reduction in the number of illness-fighting cells in the immune system. Same thing in people living near a nuclear power plant at the time of an accident, people taking care of Alzheimer's patients, and students taking medical school exams. Depression showed its own cellular effects.

What all this means at the clinical level is still a matter of intense research. Dr. Arthur Stone of the State University of New York at Stony Brook found that the positive effects on the immune system of a pleasant experience persisted longer than did the negative effects of a stressful event. Criticism by the boss can drop the bottom out of your immune system. But fishing or a pleasant family experience will give your immune system a boost that lasts far longer than the downturn after your boss's ragging. Stone found that criticism at work weakened the immune system for that day but that having friends over enhanced the immune system for two days. The converse is also true: Reducing the usual number of pleasant events in your life raises susceptibility to some illnesses more than does an increase in stressful events. So in all seriousness: Keep up the pleasure in your life, especially if stress is increasing. Eat, drink, be merry, and feel better.

Yet stress has been found to increase the risk of upper-respiratory infections such as the common cold. In a study we discussed back in the germ chapter (don't get stressed—it was Chapter 8), researchers purposely inserted cold virus directly into subjects' noses; the more stress in their lives, the more likely they were to develop a cold. Another experiment monitored naturally occurring colds and upper-respiratory infections. Life events that were stressful and even the number of hassles suffered increased the risk for getting sick. A unique part of this study revealed that an "avoidant-coping" style— basically, distracting yourself—reduced the impact stressful events had on the chances of getting sick.

Now we wander into the believe-it-or-not funhouse. One powerful study assessed wound healing and stress with truly amazing results. Don't ask how they talked volunteers into this, but researchers at Ohio State University found thirteen women caring for relatives with Alzheimer's disease. The volunteers allowed doctors to punch a deep hole in their skin. A control group of thirteen women allowed the same wound to be made on their forearms. The caregivers healed in 48.7 days, the noncaregiving controls in 39.3 days. A similar study was conducted with dental students. Wounds inflicted on their palates as they faced their toughest major exam took 40 percent longer to heal than wounds inflicted on them six weeks earlier.

What of the effects of stress on cancer? That is much harder to determine. All people with cancer feel stress. A study with post-surgery breast cancer patients found a correlation between stress and the function of their anticancer immune cells. Whether this correlates with metastasis, survival, and death remains to be seen. The next phase of the study will objectively assess whether psychological therapy designed to relieve stress will increase survival. Unfortunately, previous attempts have been disappointing.

As with heart disease, there have been many efforts to link the progression of cancer with an array of different psychological states, from anger to depression. Research again has focused on optimism and pessimism. Among 238 patients, most with lung or breast cancer, researchers found that optimism and depression had no effect on death rates or survival. But pessimism increased mortality and decreased survival, especially in those patients under sixty.

Stress has been related to less life-threatening disorders like gum disease. More stress, more periodontal disease. Other studies have found that stress in rats caused them to store energy more as abdominal fat than as fat anywhere else on their bodies. That's right, stress and your potbelly. Thankfully, this is only in rats so far. But it's worth remembering, as you surely will from our superb chapter on fat, that abdominal fat can predict illnesses, including diabetes and heart disease. Don't worry, though. You don't want to pump up that potbelly.

IT'S NOT *ALL* BAD

A certain amount of stress is unavoidable in life—just being human and alive is stressful, isn't it? The cascade of events and reactions that your body experiences under stress are supremely important to survival for you as an individual and for us as a species. Danger, hunger, and environmental extremes must all be handled. Without the ability to cope, we could not feed or protect ourselves. Rats put under a little stress in laboratory experiments lived longer than rats given none. At the very least, a stress-free life would be boring.

But where do we draw that line? When does stress harm us? Again, unfortunately, that line is different for every individual. Each is uniquely equipped—or unequipped—to deal with life's challenges. Confronting different stressors, some of us just do better, or worse, than others, and even that can vary from one day to the next with each individual. In this, as in all things, you must beware of the one-approach-fits-all gurus.

Even the research on stress can be deceptive. The classic stress-maker is job strain, with heavy psychological and time demands, which causes heart attacks and kills people. Yet when Duke University researchers examined 1,489 patients who underwent coronary angiography to check for blocked heart arteries, they found that job strain was unrelated to how they fared. Those in low-pressure jobs suffered as many heart attacks as those in high-pressure jobs. Job strain even varied among patients who had the same job. One person might view a job as challenging and fun while another saw it as stress-ful and tense.

This heterogeneous reaction is important to the species. With a given environmental stressor, some in a group would thrive and some would succumb. If all members of the group shared the same reaction, the whole tribe would perish; obviously not a good design. We must look at the characteristics that alter our individual reaction to stress. Hostility and anger, for instance, are under intense study now as fac-tors that define who does well and who does poorly with particular types of stress. It seems that our twin friends, optimism and pes-simism, are at play here as well. Rather than the power of positive thinking, we want to emphasize the avoidance of negative thinking. Pessimists reported more stress and poorer overall health after a year. Optimists did not show a large improvement.

THE HEART THAT BURNS

Researchers at Stanford University wanted to know which was worse for the heart: stress, anger, or just plain exercise. Mental arithmetic and speech-making are the standard ways researchers induce stress in studies. So at Stanford subjects with heart disease took an arithmetic test (subtract 7 serially from 3,505 for six minutes). The heat was

on. They were told to hurry up, corrected with each error, and warned that they would be tape-recorded and rated for speed and accuracy. In the next stage they were asked to imagine that they were in a department store and accused of stealing the belt they were wearing. They were given three minutes to prepare a response and three min-utes to defend themselves to store security. All this reliably caused a rise in blood pressure and heart rate.

Next they were asked to recall something that had made them angry in the last six months and that still made them feel frustrated, angry, irritated, or upset. Subjects were asked to recreate the incident with all the gory details. In this experiment, the anger segment won hands down, putting the most pressure on heart function.

The American Heart Association confirms the links between anger and strokes. Men who experienced outbursts of anger had twice the risk of stroke. "Although blowing off steam can be hazardous to men's health," its report said, "the message of this study is not to suppress anger, but to manage anger so that it does not get to explosive levels." These angry guys had outbursts of rage, slammed doors, lost their temper, became annoyed at minor stuff, and used nasty language. Sound familiar? These men also reported higher levels of job stress.

Another study in Boston found that "grumpy old men" who reported "being irritable, hotheaded, and sometimes feeling like swearing or smashing things" had three times the risk of heart disease. They measured rates of heart attacks, deaths, and angina and found a dose-response relationship—the more the anger, the higher the chance of your body paying you back with heart disease.

The risks here go beyond anger to emotional arousability itself. Men who experience strong feeling of excitement, anger, fear, or grief are twice as likely to succumb to sudden cardiac death, according to a Yale University study. These are components of the classic type A personality, the time-urgent workaholics. Those patients who appeared intense and excited just during conversation were at high risk. It is the abrupt onset and intensity of emotion, not only its nature, that counts in this study. Anger was important but by no means the whole picture. Rage, grief, fear, humiliation, and, yes, even joy—watch out for that one. Sudden death has been recorded in people jolted by devastating news or overly excited from watching a sporting event. Win the lottery and die. Between 30 and 40 percent of sudden cardiac deaths may be attributable to emotional factors.

What can you do? Overall moderation of emotion seems to be critical, says Lynda Powell, a coauthor of the Yale study. "Emotional people should learn to accept that life is filled with minor annoyances and that it is not worth it to get upset by each one," she warns. "They should expect to become emotionally aroused at sporting events and should stay away from high-fat foods and alcohol, which exacerbate risk."

In case you think that shy types have the safest, toughest hearts, check out this work from Belgium. Researchers came up with a new personality—type D, for distressed. These are folks who suppress and inhibit self-expression in social interactions and are more likely to be socially alienated and depressed. They tend to worry and take a gloomy view of things, often feel unhappy and irritated, keep others at a distance, inhibit expression of true feelings, and have low levels of perceived social support. The Belgians set their chance of dying at four times higher than the average. Are you understanding yet that, much as we want to crisply define personality and heart disease risk, it's not so simple?

One last note about your heart and then I'll let it beat in peace. No one knows the exact mechanism by which stress affects heart disease, although we have investigated all the markers of heart disease and their reactions to stress. But research has picked up on the fact that your cholesterol and blood fat levels can vary a lot, just in the course of one day. Acute mental stress causes rapid elevation of cholesterol and thickening of the blood. Neither, of course, are good for your heart.

CHILL, BABY

Whether you suffer from stress or from anger, you must learn to relax. Do it effectively, strike the healthy balance between tension and calm, and I promise that your stress levels will fall. You should schedule your individual relaxation program at a reasonable level, the way you schedule everything else in your life. Just remember that the point is to *relax*, not to become obsessed with relaxing. I once dated a woman who suddenly broke into a sweat during dinner. "Oh my God," she screamed, "I forgot to meditate." We had to hotfoot it home so she could squeeze in the second of her twice-daily sessions. That kind of anxiety should signal that this relaxation program is not working.

Whatever technique works for you, try it. I have no problem if you love your mantras. You can do formal Transcendental Meditation. You can try a more spiritually neutral relaxation response by focusing on your breathing. You can do full-body massage or biofeedback. As you like. I believe that if we did the research, we would find that for some people, sitting at home quietly sipping a glass of wine and listening to their favorite music would be as beneficial as meditation. Hobbies, hot baths, entertainment, and naps count. Do not be bullied by all the promoters who want to ritualize and charge you a fee or sell you a book for their particular brand of relaxation. Like exercise, if it isn't fun, you're not going to do it.

I believe, and can support my belief with some research, that just the act of refocusing your mind from the normal stressors of your life to anything else is the actual mechanism by which relaxation works. Meditation is focusing on nothing. As far as your brain knows, focusing on a hobby or music performs the same function.

I saved some nuggets from the exercise chapter because they support me here and explain why exercise can help with stress. Exercise is simply another way to get your mind off your routine life. It reduces anxiety by giving you something to think about other than your problems. I have a writer friend who swears that just knowing he has weekend soccer games coming up often gives him the psychic energy to get through the week. "The reason people feel less anxious after exercise is because they get a time-out, or a break, from their usual cares and worries," says Patrick J. O'Connor, a research scientist at the University of Georgia.

O'Connor and his team conducted an experiment that proved that exercise reduces anxiety by taking people's minds off whatever made them anxious. Studying for an exam while on an exercycle canceled the anxiety-relieving effects of exercise. Beyond that, it is still possible that with heavy exercise, brain endorphins—morphinelike chemicals—could allay anxiety. Different exercise may have different effects. The rhythm of aerobic exercise, for example, may help to distract a worried mind and reduce anxiety more effectively than weight training, which lacks that rhythm. One psychiatrist who prescribes exercise to anxious patients, Dr. Ronald Kamm in New Jersey, offers this wise hint: Willingness to take time for oneself is one of the biggest predictors of whether a person can cope with stress.

I cannot think of a better way to say it, but I would broaden the thought to all manner of relaxation. Take the time. It doesn't matter much what you do, but do it. Changing your environment and patterns seems the key. An example on a grander scale is one close to my own heart: recreational vehicles. One survey presented at an American Anthropological Association annual meeting found that RV enthusiasts are healthier, happier, and more mentally alert than others. One-quarter of those surveyed insist their health has improved since they hit the road. According to the psychologists who conducted the survey, it is an activity that offers "opportunities to perform interesting and challenging tasks, control over one's life in the form of making one's own decisions, and environment conducive to establishing a social network beyond one's immediate family." Those all sound to me like criteria for successful retirement.

I don't want to get personal, but I do own a 1952 Flxible bus, which I converted to a one-bedroom apartment thirty years ago and lived in with my family. I rarely get a chance to get out in it these days, but my time is coming. There is almost nothing else that gives me that feeling of renewal. But you don't need to go anywhere for that feeling. I find it in hobbies as well. I'm a great believer in hobbies. Mine is collecting, and when I sit down to play with my collections, I feel as if I have traveled to the ends of the earth. I am refreshed and energized and ready to take on the craziness of life for another day.

Still need help? How about some other, less obvious ways to help your brain unwind? Pets offer a proved benefit. Cats, as opposed to people, show unconditional affection and love. Studies of stress and dogs find that people sometimes feel more stress around other people than they do around their pet dogs. (I have to share this one with you: On an arithmetic-as-stress test, people were tested while accompanied by a spouse, a friend, and a dog. The lowest heart rates were measured among subjects when Fido sat nearby.)

How about laughter and humor? Loads of research has been conducted on the healing power of these gifts to mankind. For instance, a hundred laughs equal ten minutes of rowing in energy expended. Laughter can relieve pain. Then there's the side benefit that humor helps us to see life's ironies, and its realities, clearly.

Music is another indisputable route to mental comfort. Studies of both depressed and nondepressed individuals found marked improvements in mood and reductions in stress levels from listening to music. Another study, of surgeons in operating rooms, proved that music increased concentration, improved vigilance, and reduced fatigue. Even speed and accuracy shot up.

Perhaps the most encouraging treatise on the subject comes from Sweden. Scientists say that attending cultural events, reading, making music, or singing in choirs significantly increased survival rates. The researchers allowed for the influence of education, income, social networks, exercise, and bad habits—and still came up with the same results.

So, once again, relax. You'll live longer and be happier.

ONE, TWO, THREE, WHAT ARE WE FIGHTING FOR?

When you get right down to it, much of what we are all about is the desire to live forever.

Many people seem to think that if they could somehow attain longevity, if they could only live to be a hundred, well, *that* is the definition of a good life. They believe that longevity adds up to happiness and success in life, that the great score card in the sky is simply the number of years you live. It's the spectacular examples that keep us hoping. The oldest person for whom a birth certificate has been authenticated was Jeanne Calment, a Frenchwoman who died in 1997 at the age of 122. She lived in her own apartment until she was 110, rode her bike until she was 115, and remembered once meeting Van Gogh.

In the Greco-Roman era, the average life expectancy in Europe was twenty years. By the year 1000 it was up to thirty. Not much changed until recently. By the mid-nineteenth century, the average American could count on making it to thirty-nine. Nowadays some countries can count on the average citizen closing in on eighty.

What can you do to get yourself on the far side of those averages? That's easy, just get the right genes. One study looked at the siblings of centenarians and found the obvious. Researchers compared those whose siblings died at an average age of seventy-three with those whose siblings lived to be one hundred or older. A female with a sibling who died at seventy-three herself lived to be seventy-four. But if her sibling lived to be one hundred, she lived to eighty. A male with a sibling who died at seventy-three lived on average to seventy-three and a half, but if the sibling lived to one hundred, he lived to seventy-six. So your best bet is to try to get yourself a one-hundred-year-old sibling.

Out of billions of people on the earth, Jeanne Calments happen rarely. The secret is a rare combination of genes, environment, and luck. All the right molecules in all the right places in just the right body. Taking a vitamin pill is not going to duplicate the incredible fortuitous combination of events that let Ms. Calment live to 122 and to do so with such vitality. Fantasy aside, be warned that the reality of extreme longevity may not be what you really had in mind.

You might think that ascetic lifestyles are one path to foreverdom. True, studies of religious groups with prudent lifestyles, including Mormons, the Amish, and Seventh Day Adventists, show longer lives and lower death rates. But no one has looked at morbidity and disability in these communities. Researchers in the Netherlands studied Trappist and Benedictine monks who were in monasteries for an average of forty years. They were surprised to find that rates of chronic conditions were no different from those of the general population, but disability rates were actually higher among the monks.

Because more and more of us will have the fortune—or misfortune—of reaching one hundred years of age, interest in this elite group of centenarians is growing. One in ten thousand living Americans will celebrate their century. Between thirty thousand and fifty thousand of them are around now, so many that there is a waiting list to get their birthdays mentioned on the *Today* show. What does life have to offer at that stage? One study of nine Dutch centenarians found that all required nursing care because of their various disabilities. Eight of them had a "clear deterioration of memory and function"; four were in an "almost vegetative state." Conversation was possible with the four least affected individuals, but researchers say that memory loss and verbal fluency were seriously impaired in them all. Only one of the nine could do a standard test used for dementia: draw a picture of a clock. It took her three tries to get the numbers. She could not draw the hands.

Now that was a small European study. Here things are a little brighter for our most senior of citizens. Almost one-third have fairly full faculties and live in the community; nearly half are disabled to a varying degree; and the rest are extremely disabled and dependent or demented. Yet according to the *New York Times*, most of you want to take the chance and live to be one hundred. Says Dr. John Rowe, chairman of the MacArthur Foundation Research Network on Successful Aging: "I'm all for living to 100, 110, as long as we're not prolonging dependency. We want to prolong active life expectancy. If we are going to get ten more years of life, and eight of them are dependent, then I consider that prolonging dying rather than prolonging living."

It's easy to keep track of the number of years but to discern the quality of life as defined by health is a bit more elusive. Traditionally health status has been measured by looking at how a person is functioning in various arenas: physical, social, and mental functioning, pain and vitality, and ability to perform the ordinary activities of daily living. Can a person bathe, dress, eat, and go to the toilet independently? It sounds crude, but it is straightforward.

Then there is "time trade-off," a way to quantify your individual preference for quality or quantity of life. Actually, very little is known about the health values of very old people, which made even more interesting a recent project at the University of Cincinnati. Researchers wanted to know whether frail and elderly hospitalized patients—

eighty-plus years old—preferred to live as long as possible or to live shorter but healthier lives. How many months in perfect health would they consider to be the equivalent of a year in their current state? Overall, the group of 414 patients equated living 12 months in their current state with living 9.7 months in excellent health.

But the scores varied widely, surprising the investigators. Almost half were unwilling to give up any time in exchange for excellent health; less than one-third would only give up one month. At the end of the day, it seemed that most patients had a pretty strong will to live—whatever the state of their health.

Is living to one hundred worth pursuing if it has been a miserable life? Certainly poor health can make you miserable, but being miserable can also bring poor health. It's not worth making yourself unhappy by living right just to pursue longevity. If you just love eating sprouts and working up a sweat, that is another matter. Most people do not. So many people these days seem obsessed and neurotic in their pursuit of the latest overhyped longevity supplement or herb. I always wonder whether the anxiety that drives them to the latest fad diet or pill decreases their life span more than any possible gains from the nostrum itself.

One last note about the pursuit of digits. Keep in mind that the older you are, the more likely it is that you will live without a spouse. Two-thirds of those between sixty-five and seventy-four are married, compared with one in six over age eighty-five. And one-third of us can expect to spend our retirement taking care of aging spouses and family members.

I am not at all suggesting that aging is bad. It's just that extreme longevity is not what it's cracked up to be. The point is *quality* of life, not *quantity*. Meanwhile, there is no reason to fear getting older. You may not want to hear this as you jump on every fountain-of-youth scheme that comes along, but many surveys find that the senior years can be the happiest. A time to look forward to even. Asked about their favorite period in life, four hundred older Californians offered an optimistic view for many of you out there fretting about your frown lines and saddlebags. Their single favorite decade of all was the sixties (no, not *those* sixties); others named their fifties, and 11 percent even claimed the seventies. The teens were the least popular. Other surveys have supported this trend in thinking.

One investigation by Fordham University went to the heart of the matter and found, according to the New York Times, that "the older the respondents, the more frequently they reported feeling positive emotions like cheerfulness, good spirits and happiness within the past 30 days." It seems like it's practice, practice, practice again. Older people may be happier simply because they have more experience handling their emotions. Also, when you're older, with fewer years left, you are forced to live in the moment rather than dwell on past misfortunes and future anxieties.

THE FAT LADY SINGS FOR US ALL

No, I am not going gloomy on you. Really. Look again at the cover of this book. I want you to enjoy life. I *urge* you to enjoy life now. I like happy people. Living longer comes at the end of your life, when you may not think all that you gave up to get there was worth it. Living well, with pleasure and joy, versus living longer just for the sake of living longer? For me, it's a no-brainer.

Lots of us people live in the delayed gratification mode. Some emotional and financial nirvana is waiting for us when we finally save up the money to afford the luxury of doing the things we promise ourselves we will do one day. Of course, that assumes we will live that long. I am always hit hard by the stories of people who work all their lives and on the eve of retirement drop dead. I always hope they took the time at some point in their lives to grab some joy for themselves.

I know a delightful older gentleman of eighty who is quite well off. Most of his life he worked extremely hard and never took time for much except his career. His wife died suddenly six years ago, and everything changed. He went out and bought his toys—planes, boats, cars, RV, houses—and spends his time playing like a kid. One day he looked at me wistfully and said: "Take the time now, when you're young." It got me thinking about how I'd lost track of all that I had once grasped so easily. After all, wasn't I the guy who astounded friends, relatives, and colleagues by walking out on my surgical practice to go live in a bus and travel around the country? Where is that person? Can he really still be inside this stressed-out workaholic? I thought back and realized I hadn't had a vacation in over a year and probably wouldn't take the time for at least another year.

Certainly some of us enjoy our work and our careers. Others never had the luxury to choose. Slowing down or retiring is not in their vocabulary. Often when hardworking people finally do drop out, they wind up bored and drinking too much. Forgive me a maudlin moment, but life is an extraordinary experience. We get one crack at it, and we squander too much of it. One would think that in a country where the physical needs of the average citizen are more than cared for, the proceeds would be a life more enjoyed.

What are we missing? I have no easy answers, except some clues that work for me. Sometimes when Sharon and I have one of those perfect weekends, we look at each other and remark that this is truly as good as it gets.

It is often during one of those magical weekends up at our cabin. We swim in the river, sit in the sun, take walks in the magnificent forest. Simple things that rub out all the other routines of life. We eat meals there, the same recipes we make at home in suburbia, yet they taste exquisite. We drink the same wine and taste flavors that seem new. We take twice as long to finish the meal. We are not rushing so the kids can get to bed. We silently stare at the view out our window, watching the redwoods. Lovemaking is savored and sumptuous, not crammed between sleep and other family needs. As we drive back to the city on Sunday nights, we reflect on how lucky and privileged we are to enjoy these moments. What more should we expect from life? It's almost a painful conclusion, wrested reluctantly from the stress and struggle of the everyday.

Monday morning and the coffee tastes bitter. Off to work. Will the commute be a bear this morning? The e-mails, the faxes, the voice mail, the phone calls . . .

Of course, a weekend in the country isn't available to everyone, isn't everybody's cup of tea, and doesn't have to be. You can find it watching the kids in a play or a baseball game, listening to great music, going to a movie, laughing with friends, throwing a stick for the dog, or volunteering to help the less fortunate. There are plenty of the *other* kinds of moments in life. Your life is a necklace, experiences strung together like beads. Your memories of these beads really define how you feel about your life at any given moment.

How do we develop that joy, that ever-elusive joie de vivre? Would it help if you knew you were dying? During my medical training, I once talked to a patient, a young poet whose life and career were about to be clipped short by leukemia. He talked to me about the joy of being free from ambition. He no longer felt encumbered by the fears that plague most of us. He expressed his love to those he cared for and built the bridges he had avoided before the onset of his illness. He spent the time he had left in a genuine state of wonder, not unlike that of a child. He said that he was actually glad for the experience and the lessons taught him by a fatal disease. Given the choice, he said he might choose this illness over health.

I've never forgotten him, and to this day, whenever I feel overwhelmed by my life, I ask what would I do in that situation? A few years ago, a coworker of mine, a man in his mid-thirties, found a suspicious pigmented lesion on his thigh and ran to the doctor. The biopsy showed a malignant, particularly nasty, and probably fatal melanoma. He took a few weeks' leave from his high-pressure media job and set out to undo the wrongs in his life.

Several weeks later, he got a call from the doctor. To be safe, the clinic had sent his biopsy off for further analysis and—can you believe it?—turned out his lesion was benign. The earlier report was a false positive. How long do think his new attitude lasted? A few days later, he was back full-swing in the pressure cooker, smoking and drinking too much and as depressed as before. The joy-and-peace thing had popped off his chain of beads.

I think we are just plain stuck with the struggle. I used to believe that there was some permanent state of nirvana to be reached if I was a good boy and meditated enough and ate my veggies. After all, isn't that where the gurus reside? They don't get depressed or angry or stressed, do they? I no longer believe that such a state of being is practical, possible, or desirable for most humans. The struggle—the triumphs and the defeats—keeps us going. We curse the downturns and cherish the victories. We accumulate the beads. The losses make the victories sweeter, and the victories make the losses less bitter.

If there is an art to it all, as far as your health goes, it is in avoiding those behaviors that science is beginning to find can make you unhealthy as well as miserable—stress, anger and hostility, exhaustion, depression, and loss of control. These are among the traits that have been linked to disease and early demise, as well as misery. Yet expectation of a state of permanent bliss is naive, frustrating, self-defeating, and boring.

So eat, drink, and be merry. Don't obsess about things you can't control, and be smart about the things you can. In short, my prescription is that you follow the advice of the codfish (the whiting) in the tale sung to Alice by the Mock Turtle in her fabulous *Adventures in Wonderland*:

"Will you walk a little faster?" said a whiting to a snail,
"There's a porpoise close behind us, and he's treading on my tail.
See how eagerly the lobsters and the turtles all advance!
They are waiting on the shingle—will you come and join the dance?

Will you, won't you, will you, won't you, will you join the dance?
Will you, won't you, will you, won't you, won't you join the dance?

"You can really have no notion how delightful it will be
When they take us up and throw us, with the lobsters, out to sea!"
But the snail replied "Too far, too far!" and gave a look askance—
Said he thanked the whiting kindly, but he would not join the dance.

Would not, could not, would not, could not, would not join the dance.
Would not, could not, would not, could not, could not join the dance.

"What matters it how far we go?" his scaly friend replied.
"There is another shore, you know, upon the other side.
The further off from England, the nearer is to France.
Then turn not pale, beloved snail, but come and join the dance.

Will you, won't you, will you, won't you, will you join the dance?
Will you, won't you, will you, won't you, won't you join the dance?"

INDEX